User Experience Management

User Experience Management

Essential Skills for Leading Effective UX Teams

Arnie Lund

AMSTERDAM • BOSTON • HEIDELBERG • LONDON
NEW YORK • OXFORD • PARIS • SAN DIEGO
SAN FRANCISCO • SINGAPORE • SYDNEY • TOKYO

Morgan Kaufmann Publishers is an imprint of Elsevier

Acquiring Editor: Rachel Roumeliotis
Development Editor: David Bevans
Project Manager: Danielle S. Miller
Designer: Alisa Andreola

Morgan Kaufmann Publishers is an imprint of Elsevier
30 Corporate Drive, Suite 400, Burlington, MA 01803, USA

Library of Congress Cataloging-in-Publication Data
Lund, Arnie.
  User experience management : essential skills for leading effective UX teams / Arnie Lund.
    p. cm.
  Includes bibliographical references.
  ISBN 978-0-12-385496-4
  1. User interfaces (Computer systems) 2. Teams in the workplace. 3. Mentoring in business.
I. Title.
  QA76.9.U83L86 2011
  005.4'37—dc22   2010050658

British Library Cataloguing-in-Publication Data
A catalogue record for this book is available from the British Library.

ISBN: 978-0-12-385496-4

Printed in China

11 12 13 14 15   10 9 8 7 6 5 4 3 2 1

For information on all MK publications visit our website at www.mkp.com

Contents

Dedication

Dedicated to my wife, Marlene, and daughters, Anna and Sonja, who put up with me going on and on about this project, to many wonderful managers and some perhaps not so wonderful who I have learned from, and to my teams who I have learned from. I am grateful for the advice, insights, collaboration and encouragement from many wise friends and colleagues, not just about this book and the ideas within it but throughout my career. Finally, as a man of faith I have been energized by the fundamental hope that we can and should work to make the world a little better during our time here. Management and leadership can be part of that journey, and this book is part of mine.

About the Author

 Arnold (Arnie) Lund, PhD, CUXP, is a Principal Director of User Experience at Microsoft. He began his career at AT&T Bell Laboratories in applied research, and helped build the science and technology organization at Ameritech. He managed design and exploratory development teams at US West Advanced Technologies, and served as a director at Sapient (where his focus areas ranged from information architecture to leading a global program in emerging technologies). Arnie is a member of the ACM SIGCHI Academy, and co-chaired the CHI conferences in 1998 (Los Angeles) and 2008 (Florence, Italy). He is a Fellow of the Human Factors and Ergonomics Society (HFES), and served on the HFES Executive Council. He has long been engaged in human computer interaction (HCI) standards and in the area of accessibility and emerging technology, including chairing the HFES Institute and overseeing the HFES-200 standard and its approval as an ANSI standard. He is a certified user experience professional and served as president of the board of directors for the Board of Certification in Professional Ergonomics (BCPE).

Arnie received his BA in chemistry from the University of Chicago, and his PhD in experimental psychology human learning and memory from Northwestern University. He has published widely in R&D management and on research in natural user interfaces, and has a variety of patents. He has been on the advisory and editorial boards of various journals (e.g., *Journal of Usability Studies* and the *International Journal of Speech Technology*), and served on the board of directors for INFINITEC (focusing on infinite potential through assistive technologies). Arnie has taught user-centered design and related topics at Northwestern University and the University of Washington.

Introduction

1

> Management is efficiency in climbing the ladder of success; leadership determines whether the ladder is leaning against the right wall.
>
> **Stephen R. Covey**

ONE MANAGER'S PERSONAL HISTORY

Imagine you are a freshly minted graduate student from one of Northwestern University's old cinder block buildings with the pale green paint on the walls, the smell of years of classes, and the beat-up furniture in the lab and the graduate student offices. In a blink of an eye, you are transported to a glass box building designed by Eero Saarinen, walking down a hall lined with private offices to talk with your new boss (see Figure 1.1).[1] You have just been transferred to her team and you are about to have your first meeting. She has a big reputation, both in your field as well as among the human factors community at AT&T Bell Labs where you have just landed a job. As she sits behind the desk, it seems a lot larger than it probably is. You ease into the guest chair, anxious about this conversation and wanting to make a good impression. She turns to you and asks "So when do you want to sit in *my* chair?" What a question! It not only changes the way you have thought about your career, but the way you see yourself. Up until then you have been defining yourself as a researcher who only recently was planning to be a professor, and she is asking if you want to become corporate. One day you are happy as a member of the technical staff studying people, designing things, and solving problems, and the next day you are wondering what it would mean to lead a team and make big things happen.

---

[1] http://en.wikipedia.org/wiki/File:Holmdel-cropped.jpg from Wikimedia Commons.
http://en.wikipedia.org/wiki/File:Kresge_Centennial_Hall_Northwestern.jpg.

User Experience Management.

FIGURE 1.1

Northwestern to Bell Labs.

This particular boss, Judy Olson, was my third boss in two years, and in many ways I was still finding my place within what was then considered the biggest company on Earth (Kleinfield, 1981). It was thrilling to be one of the "wizards" of Bell Labs (home of the transistor, the laser, fiber optics, the solar cell, speech synthesis, radio astronomy, and the Princess Phone) and speculating about the mark I would make at this company. Judy is now the Donald Bren Professor of Information and Computer Sciences at UC Irvine, but at that point had recently arrived at Bell Labs from the University of Michigan.

Her question had more impact than she realized. Earlier in my life I had been a manager trainee, but had explicitly given that path up when I entered graduate school where I focused on teaching and research. The last thing on my mind was managing people. Judy's question opened another possible path and raised the questions: "Do I have the skills and the desire to manage? What would I want to accomplish if I was managing? Do others see something I don't yet see in myself? Do I want to do it?"

At that time within Bell Labs, many managers became managers not because they had management skills but because they had demonstrated great skill as individual contributors. Typically they had reached a level where if you wanted to make the next major jump in pay you needed to move into management. While there were efforts within the company to grow a few individuals based on their management talent, the experience of many employees was that often we were surrounded by management that were classic examples of the Peter Principle, because they had already risen to their level of incompetence. For me, management was not attractive because of the pay (after all, I was still fresh from reconciling myself to the expectation of an academic's salary and the long pursuit of tenure); it was about the opportunity to influence and in some way change the world.

As rumors started that a more senior colleague of mine was a candidate for taking Judy's place when she went back to academia, Judy's question regarding management and rethinking my own path led to the question: "Why not me?"

With a new found perspective, I have to admit I could not help feeling a little jealous (fed in part by comments from some of my peers). But I turned the jealousy into motivation. To help get an independent view, I began to build more formal mentoring relationships with managers I admired, and to think about and discuss questions that went beyond the immediate designs on which we were working. These questions became more strategic and were about defining the direction for the work. Many of those conversations happened over beer after racquetball with several of those mentors.

Moving into a lead role at Bell Labs was an opportunity to practice managerial skills. The joy was in the responsibility and the chance to think bigger. With the role the problems were more challenging. Because one person alone could not solve them, a team had to be created. My second manager gave me a piece of advice that I still follow. His recommendation was based on where he saw my strengths and where I was energized. He argued that I should get in the middle of apparently impossible problems, figure out how to make sense of them, come up with creative solutions, and drive them to closure. The most interesting problems often require being a lead or a manager in order to solve them. You need to assemble, grow, and leverage the talent that enables you to rise to the occasion. Furthermore, it is simply fun to work together to come up with and flesh out innovative ideas in the course of solving a problem.

When speaking to students as part of career panels, one of the top questions asked is some variation of whether to pursue an academic career versus a career in a corporation. Once students start their career in a corporation, their next question is usually whether they should try to become a manager. Recently at a retreat for the DUB group at the University of Washington (this group works in the area of human computer interaction), the question about becoming a manager came up again. In one of the breakouts, a graduate student asked what it means to be a manager of a user experience (UX) team in a large corporation, especially an engineering organization with all of the implied cultural tensions.

For many of us the joy of being a manager is not about power. It is not about money. It is not about the politics. I find it is about impact. It is about solving problems and accomplishing things that you cannot do by yourself. It is about having partners in achieving something important that you believe in. It is about working with great people who share a vision and passion for reaching the goal and helping enroll them in that vision and stimulating that passion. It is about playing in the creative world of design, as well as in the domain of emerging technology where everything seems possible. It is about being the person who reaches across roles and boundaries and makes the idea work.

Since starting my career, I have had many management roles. At Bell Labs, after moving from researcher to manager of a small human factors team, I was eventually asked to manage a broader set of responsibilities. At that time, to move up the management ladder you needed to demonstrate generic management skills and prove you could manage any discipline. The career path I was encouraged to pursue by more senior managers was managing a human factors department. To show I could do the job, I accepted an offer to manage the systems engineering and project management work for the 800 and 900 families of services at AT&T. This included project managing the human factors work from the team that I had previously been responsible for, which was directly managed by Mary Carol Day. As both a friend and a colleague from when we worked together on a project a few years before, I was looking forward to working with her and making even better things happen for this critical part of AT&T's business. The 800 and 900 families of services accounted for a major portion of AT&T revenue at the time, and they had just lost much of it to MCI. Unfortunately, after a few months in my new role (and despite having very talented engineers on my team) I discovered I was not exactly bounding out of bed looking forward to working on systems requirements and communications protocols. I was most excited creating and facilitating new feature ideas and visiting Mary Carol and hearing about what her team was doing with the user experience. This lack of excitement at work was one of the things that caused me to search for a challenge that was closer to my heart. My wife and I had a baby on the way, and I realized that I was not all that excited about raising a child in a town that raffled off Jaguars to raise funds for the local high school. It was time to re-center myself and my family.

The next opportunity came from Joel Engel at Ameritech (one of the Baby Bells emerging from Divestiture and covering the Midwest). He was charged with forming Ameritech's version of Bell Labs, since Bellcore — the research lab created to serve all the Baby Bells — was not able to meet Ameritech's unique needs. Joel, while an engineer, had managed a human factors department at one point in his career. He was an amazing man who held patents on some of the basic technologies that enabled the modern cellular network. He visualized a science and technology department with senior directors for each of the technologies that represented the future of the business. Because of his background, however, he also believed that user issues and needs were as critical to the future of the business as the technologies, so he was looking to hire a Senior Director of Human Factors. In Chapter 3, I will talk about the importance of champions. Joel was clearly one of those champions who created an environment that allowed our group to impact the transformation of a major corporation.

I accepted Joel's offer. This position allowed me to hire anyone I wanted, I had a virtually unlimited budget, and I could define the work plan for the organization. Since then, I have never been in another position with such an opportunity to demonstrate what user experience can deliver. Over time, we became so successful that when one of the senior directors who had engineers working on several of the emerging technologies most related to creating new user experiences (e.g., AI, speech processing, and image and video processing) left, his team was combined with mine. With the added engineers, we were in a position to research and uncover new applications, incubate them, and then deploy them — even as we continued to support a variety of new Ameritech products. When the general manager was moved into the emerging cable business, I served as acting general manager of the product development organization until a new permanent general manager was hired. This spoke volumes about the excellence of the UX team's work, the impact it was having on the business, and how the business came to see the skills of the team as being a core competency enabling the business to compete.

Good things have a way of ending, however, and as the direction of the company changed (later to be taken over by SBC), I moved to US West Advanced Technologies. I became a distinguished member of the technical staff — an individual contributor responsible for helping US West move into the e-commerce area. In Chapter 7 I will talk about the importance of keeping yourself fresh, and while it was exciting to manage the corporate move into the Internet and interactive television at Ameritech, I found I did not have the skills that my team members had who were working on the projects directly. I wanted to get hands-on experience with the Web so I could provide meaningful coaching and advice as a manager. Not long after, however, I was asked to take over management of one of the human factors groups, and shortly after that to become the acting senior director over the exploratory development team (including my former human factors team). When a new head for US West Advanced Technologies was found, I went back to managing the new media design and usability team.

Once Qwest acquired US West and the handwriting was on the wall for the eventual demise of Advanced Technologies, I left to become a Director of Information Architecture for Sapient. This was during the explosion of the Web and Sapient had a unique user experience culture, with a Chief Experience Officer (Rick Robinson) and a Chief Creative Officer (Clement Mok) advising the CEOs. It is one thing to have a champion for user experience, but when you have executive UX people whispering into the ear of the CEO, and driving their experiences and perspectives into the strategic conversations that happen at the most senior levels of the company, you are really in a position to change company culture.

At US West, one of the exercises I ran to grow my team's skills was to search the Web for great sites and to share their analyses of what made them great. Sapient was the company producing most of those sites, so it was particularly exciting to join that team. Sapient had attracted some of the best talent in the industry and was producing many of the most innovative and effective Web sites among the Fortune 500 companies. Within Sapient I looked after information architects who were distributed across the western United States in a matrixed reporting organization (the individual information architects reported directly to the projects on which they were working), as well as helping develop business and providing creative director-level oversight for specific projects.

Part of the role of a manager within a consulting firm like Sapient was to help grow the business. The reason the Sapient office had been set up in Denver was to go after business with SUN, IBM, HP, AT&T, Qwest, Lucent, and other technology companies with major offices in the area. Unfortunately, shortly after joining Sapient the Internet bubble burst and business was hard to come by in Colorado. I began to manage Sapient's global R&D effort, including developing new practices (e.g., for mobility and speech). Additional reorganizations in response to the economic climate resulted in my becoming a Director of Research as we began to chart a new course for research within Sapient. Eventually, there was not enough business to sustain the kind of office we were trying to build in Denver. I was caught in the third wave of Sapient layoffs. Through both the experiences of laying off and being laid off, however, I acquired a sensitivity that has made me a better and more compassionate manager.

Through an introduction by a colleague, I was hired by Microsoft. This again demonstrated the importance of a vibrant network of professional colleagues. Initially the role at Microsoft was to manage a team of usability researchers, but before the interviews were over the general manager reorganized the user experience team so that I would become its director. In this position, I had several user experience managers reporting to me and the department was organized based on discipline (design and user research). The challenge was to deal with a variety of personnel issues, and to rethink how the team was supporting a very diverse business. The team was redesigned so there were managers focused on each product area. The user experience team was inside a larger organization that focused on writing and editing technical documentation for servers, rather than positioned in engineering teams, as most of my previous roles had been. After I moved into my next position at Microsoft, one of the talented people who worked for me stepped into my position. Eventually the entire organization was restructured and the teams supporting the product groups were absorbed into those groups.

From servers I moved over to manage user experience for the Tablet PC area, and the notebook computer user experience team was placed under my direction as well. At that point I had a design team, a user research team, a content team (writers and editors), and a team of technical writers and developers creating software development toolkits. I also had a former peer who expected that I would be reporting to him, who was now reporting to me. That led to issues long after the merger of the teams. This experience convinced me that when this happens the most senior manager over the merger needs to take steps to clearly define the new situation and support the healing process.

The Tablet UX team worked on a major release of Windows and also did research to help drive a new form factor of personal computing devices. Once the target version of Windows was released, the Tablet team was largely absorbed into the Windows team and its related projects. A user experience general manager who had a background in industrial design was brought in to lead the new team. The general manager and I agreed that it was time for me to find a new gig, because someone more senior was now sitting in what had been my chair.

I moved into the Microsoft IT organization as a user experience architect. The goal was to begin transforming IT to be more user-experience oriented (Lund, 2010). As it happened, a designer from my server team (Pam) persuaded the organization to hire her, and she became my "team" even before I arrived. She has continued to be a critical source of energy for the team, as well as consistently winning great reviews and helping us grow demand through her design work. Since then I have built a larger team, gone through downsizing, re-grown the team with a different mix of skills, and worked closely with the other major user experience team and individual user experience professionals scattered across IT as a UX community lead.

As I write this, I am in an IT organization whose goals have changed significantly from those that first attracted me. A key champion at the vice president level has moved on, and I have my fifth boss in three years. We are yet again trying to educate an organization about where user experience value is delivered and to speak to people who are mostly focused on scorecards and who view user experience as nice to have but not necessarily critical to business success.

I have invested the time to share my history in part because it illustrates the diverse paths a career in management can take as well as the need to grow a toolkit of skills that can be drawn on as work contexts change. I have been fortunate to work at a series of great companies, in a wide variety of roles — sometimes starting new groups, and sometimes finding new and better directions for the groups I was given. As one of my earlier managers coached, I find myself energized by jumping into difficult situations and turning them around. I also continue to fight for my vision of excellence and for advancing the UX field even when it conflicts with some of my managers. Sometimes it works out and sometimes it does not, but it definitely adds spice to life, and each context has had its own unique characteristics.

It is worth looking at the history of different teams for the lessons that can be applied in a new role. Israelski and Lund (2002) wrote a history of user experience in the telecommunications industry that captured many types of groups and their fates. One older book edited by Michael Wiklund is still a great source that illustrates how major companies built their user experience programs (Wiklund, 1994). The story of how the program at Ameritech was grown is one of the chapters in that book. It is telling and sad that only a couple of those programs still exist, although the lessons have a way of continuing to be relevant. More interesting is that many of the managers who wrote chapters in Wiklund's book have continued to grow new groups or improve programs as they have moved from company to company. Some have moved very high in the companies they have joined, transforming the focus of those companies in ways that were important in growing their business.

QUESTIONS YOU MIGHT BE ASKING

Members of various discussion lists and social networks for human factors, human-computer interaction (HCI), and other UX professionals were invited to nominate managers they felt were highly experienced and successful. These managers in turn were surveyed. They were asked about the questions most often posed by new or aspiring managers in the user experience field. The questions they identified tend to come up in a variety of forums where management careers are discussed as well as in mentoring. The categories of questions include:

- How should I decide whether to become a manager? Can I change my mind if I don't like it?
- Is there a preferred background for being an effective user experience manager?

- What is unique about managing creative people? How do I motivate and grow them?
- What does it mean to balance my individual contributor and management responsibilities as I influence design? Do I have to stop doing what I enjoy?
- What does success look like? How will I be compared to those managing engineers?
- What do I need to know about the business and about technology to be most effective?
- How do I help my team to have impact? What should I be doing politically in our engineering culture?
- What do I do when the demand exceeds the people I have available?

While one perspective is the new or aspiring manager's questions, equally interesting are the questions the experienced, successful managers wished they had asked when they were just starting out. The questions from new managers will certainly be addressed throughout the course of this book, but the questions formed by years of experience provide a unique window into the context of what it can mean to be a manager. They will also be addressed. These questions include:

- Should the job be about being a creative director or about managing people and their assignments?
- How do I communicate messages to my team that I don't fully believe and that may not reflect my commitment to user experience?
- What are the top three to five things I must focus on and never let slip?
- What should I look for when hiring stellar designers, researchers, and other user experience people?
- What management skills are valued for getting to the next level of management, and how do I demonstrate them managing a user experience team?
- Where do I find support when I am managing people outside my domain of expertise?
- How do I handle complainers and whiners and get them to be positive, productive contributors while working in an engineering culture?
- What level should a user experience team report to and how do we get there?
- How do I position my team to lead in defining the experience rather than as a reactive service provider? How do I implement a 3–5-year strategy when demand has a 6-month horizon?
- How do I influence senior-level managers with my vision of what needs to be done to drive a user-centered process?

Throughout this book we will discuss all of these questions from different perspectives. Some questions will be covered more and some less. They will come from the lessons gained from my experiences and from those of other successful managers I have known. As a user experience manager, you are in a unique position to change the world of your users, and certainly to change your company. The user experience is the lever through which business is done. When it is designed poorly, everything and everyone may suffer. Done well, the return can be tremendous. The user experience manager is the person who — while often unsung — is the hero of the story of much business success, as those businesses and organizations impact people's lives and help them achieve their goals.

This book is part memoir and part handbook; however, it is not a cookbook. It documents ideas that have worked and lessons learned from failure. It contains approaches that have been tried and their rationales. It contains personal opinions that may be controversial. It should provide a framework for new managers and leaders as they lay out a plan to achieve their goals. Hopefully it also contains a few nuggets for more experienced managers about areas not yet considered or that may be forgotten in the pressures of day-to-day work. To fill in the gaps, the best advice is the approach that led to this book — establish a network of mentors who can share experiences and perspectives as you face some of these questions throughout your career.

HINTS FROM EXPERIENCED MANAGERS

Leadership is not granted with a management title. You still need to earn it. If you cannot, or, more importantly, if you do not try to earn the respect of those around you as a leader the title will not help. Likewise, getting a manager title won't make many of the cross-group, people, etc., challenges go away.

Take risks. It is very easy to get into a management track and use "the formula" to make safe decisions. While that may be the easy path to stay on to move up, it does not have impact. If you don't have impact, you are not being effective and you won't develop a fiercely loyal team.

Andy Cargile, Director of User Experience, Microsoft Hardware, Seattle, WA

- Don't forget why you are in UX. Have a point of view and learn to articulate it using the tools you have.
- Don't worry about your idea. Make it theirs. Your success is about how well your team does.
- You can have way more impact with a team of people than you can by yourself. So focus on learning how to communicate what you want as opposed to doing it yourself.

Thomas Bouchard, Design Director Office Communications Group, Microsoft Corporation, Seattle, WA

Never rule by rank. "Do it cuz I am the boss and I said so!" is the end of the road for a manager.

Robert M. Schumacher, PhD, Managing Director, User Centric, Inc., Oakbrook Terrace, IL

Sometimes you need to learn to "under share." It is a challenge to develop a "need to know only" communications style.

Luke Kowalski, Vice President, Corporate Architecture Group, Oracle

---

INTENDED AUDIENCE

The audience for this book includes anyone who is leading or managing user experience groups or who may want to lead in the future. People involved in creating user experiences may wear many titles (as shown in Figure 1.2). They share the

	Communication Design Communicating the Value Proposition		Product Design Creating the Value Proposition	
Analogue Medium	Product Marketing Managers Brand Strategists	Business Strategists Publishers		Product Managers
	Program Marketing Specialists Marketing Research Specialists	User Researchers Publication Designers		
	Media Planners Writers Packaging Design Specialists	Retail Environment Designers		Industrial Designers
	Illustrators Photographers			
Digital Medium	Advertising Art Directors Graphic Designers Information Designers	User Interface Designers		Software Designers
	Animators Filmmakers Sound Engineers Interaction Designers			Software Engineers
	Audio Musics Composers Usability Researchers Information Architects			O/S Specialists
	Direct Marketing Specialists Broadcast Designers Game Designers Database Specialists			Hardware Engineers
	Audience Development Specialists Content Management Specialist			System Architects

FIGURE 1.2

User experience skills (Mok, 2000).

responsibility, however, for designing the experiences people have with hardware and software systems and products.

In the early 1980s, people working on creating user experiences were typically known as human factors professionals. They often became affiliated with a group known as the Human Factors Society. Reflecting the changing times and a more global perspective, in 1992 the Society changed its name to the Human Factors and Ergonomics Society (HFES, 2010). The Board of Certification in Professional Ergonomics that certifies people in the field offered alternative titles for the certification; you could either be a Certified Professional Ergonomist or a Certified Human Factors Professional. Recently, however, the board has introduced a third alternative, the Certified User Experience Professional.

ACM SIGCHI (Association for Computing Machinery Special Interest Group on Computer Human Interaction) was formed in 1982 to serve the needs of those specializing in computing systems (Grudin, 2005), and subsequently the UPA (Usability Professionals' Association) was formed in 1991 for usability professionals. To create a user experience, however, requires a variety of skills. When UX work is discussed, people are typically thinking of designers and user researchers, but writers and editors also are critical to creating great experiences. The field may also involve specialists in interface development and testing, producers, and others. Even within each area there are specialist skills (summarized nicely in Figure 1.2, which was created by Clement Mok, 2000, and published in *Gain*). This book is intended to be useful for leads and managers of teams made of any combination of these skills and titles, but the focus is on the general challenges posed by teams designing user experiences.

This book is not filled with generic management advice. There are many books published regularly on how to be an effective manager. This is a book about the specific issues associated with managing the diversity of UX skills, typically in corporations that have a largely engineering culture. Managing UX teams brings unique challenges. The process of creating great user experiences involves working with both business and engineering. It requires partnering with engineering, and the kind of rigor associated with many development processes and the engineering culture is often at odds with what may appear to be more art than science, the apparent ambiguity in dealing with human feelings and needs, and the uncertainty of the creative process. Many of the challenges faced by UX managers involve creating a vibrant and effective design environment and enabling it to function within an engineering culture. It often involves working with personalities that chose a creative and user-centered path, rather than a more technical path, and yet serving as a bridge to support effective collaboration across the different cultures.

In addition, this book is not a how-to book of UX work. There will be some discussion of process, and how to sell the concepts of UX and deal with the politics as well as other topics, but again there are many excellent books that concentrate on the individual topics of practicing as a UX professional. The focus here will be on what it means to lead a UX team and the management issues faced in that position.

Two questions that you may be asking are: "Do I need to be a UX person myself?" "Do I need to have a degree in design or HCI or a related discipline?" The answer is generally no, but there are a few caveats. Most of what is described throughout this book does not require a formal background in any of the various aspects of UX. My formal training, after all, is in chemistry and psychology. There are talented designers working for me whose educational background is computer science and brilliant researchers who entered the field from business, counseling, and other areas; all could be effective managers. There are strong managers of UX who came from project management. One of the most effective evangelists and thinkers about UX topics in Microsoft's IT organization who managed a UX team and led virtual teams on user experience topics came from field sales and support.

UX professionals do best when they feel their manager understands what they do, and can evaluate their work fairly. They often want a manager from whom they can learn more about user experience and who can contribute to the quality of their work. In general, they want to work for a manager who understands their job and advocates for it effectively and passionately. When they feel they are misunderstood, these professionals will complain they are assigned to tasks they do not particularly want to do and/or that do not make the best use of their skills. At other times, as individuals they may indeed be successful in turning their boss into a champion, but in some cases it is clear that they are rewarded more highly than user experience professionals at the same level but who report to a manager who understands their work. At some point individuals who complain are likely to run into difficulties when they try to move into another job.

Since even those trained in different areas of UX generally do not excel in every part of the user experience profession, it is clear that the knowledge and experience needed is not necessarily identical to the deep knowledge acquired by individual members of the team. Indeed, even trained UX managers are trying to hire people who are better than themselves. You should show up with passion for the user experience, and articulate an effective vision. If you are coming into the field to manage UX your goal should be to grow your own design thinking skills. Growth will come from creating a personal training program through reading, formal training, immersing yourself in the world of UX, and mentoring and coaching from professionals in the area. You will be rolling up your sleeves and taking on UX jobs, getting critiqued, and seeing the feedback of your work as it goes into practice. You will learn by doing.

Finally, one excellent point that Dan Rosenberg (2007) made is "There are no 'one-size-fits-all' recommendations that can be made, because every management situation varies by company culture, product domain, competitive market place, and international location."

NAVIGATING THE BOOK

This book gives you plenty to think about on your first day, whether you are sitting by yourself and planning on how you will build a team or whether you have inherited a team and have to make the best of it. It will also give you ideas about day two, day three, and beyond. It lays out some of the major topic areas that unfold over time. It also covers the situation when a manager is brought in to run an existing team and has ideas for running a virtual team.

Chapter 2 will cover one of the most important things you will do as a manager, hiring, and the rarer events of firing and downsizing. It will help you think about the combination of skills you want on your team and the structure of the team you are building whether it is a new team or whether it represents where you want to take your existing team. A common question that senior managers ask a prospective manager is, "What kind of team will you need?" Over time, issues come up about how you should structure the team and about how it will be funded. In fact, these issues are likely to come up over and over again. Many of these are covered in Chapter 3. There are practical questions about where your team should sit physically and organizationally. You will need to fight to get the resources your team will need to be productive, and these needs often will seem quite foreign given the experience of the engineering team in which you are operating (Chapter 4).

Once you have a team, the goal is to provide the leadership that drives the change you want to make happen. This is covered in Chapters 5 to 7. You will need to help your team to be as effective as possible by:

- Defining a strategic framework with a vision, mission, and elevator pitch.
- Creating team identity and identifying and shaping the values your team will share.

- Growing the team as individuals, as well as helping it grow as a team.
- Dealing with conflict within the team.
- Balancing work and personal life for your team and for yourself.

Chapters 8 and 9 address transforming the organization. A foundation for this transformation is the return on investment narrative that emerges from your strategic framework. The goal is not to defend; the goal is to drive your organization or company to higher levels of UX maturity. An approach to transforming an organizational culture is shared along with hints drawn from successful experiences and the periodic failures.

While I have had a broad range of management experience throughout my career, the experiences have not been exhaustive. The survey used to obtain the questions common to new managers and questions that experienced managers thought were important was also used to identify experts in management areas that I may not have experienced firsthand. These managers include those running consulting companies, UX senior executives, managers of international and globally distributed teams, and experts in specific UX management topics as well as others. Essays, case studies, and hints from these experts are distributed throughout this book. Research, articles, and books by many of the experts are referenced as well.

1.1 HIGHLIGHTS FROM THE 2010 SIGCHI PANEL "MANAGING USER EXPERIENCE — MANAGING CHANGE"

By Carola Fellenz, Thompson Senior Director of User Experience, Mindjet

For the CHI 2010 conference, I assembled a panel of successful UX managers to talk about their work. The topics we covered included working with adjacent domains, collaboration, positioning user experience, and innovation. The panel was called Managing User Experience — Managing Change, and the panelists included Irene Au, Director of User Experience at Google; Catherine Courage, Vice President of User Experience at Citrix; Nida Zada, Director of User Experience at Plaxo/Comcast (Social Media Technology); and Arnie Lund, Director of User Experience of Microsoft IT. I've captured some of the highlights of the panel, but I encourage you to see the full recording of the panel at http://tinyurl.com/chi2010mgmtpanel.

Crashing Into Adjacent Domains

Development teams are adopting Agile methodologies where user stories sound a lot like the user scenarios in user-centered design. We've seen books like the recent *Tuned In* from Pragmatic Marketing, advocating an approach similar to user-centered design but defined in marketing terms. What implications does this have for our work?

From her experience at Salesforce.com Catherine sees the introduction of Agile as a good thing for user experience. The increased focus on the customer and the user experience is a big benefit. The challenge lies in the fact that things are moving a lot faster, making it difficult to do holistic design. For smaller projects, fast iteration on design with embedded testing works, whereas for bigger projects you need to work a sprint or two ahead of the team to ensure cohesive design. Irene Au said this so perfectly:

The more the company and stakeholders care about the users and user experience, the easier my job becomes because then we don't have to evangelize and talk about why it is important and why you should care. Everybody already cares. So then we can just get on with creating great products.

Google has made a significant investment in teaching engineers and product managers design so they buy into the process more. They teach a course to all new hires called *Life of a User* to encourage empathy for the end user as well as courses in design and prototyping.

With regard to engaging adjacent domains, Irene makes the point that one size does not fit all. At Yahoo!, her lever to build empathy for the user and ultimately demand for her team's services was the usability lab. Lots of people were designing prototypes, but they had never seen real users interact with their designs. She first "up sold" them to research user needs earlier in the process, and then she finally "up sold" design skills and design thinking. Since Google already had an established culture with a focus on users, her hook there was to help engineers realize their design ideas by offering design and prototyping services. She adapted her approach to the company culture and needs.

Collaboration

Another trend we are seeing in the business press is in the area of collaboration and how critical collaboration is for the success of teams. Nilofer Merchant and Morten Hansen have both written books on the subject. Engaging effectively with adjacent domains is a form of collaboration, but there is something else that comes to light as we talk about the UX team's role in cross-functional collaboration.

Arnie notes that at Microsoft collaboration is an identified corporate value, but how an individual's contributions are recognized often works against this value. A key value that his team brings to the table is facilitating collaboration between functions.

When Catherine started at Citrix she introduced cross-functional kick-off meetings. These meetings brought people together from all over the world to a single location to meet face to face and involved everyone on the team from day one. She observed that these face-to-face workshops had a positive effect on collaboration that went beyond the workshop. Conference calls where everyone was once silent turned into working meetings where real issues were addressed.

Nida capped off the discussion on collaboration with a great quote:

Design isn't any fun if you don't collaborate.

Given the increased importance placed on collaboration by businesses, UX seems uniquely positioned to help businesses achieve a higher degree of success.

Positioning UX and Getting Recognition

User Experience Design is different from other design professions. Unlike design for visual communication or architecture, we don't have annuals and don't typically receive recognition for our work from awards. Instead, we receive our recognition from the companies we work for and our users directly. This difference has implications for our models of design practice in how we measure success and get credit for the work we do.

Arnie suggests that UX should be positioned in terms of the value the team can deliver and that it's important to find out what is important to the company and articulate UX value in that context.

Irene said that she isn't worried about getting credit. Executives know that the results these teams are getting wouldn't be possible without UX. As a manager, she has to work on ensuring team effectiveness. Sometimes work practices can get in the way. If people are happy and engaged and working effectively as a team, good things happen for the products they are working on.

Innovation and Design Strategy

We are seeing an emphasis put on design in Business Schools, especially those focused on innovation and strategy. Are we seeing more innovation being driven by design groups?

Catherine's team would like to be involved in more strategic, longer term projects, but the challenge is that her team gets pulled off onto the near-term tactical projects. The rest of the panelists echoed this.

Irene noted that just like user experience, innovation is inherently collaborative. By bringing together a cross-functional team with different perspectives you can create something that has never been done before. You also have the added benefit that everyone has bought in since they participated. Creating a separate group for innovation isn't as effective for a high rate of innovation as building it into the daily work practices of teams.

Arnie advocated doing deep ethnographic work to inspire innovation. Involving the entire cross-functional team in the research as well as the synthesis and design enables them to create a compelling vision that has a natural gravity that everyone snaps to. User scenarios are a powerful tool for communicating product vision.

Arnie also reminded us that the ideas generated are intellectual property. By filing patents on the ideas we generate, we show the value of UX.

Building the Team

2

HIRING

I have hired a lot of people, but still remember the start of my career each time I talk to a candidate. When I finished graduate school and went through the interview process at Bell Laboratories, I experienced all the emotions a new graduate would have with the chance to join the most prestigious corporate research organization in the world. After all the preparation and interviews in New Jersey at the incredibly impressive Holmdel site (there is a water tower designed to represent a giant transistor), all the pressure and anticipation of their decision had built to a boiling point. I remember my wife and I were in the graduate student housing where we lived in Evanston, IL. It was one of those old brownstones, with lathe and plaster and hardwood, and a slightly aging musty smell. One night the phone rang; it was Bell Labs. They congratulated me on a successful interview and made a salary offer. The offer was about two to three times what I had been expecting from the academic jobs I was considering. I was so overwhelmed; I choked a little and was shocked into silence. I think they thought I was disappointed and said something like "Wait, wait, I think we can do a little better." They immediately came back with another few thousand more. As you can guess, I immediately accepted and we went out for an excellent dinner!

Identifying the Skills Needed

When building a team there are four things you want to achieve:

- Getting the right skills to accomplish the charter of the team
- Creating diversity within the team
- Pulling a team together that has at its core a spark, an energy around making things happen
- Hiring people who are great collaborators

Each person on the team does not need to have identical skills. To ensure the most creative diversity team members should have different collections of skills. This means you are putting together a portfolio of skills. The choices you make about new skills, experiences, and styles you are adding are determined by the skills, experiences, and styles that already exist.

Diversity is important not only because it is the right thing, but because it is at the heart of building a creative team and baking innovation into everything the team does. The literature is full of research that demonstrates the power of diversity in driving creativity. For a UX team it is especially important as it brings with it a richer set of perspectives for understanding your users, for relating to the diversity of people you are collaborating with across the business (and for solving collaboration issues when they arise), and to enliven the design process. This diversity includes skills and experiences, race, cultures and gender, disabilities, sexual orientation, age, new hires, senior people, and more.

Coupled with collaboration skills, the healthy give and take from different perspectives and backgrounds also contributes to the energy of the team. I have found the more diverse the team the more fun we tend to have. Each person should have a can-do attitude, curiosity and imagination, and the willingness to be ready for any challenges faced by the team. Team members should be able to put together a point of view and move it forward. They should be willing to grow and take coaching. Each member may express it in different ways. Some will be quieter and some more outgoing and some will bring different cultural backgrounds and personal styles to the table; ideally each member will have an energy that adds to the whole. With this energy and diversity, however, there will inevitably be some tension. It is important to turn it into creative tension and make it work for the team so people are able to work collaboratively and have the greatest impact.

A colleague from Microsoft's office in Israel visited and asked what skills they should look for if they could only hire one person. Who should be first in after the manager (especially if the manager is not a UX person)? A good choice is an interaction designer since this position is typically a "tweener," spanning both design and user research. Interaction designers usually come out of human-computer interaction (HCI) or human factors programs, can prototype, can create interaction design and basic wire framing, may be able to do reasonable visual design, and can perform user research to validate and shape the designs if needed. The most important driver of user satisfaction is usefulness, which is largely reflected in the interaction design.

The interaction design has to be incorporated at the deepest level of the software architecture and it is often the most expensive to change late in the process.

The biggest demand from development teams is for visual design. Many developers would prefer to do something other than design, although there is an ongoing conflict with developers who believe their sense of design is equal to that of experienced designers. However, in order to deliver value to users and the business and to get the interaction design right, it is important to have user research skills on the team. Engaging users in the design process, centering design on scenarios coming from the users, exposing engineering teams to the users, getting feedback on designs throughout the process, and other activities of a user researcher are terrific sources for demonstrating the value of UX work. Interaction designers are often capable of both design and research skills, but if they are not or if the demand far exceeds their ability to deliver in both areas, adding a user researcher could be worthwhile. Figure 2.1 contains a sample job description for a researcher.

Once the team has interaction design and user research skills, then typically great visual design skills are needed (see Figure 2.2 for a sample job description). It is the visual design that makes the user experience work the most visible. In the early 1990s visual design became important to successful software products, moving it from a luxury to the necessity it is today. As the Internet started to be widely adopted, the design bar moved higher and people began expecting an aesthetically pleasing experience along with functional value. A great product designer can drive people's emotions and trigger a WOW! Research has shown that great design builds user trust and triggers expectations of ease of use and value. Coupled with the interaction designer building in the value and the user researcher who can identify changes needed in the design to enhance usability, the visual designer brings the design over the finish line. The visual design carries the branding for the team's value, and a great designer is typically recognized by everyone as having skills that the developers do not have. Creative visual designers enhance the skills of the interaction designer and the researcher as well. They help everyone communicate their ideas in a more compelling way and are a unique source of innovation in how the interaction design is implemented.

Beyond the basics, it can make sense to grow the number of visual designers faster than the interaction designers and user researchers (since they move between each other's roles and support several visual designers). Some teams try to match researchers and designers 1 to 1, but for many teams 1 researcher for every 2 designers seems to be good ratio. Corporate cultures differ in whether they try to keep design and research roles separate, and the degree to which they differentiate specialists within the skills. In practice it is possible to find both specialists and generalists, and academic programs are producing both.

Figure 1.2, created by Clement Mok (2000) and shown in Chapter 1, illustrates many of the skills and job titles in the user experience discipline. Design includes the interaction and visual designers that have been discussed, information architects, graphic designers, art directors, industrial designers, ergonomists and human

---

Researcher

Microsoft IT UX is seeking an experienced user researcher with a broad range of research and modeling skills, and an ability to provide leadership in creating a deep understanding of users and how we can build relationships with them. We want someone who can partner with designers and content publishing professionals to create compelling, valuable experiences, experiences that drive the "wow" we want in every user touch-point. You will help achieve the right balance of user, technology, and business/market needs, and drive insights that lead to design innovation and transforming the relationship Microsoft has with its customers and our ability to bring them value. You will bring insights and leverage your skills to help shape business and product strategy and planning, informing business decisions, as well as shaping the user centered design approach for design and user research activities within IT. You will be engaging a variety of audiences and cross-functional groups as you stimulate collaboration, communication, and impact. Additional responsibilities can include user research, design standards definition, solutions that inform business requirements, innovation, and prototyping; and managing projects and people to provide these functions. The potential impact of these efforts, as you can imagine, is huge for Microsoft and its customers. Clearly we need someone with the vision, skills and intelligence to influence experiences that will touch nearly every Microsoft customer around the world.

Qualifications include:

- Three or more years of work in the area of user experience, especially usability research.
- Project/product management experience is highly desirable, as is experience in field research and guidelines development.
- Minimum of a Master's degree in a social science area (e.g., HCI, cognitive psychology, etc.) or equivalent.
- A solid knowledge of HCI principles and methods with related applied professional experience is desired.
- Thorough knowledge of user research methods and techniques, including strong research design (ideally both qualitative and quantitative), data analysis, and results interpretation and modeling, inferential statistics, site visits, interviews, card sorts, focus groups, user flows, user profiling and task analysis; and has demonstrated an ability to apply and adapt the appropriate method to specific development stages and design questions.
- Required experience includes developing and managing studies from writing the research protocol for an individual study through the final written report with prioritized recommendations and delivering impact for diverse audiences and stake-holders.
- Proven experience influencing product designs and direction based on customer needs. Be prepared to share examples of research that demonstrates this influence.

FIGURE 2.1

Example research job description.

factors professionals, brand specialists, producers, audio designers, experience architects, and others. Researchers include specialists in usability, quantitative research, statisticians, ethnographers, market researchers, and more. The particular mix of skills that you add to a team depends on the focus of your organization, your strategy, the size of your organization, and the demand for its services.

Technical writing and editing of the text within the interface is often overlooked when thinking about staffing a UX team. This is distinctly different from the writing

Designer

Microsoft IT UX is looking for a highly creative conceptual designer to play a strategic role in helping us define, design, and develop innovative user experiences. This role requires a multi-disciplinary skill set including the ability to understand and synthesize broad business goals, product and technical content, visual and interaction design, and brand strategy to create engaging personalized experiences for our users.

Microsoft IT UX is establishing a creative culture and production framework for sustained design innovation. A qualified candidate should be able to present a body of work that demonstrates a passion for experience design. They should have a sense of urgency and energy to explore and expand the boundaries of design as they solve complex communication and interaction problems. The successful candid will exhibit strategic breadth, attention to detail, and a sense of aesthetics, innovation and usability. They will be able to show experience with diverse content messaging intended to support key business goals and they will be able to illustrate a deep understanding of user flow and user behavior as it relates to design. A qualified candidate must share our belief that design is as much about behavior and emotion as it is about utility and ease of use.

A Bachelor's degree is required. An advanced degree in graphic design, interface, information, interaction design, design planning, communications, marketing, humanities, social sciences (Anthropology, Sociology, Psychology, Linguistics), or human-centered design is preferred. Significant relevant work experience in any of the above areas may substitute for an advanced degree.

Other qualifications include:

* Minimum 3–5 years of related work experience.
* A compelling portfolio of past design work.
* Demonstrated understanding of how substantial business value can be delivered via innovative design solutions.
* Leadership ability in design and solution development with expertise in many of the areas listed above.
* Experience in managing several projects simultaneously.
* Strong prototyping skills are required.
* Excellent problem-framing skills and diagrammatic sensibility with a strong orientation toward "modeling." Visualization skills or the ability to leverage design resources to visually articulate models will be important.
* Excellent verbal and written skills.
* Strong sense of process and the ability to innovate in process, tools and conventions.
* Ability to work collaboratively on multi-disciplinary teams critical.
* A demonstrated commitment to mentor and share knowledge across the team and company-wide is a plus.

FIGURE 2.2

Example design job description.

HINTS FROM EXPERIENCED MANAGERS

Don't hire people who are exactly like you. You'll be tempted to because you'll feel like you can understand them better. But, you really want to hire people who have strengths that mirror your weaknesses and have weaknesses where you have strengths. The team will be stronger because you have balanced out their skills and expertise with yours.

Julie Jensen, Principal User Research Manager, Microsoft, Redmond, WA and editing of marketing content, because it focuses on the embedded assistance in the design and the discoverability that it supports. Everyone has seen examples of poor content writing and editing. A recent design my team was trying to salvage began with prompts and explanatory text that developers wrote as they produced the interface, was modified by marketing people who wanted to make sure all the right words were included that would convince people to buy more products, and then was extended by lawyers who wanted to make sure that every possible liability was covered. The resulting design was virtually unusable. Designers and researchers can often write well, but they are not the word masters that a good technical writer and editor would be. Occasionally there will be successful writing from designers and researchers, but there is no substitute for a professional and specialists in the technical writing field are very good at what they do. If you cannot have content people on the team, ideally you should try to have access to them. As your UX team grows beyond the size of a group, the importance of having these specialists grows.

For larger teams it can make sense to start growing specialists in key areas that can work across projects. A critical specialist is an expert in accessibility. Obviously everyone should have this issue close to their hearts and built into their toolbox of skills, but practically speaking I have noticed that this works best when there is one person who is really passionate about it and works as an evangelist across the team. Similarly for products that will be deployed globally, having someone who is a passionate expert on globalization and localization can bring tremendous benefits. As the team grows, and as you start to have a group of researchers and research that happens on an ongoing basis, having a technical support team member or access to technical support for the user research lab, design and research tools becomes important to ensure that the team can be maximally productive and not waste their time on overhead activities. You may need someone just to handle the recruiting of people for user testing, gratuities, and to maintain the database that tracks who has already been tested. Beyond that, building out interface development and prototyping skills, the skills of an experience producer or equivalent, and market research skills can enable various strategies. Past teams I have managed have included writers and developers specializing in producing software development kit (SDK) content for the design patterns and code samples we were creating, and Web developers working on our team site and interfaces to our guidelines. One colleague had ontologists on his team who were helping create a particular user support experience.

An alternative to growing a user experience team that owns most or all of the interaction design is to grow a team whose strategy in part is to scale up by enabling others to produce effective experiences. The way to do this is to grow the design skills of everyone involved in the user interface (UI). The goal is to create a virtual UI team with shared responsibility for the user experience. Andreas Hauser (2007) described this well in the article "UCD Collaboration with Product Management and Development." The argument is that the user experience team helps bridge the relationship between product management and development by representing the user's task-specific requirements, providing design leadership, creating process controls, and educating others to perform key tasks needed for the design and development of the interface. Hauser argued that in one view of the ideal model

> … product managers with direct user research data and deep domain knowledge create accurate use cases that describe the user requirements. Then UX specialists transfer these requirements into superior UI designs that meet a full range of additional corporate requirements for suite behavioral consistency, corporate look and feel, and accessibility. In addition, they do the necessary validation activities with users of these designs.

Some companies are beginning to grow project managers who specialize in the user experience area. At times they are called producers and their role is to clear the way for the UX work and support it, to amplify the impact of the designers, and to work through the technical issues necessary to deliver on many of the user requirements. In one product group these specialized project managers are responsible for much of the scenario definition and interaction design, and they work closely with the user researchers as the interaction is defined. The project managers also reach out to the visual designers to implement their designs in a consistent and compelling way.

Some want to create developers who are generalists that can be shifted from project to project as needed. It can be effective to create UI developers who understand the technologies needed to create great user interfaces and who are experienced in working with designers. This is especially true as more and more tools are created that blur the lines between design and development. Testing is one of the final links in the chain. Like user experience professionals, testers also want to get involved earlier and be treated as partners and collaboratively create test plans. If UX and testers work together on test cases that appropriately reflect the targeted users and the top priority scenarios, better experiences will result. To grow each of these disciplines involves rethinking traditional roles and responsibilities, relinquishing control of some tasks that UX might otherwise take on, and training and mentoring the members of the virtual UI design team.

The Myers-Briggs method of characterizing differences among people is commonly used in companies as another way to describe the diversity of people on teams, and both the challenges and virtues arising from that diversity. Some leadership training courses recognize that personal styles differ between normal and conflict situations. Another way of looking at the diversity that can be designed into teams through hiring is to focus on problem-solving styles (Basadur, 2004; Basadur & Gelade, 2003). Much of what UX people do is problem solving. In this scheme, there are innovators, conceptualizers, optimizers, and implementers. Innovators love to come up with new ideas. Conceptualizers are about looking at diverse data and make sense out of it. Optimizers like to put things together in a way that drives efficiency (and they are typically the people who look at a large spreadsheet and immediately see the numbers that do not fit). Implementers ensure projects get done and are excellent at creating and driving plans.

User experience people tend to fall mostly into the innovator and conceptualizer categories, while many engineers are optimizers and implementers. It is not too surprising then when misunderstandings between people in different roles occur, since each person has different goals and values. To get a project done and for a team to collaborate most effectively, you would like to have team members in each of these categories. Most people have a preferred style of problem solving but have some skills in the other styles as well. One thing Basadur noted is that people can move into different areas depending on situational needs.

As your organization grows you will need to start hiring leads, managers, and perhaps even managers of managers. Here the focus is on many of the topics being discussed throughout this book. At this point you are looking for leadership and the ability to attract a following. Look for strategic thinking. Project management and experience leading teams will be important. The ability to communicate effectively is essential when selling ideas and negotiating to overcome conflict. Much of what you are looking for in individual contributors in the soft skills area becomes the hard skills for leads and managers.

Interviewing

At many companies, the process begins with an approval to hire and enter the job opening into a system that tracks personnel. Often there is an administrative assistant in the organization who serves as the interface to the personnel system. Entering the job opening into the system triggers a variety of business processes that support bringing the person hired on board.

This process begins with writing a job description. The job description typically contains a high-level description of the role with text that gets people excited about the job and motivates them to apply. While you want to entice the right people to apply, you still want people who are not going to be a match to realize they clearly will not make it through the process or eventually discover the job does not match their interests. You want to catch people's interest but you do not want to deceive them. The job description also includes the job requirements (both the requirements that must be met and those that it would be nice for the candidate to meet). These requirements need to be verifiable and linked to successful performance, and avoid subjective characteristics. Cheerfulness, for example, would not be a good requirement. Figures 2.1 and 2.2 are examples of two job descriptions I have used before.

Part of the challenge is that many companies have career ladders where the specific responsibilities vary by level. As a hiring manager, you may have some leeway in the level for which you are hiring so the job description may need to be flexible. There are roughly four categories: entry-level people, experienced early-career people, senior people who are hired in part for their leadership abilities, and very senior people. Beyond entry level, job descriptions differ between individual contributor roles, leadership roles, and roles that require a mixture of the two.

Hiring regulations have caused some companies to require applicants to go through the corporate Web site, and for the first contact to be handled by recruiters (either internal or external) who can assure the process is unbiased. The recruiters are likely to want a subset of the requirements from your job description so they can filter resumes and so they can use them during the initial phone interview. If you have employed a headhunter, they will share your job description with candidates they are recruiting on your behalf. If you or your recruiters are finding candidates at conferences and through various job boards and sites frequented by UX people, your job description will serve as the basis for posters used at job sites. Know that UX professionals are a community, and chances are your job description will be forwarded far and wide.

Dealing with recruiters in the Human Resources Department (HR) can be quite frustrating for many managers. The process they use to recruit engineers might not be as effective when recruiting UX candidates. UX professionals may come from a wider variety of backgrounds and schools, and are often evaluated based on portfolios and criteria that may not be as important for, say, developers. It helps if you can get a recruiter dedicated to recruiting UX people. You can then invest the time to educate that recruiter about UX, what it is about, and the skills needed to effectively do the job. Recruiters may be able to join you at key conferences, where they should ideally attend a few of the sessions. As recruiters attend UX conferences and meet a variety of people in the field they can develop a better sense of what makes an effective candidate. A dedicated recruiter can also begin to build a list of relationships with potential candidates that they can leverage over time to either hire senior people who might become available or to leverage for networking to find other candidates.

Working with recruiters to better help them understand the requirements built into the job description is very important. They in turn will help you understand what they can reasonably screen for as they go through resumes, do phone interviews, and meet people at conferences and universities. Recruiting is a long-term investment, and just as you want to build a reputation with the candidates, you want to build a relationship with the recruiters on which you depend. If you can get someone dedicated to your cause you can meet with them periodically to provide advice on where they can look for candidates, you can feed them names of UX professionals that they should build relationships with, and you can give them feedback on how candidates they have recruited have worked out. This investment in time also can help during the process of negotiating an offer and it supports the candid conversations that will result in the best for the candidate, for your team, and for your company.

Students will often ask what I look for in a resume. I have shared some of the attributes in Lund (2000) and through student panels on which I have served (many of which were organized by Ron Shapiro for the Human Factors and Ergonomics Society, HFES). The questions students ask these panels as they consider applying for jobs and the responses from various hiring managers are documented on the HFES site (http://64.9.213.250/Web/PubPages/career.html). Fundamentally, the goal is to match a candidate who has the skills and passion to do the job with the characteristics of the job. These characteristics consist of both the specific needs that led to the opening and the more general needs you anticipate as your team moves into the future. Hiring someone is a long-term investment, and you should be thinking about hiring for your team *and* hiring for your company. Remember that if you do your job well, the person you are hiring today may be your boss in the future. The process, therefore, is about transparency. Both you and the candidate should be confident the fit is right.

In the 1980s and 1990s in the telecommunications industry it was common for UX applicants to have PhDs and come out of cognitive psychology programs. As the software industry has grown and the variety of skills needed has increased, the diversity of the candidates has also increased. Skills may come from formal training or through experience, and some of the most interesting candidates have traveled very unexpected paths. The approach to resumes has evolved as a result. In the beginning, the review was similar to the way you might expect to review an academic curriculum vitae. Currently the review is more focused on looking for evidence that the candidate can do the job.

When I first pick up a resume I briefly look at its design. The job is for a UX person after all so the resume should have an appropriately clean and attractive design, and should guide me to the information that convinces me the person would be a match for the job. It does not need to be fancy, but it should not be poorly designed. As I read through resumes, I will be monitoring grammar, typos, and so on. Those are clues to how the person will approach their job. I look at the schools they have attended. If they have been successful at high-quality schools in programs that I respect, that will shape my initial estimate of what they know. If I do not recognize the school, that does not rule them out, but it means I will look even harder for more evidence that their practice is grounded in knowledge. If they have some form of certification that I recognize and value, that also tells me more about what they know and about their attitude. For new graduates I look for internship experiences (and where they occurred), professional activities, and leadership positions held. For more experienced people, I look for what they have done and their professional accomplishments. I go through their work experiences looking for evidence of substantive contributions and its impact. I look for evidence of skills that predict how they will do in my work environment. If they have a Web site, I will look for similar evidence there. Finally, if they are a designer I go through their portfolio in detail. I want to see design that is compelling, creative, and reflects sound design principles. If they are a researcher I look for any examples of the research they have done (perhaps in conference papers or published articles). I pass the resumes of the best candidates to my team and seek their opinions. For candidates that may move to the next stage, I look for gaps to explore with their references and through the interview process.

For visual design candidates, the portfolio is a critical part of the process. When the job is about producing design, seeing the designs a candidate has produced is revealing. For designers I look at the quality of the designs they produce; I look at their aesthetic. The portfolio may be thin for new graduates, but those whose training is explicitly in visual design should have design to show. Recruiters unfamiliar with UX may neglect to ask for the portfolio, and will need to be reminded to do so.

It also serves as the basis for many of the subsequent conversations through the interview process around the designers specific contributions, their own design process, and how they think about design. Interaction designers and researchers may not have a rich portfolio given the nature of their work, but you can look at any publications or other artifacts they share and study the content they include in talks during the interview process.

Depending on your company's policies, either recruiting or management may do a phone screen with the candidate. If recruiting does the initial screen and gives the go ahead, then follow up and make your own phone call. The screens serve several goals: they provide the candidate with more visibility into the nature and requirements of the job, and they provide a better idea of what the candidate wants in a job. The screens also present an opportunity to explore the gaps in the resume and answer questions that may have arisen when talking to the candidate's references. They are also the first opportunity to evaluate the candidate's communications skills, and for the candidate to show their curiosity, creativity, and problem-solving skills.

If the phone screens are successful the next step is the face-to-face interview. Companies vary in what recruiting considers an appropriate process. Some years ago casual meetings between the team and the candidate over breakfast, lunch, and dinner were encouraged to make the candidate more comfortable and to explore the fit with the team culture. Now these seem to be more restricted because questioning about personal areas is discouraged to avoid even the appearance of discrimination, and interviewers are rightly cautioned to beware of their own stereotypes through the interview process. Unconscious biases might restrict the kind of diversity that creates a more effective team in the long run. There will be casual conversation and the candidate needs to eat, but these times are more constrained than they once were.

The interview process is an opportunity to share the culture of your team and company. You want the candidate's experience to be professional and well orchestrated from the moment arrangements are made for their visit, through the final filing of expenses and the completion of the process (whether an offer is made or not). You also want candidates who do not get hired to serve as evangelists for your team. A standard checklist with owners identified and activities tracked can be helpful in managing an effective experience while minimizing the workload. The interview experience should be designed based on the goals of the visit and the impression you wish to make with the candidates interviewed. The interview process will go smoother if both your team and the candidate are prepared. Let the candidate know how to dress, what to bring, and what to expect. Provide directions, and arrange or help arrange needed transportation ahead of time. If interviews and activities are distributed around several buildings be sure to allow time to get from one place to another and allow time for things to go wrong — as they inevitably will.

The interview day is not just about interviewing the candidate; it is about the candidate getting to know your team. For some companies, there is a formal recruiting interview at some point during the day where the boilerplate questions are asked. A good way to start is with a portfolio or a research review with those interviewing the candidate throughout the day. If you invite your entire team and a few other key stakeholders or knowledgeable people, these reviews can even serve as training. The goal is for the team to see how candidates perform in a group setting, their communication skills (especially their presentation skills), their ability to design their communication to have an impact, and for you to quiz them on their design or research process (simulating what might happen when they present to a project team). It also saves the interviewers from having to cover the same ground and provides material for deeper questions to be asked in individual interviews.

A good approach to the interviews is to have a variety of people talk to the candidate, including both members of the team and perhaps a representative or two from one of the teams with whom they might work. It can be effective to identify the skills and experiences you are looking for up front, and then have different people be prepared to focus on each of the areas based on their unique expertise. Distribute the topics so that each interviewer has their own set of questions, but ensure that for the key questions there are at least two people providing their assessments. At some companies one or more of the interviewers is responsible for evaluating the candidate not just from the perspective of the immediate opening but also determining whether the candidate would make a good company employee. A more senior person who has been part of successful hires before can provide valuable insight in this role.

Knowing that as the interviews proceed new questions can arise and other questions may not be completely answered, arrange for communication between interviewers throughout the day. If you can get the interviewers to agree, a very effective technique is for each interviewer to e-mail a quick summary of what they learned and questions they believe still need to be answered and send it to the other interviewers. Some companies have arranged the process so that if it becomes clear the candidate is not a match, the process can be terminated early. If this happens, the candidate will not meet with all of the interviewers. The candidate will need to be prepared to be flexible and should know the interview schedule is subject to change.

As the hiring manager, you should finish the interview day. This is the place to ask any remaining questions and answer any questions candidates have at the end of the process, as well as lay out the next steps. The final discussion is a good time to sell the team and company as well. If you believe the person is a match then this is a key point to win them over, and even if you feel there is no match then it is an opportunity to ensure they leave with a great impression of your team.

Some companies have a defined set of competencies that employees work on growing and that are leveraged throughout the interview process. These are defined by the HR organization, and if your company has something similar it is a good place to start when designing an interview process. The skills behind the competencies are common across many companies, and common questions that are explored depending on the candidate and the job requirements often include:

- How well do they communicate (verbally and in the written word)?
- How do they handle their responsibilities? What is their commitment to quality?

- How effectively do they work with other disciplines or people with different skill sets?
- Where are they in growing their leadership skills?
- How do they think? This is often explored with a design or research problem, and by reviewing their problem-solving skills.
- What skills do they have? What tools do they use?
- What are their weaknesses? How do they work around their weaknesses?
- What process do they use to ensure consistent creativity and excellence?
- How self-aware are they?
- How quickly do they learn new things? What are they learning now? What do they want to learn?
- How do they overcome challenges to collaborate effectively?
- What brings them joy? What do they want to achieve? Why?
- Are they curious?

More recently candidates are reporting that they are given "take home" problems to submit before interviewing. Other companies require designers to solve design problems during the interview process or to design a research study. There are teams that ask candidates to solve problems the team is currently facing, and others that use hypothetical problems. Some companies use team interviewing. The press has covered companies that use "impossible problems" (e.g., How many utility covers are there in the United States?) to test candidate creativity or reasoning ability. Still others have used formal tests. I personally have not seen these techniques yield better results than rich interviews and portfolio reviews, and the end results strike me as not recognizing that people may have very diverse styles and yet still be highly effective. These artificial situations seem less like simulations of real work environments and more like selecting people for colleges based on their standardized test-taking abilities. The interview process needs to be more nuanced to create a team with the greatest creative and effective diversity.

If the candidate looks promising, I try to connect with their references to see if I can get more real-world confirmation about what the candidate is actually like to work with on a day-to-day basis. One thing you cannot get from the resume or even the interviews is how a candidate collaborates. Be realistic about what information you can get from a phone screen with a reference. Clearly the candidate's references were chosen because they will say good things about the person, but I have found in talking with them I can usually get behind the "he/she is great" comments. From the resume I can often also find people who have known the person when they were at school, at previous jobs, or professionally. UX is a relatively small community and there are usually only a few degrees of separation between any of us. Those who have made favorable impressions as they have moved through their careers (however short) are those that have the kinds of skills I am looking for on my teams. Internal candidates allow you to connect with previous managers and have a more candid conversation about a candidate's strengths and weaknesses.

If the candidate has made it through all of these screens, the next step is to work with the recruiter or other appropriate HR person to put together an offer. You will want to be competitive, but you do not want to set the candidate up for frustration or even worse, failure, by bringing them in at a level or salary that is too high. It is better for them to move up quickly than to come in and stagnate in the career and salary ladder.

Finding Great People

The best way to find great people is to get great people to find you. If you already are an excellent manager and people know it, your reputation will bring people to you. People who have worked for you will want to work for you again, and they will tell others about you. If you let them know you are hiring, they will actively recruit for you. Similarly, having an ongoing professional presence where you demonstrate the quality of the work your team is doing, the impact you are having, and the excitement your team feels about their work environment serve to lay a foundation for future recruiting. I almost never return from a conference without a pile of cards or resumes in my briefcase. The most effective recruiting often starts well before you have an opening; it starts as you build relationships with potential job candidates and with influencers who will evangelize on your behalf.

Large companies often have an internal site for posting jobs. There is some pain in losing good people to internal movement, but it is often exactly the right thing for their own development and is beneficial to UX departments within companies. New ideas and best practices are brought to your team, even as your best practices have a broader impact across the company. Movement within the community allows teams to flex their size based on local need without the company losing great talent. It also creates an internal network that can be leveraged when you are looking for special skills, and gives you a natural way to discover background information on people interested in joining your team. Beware of getting a reputation as a raider. It is one thing to reach out to peers to see if they have people on their teams who might benefit from moving to your job or to publicize your job to those seeking a change, but it is quite another to be seen as poaching. The Golden Rule is a good one to apply when recruiting within your corporate community.

As mentioned, your job description should appear on the external-facing corporate career site. It is worth checking how it appears and running through the scenario of a UX person looking for your job. Some companies do not include the UX tags that job applicants look for in their site search or navigation architectures. Also make sure recruiters are actively scanning the resumes that arrive in response to your job description, and see if you can review resumes coming in for other UX jobs sibling groups have posted on the site. You may be able to negotiate to achieve the best match of candidate to job, and even have a candidate come in and interview with a couple of groups at the same time. You and the other hiring manager can then agree on a process for resolving the situation when you both want to make an offer.

Other opportunities to expose your job to potential candidates include:

- Leveraging corporate recruiters
- Unleashing the headhunters (if allowed and budgeted by your organization, since headhunter fees can be quite significant)
- Posting the job on discipline job boards (e.g., the HFES and the Board of Certification in Professional Ergonomics [BCPE] jobs databases, society Web sites, the HFES Technical Group sites, and local chapters of professional societies)
- Publicizing the job through professionals known for sharing available jobs
- Asking colleagues and former employees to help look for great candidates
- Encouraging your team to reach out to their networks of friends (and don't be afraid to be creative and try things like recruiting contests)
- Leveraging LinkedIn and other social networking services
- Participating in college recruiting activities
- Posting the job at professional conferences or setting up a recruiting booth at the conferences
- Participating in conference activities for students where you can talk about your job
- Encouraging members of your team to present at conferences and to share openings

One recent change is that corporations are working very hard to ensure that every candidate is treated equally. That means while it is okay to stimulate people to enter the pipeline or to encourage people to apply for jobs that might be a good fit for them, you have to be very careful about what is said, not to promise anything, and to make sure the candidates enter the formal recruiting process (through the corporate recruiting site). Recruiting then applies standard filters to the people in the pipeline to find the ones that match the job you have defined. It is very important, therefore, to work closely with the recruiters to make sure the attributes you are recruiting for are very clearly and objectively defined, and to identify where you have flexibility in the parameters. Companies differ as to whether you have the ability to interview two or three applicants and then pick the best candidate, or whether you must hire the first person you feel qualifies for the job.

When you start a team and are looking for your first employee, you are faced with a unique challenge. The team has no reputation yet — a team brand. Your personal accomplishments may be impressive, but from the outside it is not clear what your management style is like and whether your team will be successful. Joining your team may appear to be a risk for candidates. There may be an attraction for the entrepreneur who wants to be part of starting something new, but how do they know if funding might be cut next year and the team eliminated? At some level you will be bootstrapping your team up, acquiring the best people you can, and then taking advantage of growth and attrition to enhance the mix of skills and experiences on your team.

If you have come from another organization or another company, some of the great people from your previous teams may come to join you (or at least be interested in interviewing). If you can provide a compelling vision you may be able to attract a team who wants to join you specifically because of the uncertainty, the chance to build something new, and the chance to put meat on the bones of your vision. But you may also need to take a few risks and choose from candidates who might have the occasional flaw and who did not fit well with a previous team. They may have struggled in an earlier organization, perhaps because of a mismatch between their style and goals of that organization or because they are still growing in a particular area. What you need to decide in cases like that is whether or not you are betting that the apparent flaw was an aberration, or if it is a true growth area that will improve under your leadership and your particular strengths. Often the best people are most willing to strengthen their weak areas and those that most need to grow are often the most resistant to recognizing their flaws. You may also need to supplement with others who have strengths that complement the growth areas to create a complete team. At the beginning, getting the mix in balance is often the biggest challenge.

Interns

One of the things I enjoy is talking with students who are getting ready to enter their careers. The HFES conference has done an excellent job over the years in creating opportunities for students to see what directions their careers can take and giving them a hand up. Consistently the most important advice fellow panelists and I give to students is to get an internship. There is no better way for students to learn what working as a UX professional might be like; to find out if their future is in practice or teaching and research; and, if in practice, to discover the questions to ask to help ensure that the job they are considering is the right job for them.

Hire interns if you get the chance. Practically, you can often hire interns when you cannot hire anyone else. That is not always true — at some companies an intern may take a vacancy that would otherwise go to a full-time person — but generally it is. Interns are very cost-effective. They may only work for a short period of time (like a summer), but they are perfect for many of those tasks that your full-time staff does not have the time to take on.

Interns also add to the diversity of the team. They bring a lot of energy, they bring fun, and they add to the creativity. They also help take your team to another level; while the team is educating the intern they think about their own work in more general terms. Interns ask naïve questions and questions grounded in the latest research and both often cause your team to step back and re-evaluate approaches to problems. They also are future candidates for full-time positions. The internship gives you a chance to see them at work before they enter the full interview process.

When I interview interns, I look for the same kinds of characteristics that I look for in full-time people. I just do not expect their talents to be quite as developed. The interns obviously do not have the same level of training and experience, but they can have the spirit and curiosity I want more seasoned professionals to have. They will have skills they are bringing that can be applied to a meaningful problem

I would like them to address. They may not have evidence in their resume that looks as impressive as a new full-timer, but on interviewing them I often find experience that typifies the collaborative skills and the ability to take responsibility that I am seeking.

Vendors and Contractors

The needs of projects can vary, and in some organizations funding ebbs and flows quite frequently. When that happens using vendors and contractors can be an effective approach to staffing. It is relatively easy to bring them in and equally easy to reduce staffing (assuming the contracts are written properly). If a project walks in the door and needs someone right away you can create a team with vendors and contractors more quickly than if you hired full-time staff. Since such projects may be of limited duration, the staff is hired only as long as you need them. You can also add staff without adding the other infrastructure that comes with full-time people such as offices, equipment, and hardware.

If you need specialized skills (e.g., ethnographic research or high-end product design visioning), the best way to find those skills for the time that you need them is with vendors and contractors. In this case, those bringing in the specialized skills may not only be doing the work, but you should work to leverage them to transfer their skills to your full-time staff. Over time, your team should be capable of taking on these added tasks. There may be times when hiring an outside expert brings credibility to an argument you are making that might not be there if you use internal staff. There may be times when there are teams that want support and you do not have people available at the moment but want your team to have effective, professional UX support so in the future they will fund full-time support. During these times vendors or contractors should be considered. In general you want your full-time staff to do most of the interesting work, take on the big challenges, and build the intellectual capital that brings value over time. If you are focusing your full-time staff on the work that provides design leadership you may want to outsource the more routine production work to vendors and contractors.

As a manager, be careful to not treat vendors or contractors the same as you treat your full-time employees. It needs to be clear that these relationships are different. You do not want your full-time employees envying the life of the vendor or contractor. On the other hand, for effective projects you need to worry about how to ensure people are fully informed about what they need to know to do their jobs, that there is communication and collaboration, and that the contractors and vendors not only have a contractual relationship to deliver but share your personal vision for the excellence of the work. Great contractors who catch the excitement of your team and bring unique value also become potential candidates for full-time positions. As a result, you should try to bring the contractors and vendors into the right meetings to help ensure they are collaborating effectively with the team.

There can be a distinct difference between how contractors and vendors are handled. I am going to discuss this distinction to differentiate between two models used to supplement your full-time staff. The terms used at your company may vary, but the models are fairly common. Contractors may freelance or may be associated with a staffing agency. They typically are brought on when particular skills are needed for a period of time. If they are working with an agency the costs might be slightly higher since the agency will want to recoup the overhead of managing benefits, taxes, payroll, and so on. From a corporate perspective, however, it is often easier to work with an agency versus the individual, and contracts may be easier to set up with the agency. If you identify a particularly interesting freelance contractor and you run into barriers engaging them, you may be able to find an agency that they can work through. Contractors can be relatively easy to move from one project to the next as priorities change without needing to renegotiate contracts. Selecting contractors is similar to selecting full-time employees, although it does not need to be quite as extensive as it is easier to terminate a contractor if they do not meet your needs.

Vendors are usually engaged to take on specific projects. They may be pre-screened and need to be approved at the corporate level. If you want to work with a new vendor, it can take a long time to get through the screening process. For large contracts you would go through a Request for Proposal (RFP) process to find the best vendor for a given project. While your company may want you to focus on a few large, full-service vendors, UX work tends to be more specialized. Many of the largest vendors are not particularly strong in their design and user research competencies. We have identified sets of UX vendors that have strengths that we want to leverage. Some are particularly good at design innovation or generative user research (and they tend to charge the most). Some are good at production. There are firms that specialize in usability, contextual inquiry, branding, and graphic design. There are vendors with an international presence, and some capable of scaling to very large projects. There are small, low-cost vendors who are willing to be very flexible and responsive and large, more expensive vendors who bring brand-name credibility to projects. In large companies there is the opportunity to learn about the experiences others in the company have had with the vendors you are evaluating.

One thing to watch out for, especially where you have helped teams outside your organization to hire vendors or contractors, is to make sure they are aligned with your best practices and reusable assets (e.g., design guidelines). How they perform reflects on you even after they have left the project. Try to stay involved for quality oversight. Teams supported by vendors or contractors need to align with the way you do things because of how it reflects on your team and how it helps ensure consistency across experiences. For example, you may want to build compliance with your standards, guidelines, or best practices into the contracts that are created. You may also want to build opportunities for you to review or sign off on major milestones into the project plan. It may seem like using vendors and contractors will allow you to scale indefinitely, but it does take overhead to manage them if you are going to ensure quality, consistency, and client delivery. It is likely you will hire a limited number of vendors. Before deciding on how many vendors to hire, you need to anticipate the management overhead in your resource plans.

Interestingly, one of the best discussions of how to select a usability vendor is written by an usability vendor (Schaffer, 2004). Eric Schaffer, recognizing that initially you are trying to build your program, recommends leveraging usability vendors to help get your program started. He suggests:

- They can often do things that no insider can do.
- Bring in vendors early to help get your program going before you have the infrastructure and to jump-start the institutionalization process.
- There are many types, with different types and levels of expertise; you need to shop carefully.
- He says, "A good consultant [what we are calling a vendor] guides your strategy, sets up your infrastructure, helps develop your staff and internal organization, and smoothly transitions to a role that supports the internal group."

Schaffer laid out a nice set of weighted criteria for selecting a usability vendor in his book. His top criteria are the staff that will be on your project, the completeness of the solution they can offer, their domain expertise (which I would include in my staffing evaluation), their methodological expertise, and their available tools and templates. For each criterion he lists, he provides further detailed considerations that you can use.

In recent vendor evaluations, we have started to compare them on similar criteria. Our set of dimensions includes:

Proposal and Presentation Quality
- Complete and thorough response
- Visibility into rationale for response
- Deep understanding of topic
- Sample deliverables relevant to request
- Change control plan
- Collaboration plan

Demonstration of Expertise
- Recommendations and history of success (with similar projects)
- History of successful relationships with company and compatibility with corporate culture
- Objectives that achieve desired success criteria
- Deep understanding and appreciation of organizational process
- Quality of portfolio of work
- Demonstration of desired core competencies
- Demonstration of excellence of team skills applied to project
- Knowledge of, and experience with, targeted technologies
- Unique skills, experience, and value not available through full-time staff

Schedule and Execution
- Plan to transition intellectual capital to full-time staff
- Demonstration of project management skills and plan
- Capacity
- Risk

Value
- Cost
- Proposed deliverables

We define a scoring scheme for each item and calculate an average for the factor. Each factor can then be weighted, and the weighted average scores summed to define a total score. The total score is then used to compare alternative vendors. The scores are just a tool, and business judgment needs to be applied to the result in case an individual item or other considerations turn out to be critical to the final decision. This approach works well for evaluating responses to RFP requests, especially when the RFP provides responders with a clear vision of the requested work. Supplement this process by having the vendors present their proposals in person and respond to questions that arise as you compare the written proposals.

Costs of vendors and contractors vary considerably. Reasonably experienced freelance contractors often cost less than full-time staff, although very senior contractors may command as much as a 25–33% premium over comparable staff. Contractors obtained through an agency seem to come in at about the same as the loaded cost for full-time staff (where the loading includes the overhead for benefits, offices, equipment, etc.). Vendors leveraging staffing outside the United States may be able to get their costs to a level that competes with full-time staff but at the cost of the overhead that comes with remote workers. Vendors who specialize in local production work are often in that 25–33% premium rate over your full-time staff, and specialty vendors who are in great demand and some very large brand-name vendors may run fully 2 or 3 times the cost of full-time staff.

Currently we are testing a staff augmentation model that tries to combine the virtues of a consulting model with a vendor model. We are engaging a vendor who can provide contractors on demand. The contract will be set up so that teams can "buy" support either for specific UX deliverables or they can by blocks of hours. The hours can be used to engage a variety of skills as needed. To help the vendors in their responses to the RFP, I have defined a prototypical project with a set of deliverables through the development cycle. I have also provided a framework of the standard design and research artifacts we typically create and how much effort they take (for small, medium, and complex projects). The statement of work also includes skill descriptions that map to comparable levels in a career ladder. The vendor will provide program management office (PMO) support that handles recruiting to our requirements, managing staff in and out, and performance reviews. The expectation is that they will meet our guidelines and design patterns and other requirements to ensure that their design is consistent with the full-time staff designs. We' are able to use the staff as we would use contractors and move them from project to project as needed with easy modifications to the base contract. There will be service-level agreements about how much time they will have to staff new projects and for the quality of the work delivered. Over time as we increase our use of this type of vendor, the goal is that prices will come down but we will be able to continue to increase the quality of services. The goal of this model is to enable the staff augmentation to scale indefinitely. The hidden agenda is that we will be able to demonstrate an ongoing year over increase in the demand for these services, and that this increase will be converted to help fund full-time staff (which should be less expensive on the average and produce a greater return).

What About Certification

Over the years I have tried to get each of my managers periodically into a neutral setting to have a casual conversation about where the UX program is heading and to improve my own performance. When I was at Ameritech, at one such lunch Joel Engel (my boss at the time) asked "Don't people in your field actually know anything?" I thought this was interesting since Joel had previously managed a successful human factors department, and was clearly a champion for UX within Ameritech. Certification is one way to show that people in our field know something. It is also about the science behind the field, and it is what distinguishes the field from an art and perhaps from the craft. Our field has elements of both art and craft, so those that argue that a portfolio review is the best way to capture those aspects are right. We typically assess those skills in interviews where we try to understand the process the candidate uses to get a sense of whether they will be reliably successful in their design work. As with engineering, however, there is also a long history of research and the evolution of best practices in the relevant fields that inform user experience. While having a foundation in that body of knowledge is not a guarantee of excellence, one would hope that having the foundation would help improve the probability and reliability of making good design and research decisions as well as in interpreting feedback from users.

With this in mind, I would also state up front that I am still a little old school. I believe in doing things for reasons in addition to their usefulness. I believe in doing them because they are the right thing to do. I believe that the certification process itself should continue to drive our field to be more systematic in the excellent results we want to produce, as it forces us to think in terms of generalizable principles based on a deep understanding of design and users in context. It is consistent with the arguments we make about why and how we should be integrated into the development process. I also believe that as a user experience professional, I should test myself. When I run in a marathon, it is partly to see if I can do it. It is a test of my own ability and my training. As a professional, I want to make sure I am as fully equipped as possible to give my very best in my chosen field, and when I do research to advance it, that I am advancing it from the shoulders of the giants who have come before.

Certification is a controversial topic. It is regularly discussed in forums frequented by UX professionals. Some argue that it is impossible to certify UX people, and others argue it is critical for the credibility of the UX profession that certification become part of our community culture. For a manager, the question is whether certification is desirable for full-time staff, contractors, and vendors and, if so, under what circumstances.

Certification is intended to verify that someone has a body of knowledge or is able to exercise a specified set of skills. In a sense, some university programs are training people in the relevant skills for a job and successful graduation can be thought of as a kind of certification. Some candidates for a job, however, have entered the field from other fields and many university programs cover portions of the practice of UX but not all the areas that may be important for the most successful practitioners.

Certifications are often talked about as demonstrating the qualifications to perform a certain job or task and may be treated as a method of protecting the public interest. As a result, there are many certifications in the engineering field. There are certifications sponsored by IEEE, that show engineers have a comprehensive understanding of a fundamental set of principles identified as representing the best science in the field (e.g., the Software Engineering Body of Knowledge), and there are certifications for special areas within the engineering profession.

Certification can be controversial because it does not guarantee the quality of the work produced by those certified. In discussions among usability people, for example, you often hear "How dare they claim to determine whether I am going to be good or bad at my job! My work speaks for itself!" On the other hand, many employers and professionals in the field complain that they see many usability people who have virtually no understanding of the human factors basics that influence what makes a design good or bad; human-computer interaction (HCI) principles that specify good design; or even the proper, unbiased application of the range of formal methods they claim to use.

I cannot tell you how many times I have asked someone "Do you know how to do contextual inquiry?" and the response is "Yes, I have done field studies." It turns out they have no idea what the formal elements of a contextual inquiry are. These people feel the power and the confidence they get when doing a user study, so they are absolutely confident they are discovering truth. Without being sensitive to and practiced in the concepts of control, reliability, validity, and generalizability they may inadvertently be missing what they should be finding, and without the formal background in human factors and HCI they can make design recommendations that are less than optimal. They are confident, and because of the power of engaging people in the process they often please their sponsors. They often also find some of the most obvious problems (how could they help it), but they may not discover the most important issues. It is not too surprising that the reliability between usability researchers testing the same system is often low. If the basics were well defined, and if professionals had the foundation of those basics, the field would enjoy a stronger reputation.

At this point there is a bigger problem in the field associated with this uneven expertise among practitioners. It is hard for many companies to know the difference between good user experience and bad user experience, and what it takes to create it. That is probably part of why the staying power of UX programs depends so heavily on champions and why it is so difficult to find any kind of return on investment (ROI) narrative that is persuasive, even when we know the tremendous business impact that user experience can provide when done well. As long as user experience appears to be more art than science, and as long as some professionals try to keep it that way, it will not be viewed as predictable a business value as engineering, and companies will not look for certification to ensure people have the foundation to do the job well. At this point, certification is sought largely for jobs in the government, safety, and hardware design areas. Consultants use it as a way to distinguish themselves from competitors as well, and job candidates may similarly use it as a selling point when the hiring manager is sufficiently knowledgeable to understand what they are seeing and how to interpret it.

In engineering, certification is quite common. IEEE certifies software professionals (the Certified Software Development Professional), the Society for Professional Engineers has a certifying body, and the British Computer Society has just developed a Chartered IT Professional certification. The Software Engineering Institute has certification for security, process improvement, and software architecture. There are certifications for best practices such as the Six Sigma Black Belt. There are also corporate certifications for platforms and tools (e.g., by Microsoft, Apple, Oracle, and Cisco). There are third-party and vendor-neutral certifications (e.g., the XML Certification Program and the Linux Professional Institute).

For managers, certifications are like other records of education and training and should be evaluated in the same way. Look for the nature of the certification, who is doing the certification and their qualifications, the confidence you can have in the certification process, and what is actually being satisfied. There may be areas where you may want to require specific certifications. For most of us, certification is one of the pieces of information that helps a candidate stand out from other candidates, and suggests additional steps the applicant may have been willing to take to demonstrate what he knows. Managers may use certifications as part of career plans for their employees. It can serve as evidence that an employee has been successful in growing his knowledge in a particular area.

Certification may be a step that people outside the field use to build credibility for moving into the field. For example, I have known several technical writers who have a bachelor's or master's degree, and who want to move into interaction design, or information architecture, or even usability. I have also known computer scientists in development teams or in project management roles who similarly want to move into user interface roles. In these cases, they sometimes start by jumping in and gaining experience, educating themselves through reading and community activities (e.g., listservs), and perhaps taking the University of Michigan Human Factors Engineering Summer Conference, other conference training, or consultant-run seminars. But when they want to move more formally into the field and show what they know, they look for some kind of certification that does not require them to quit their day job. In the Seattle area, that typically means getting the University of Washington Human Centered Design and Engineering user-centered design certificate.

There are a variety of ways people can be certified. I have been involved with the BCPE, which was created as a certification driven by the profession itself. It was established in 1990 as an independent non-profit organization and aims to certify individuals whose education and experience indicate broad expertise in the practice of human factors, ergonomics, and UX in a variety of human-systems interaction design areas. It certifies, but it does not train. It provides direction through the Ergonomics Formation Model, which is designed to be an architecture describing the range of knowledge that makes up the ergonomics or user-system design field. Over 1,500 professionals have successfully met the certification criteria and been awarded one of the credentials offered representing a cross-section of active professionals who are also members of the societies that make up the field. The BCPE is governed by an elected board of leading professionals. It is managed by a full-time Executive Administrator and a Financial/Information Systems Manager. It is endorsed by the International Ergonomics Association and is a corporate member of the National Organization for Competency Assurance (NOCA), which is a U.S.-based organization that provides best practices and support to certifying bodies. In March 2009 the BCPE became accredited by the National Commission for Certifying Agencies.

The University of Washington Human Centered Design and Engineering Department offers a full set of courses designed to provide working professionals with skills in two key areas: user-centered design and technical writing and editing. A certificate in your specialty area is earned when the training is completed. This training program is less extensive than a full degree, but is an excellent complement to an already existing degree and can prepare the professional for the UX field. I have known several people entering UX from other fields who have gone through the training and have been successful as designers and researchers. There are others who have taken the training and have exercised their unique understanding of UX in areas such as project management, development, and technical writing.

Human Factors International's certification is aimed at usability analysts. The exam can be taken without the training, but training is also offered that prepares you for the exam and provides an insight into the focus of the certification. Courses include: user-centered design and conceptual design, Web design, practical usability testing, and putting the principles into action. The courses (and I would expect the exam) are designed around the approach that Human Factors International has built into their consultancy.

Figure 2.3 was created by a list obtained from the BCPE and shows a variety of available certifications. When you find a certification on a resume or explore a certification for continuing education for an employee, the questions you have to ask include:

- What knowledge is being certified?
- How credible is the testing process? Does it meet the criteria you and your company have set for objectivity and coverage of the targeted domain?
- How relevant is it to the range of tasks in your company?
- How transportable is it to future roles the holder may undertake in their career?

Sponsor	Types of Certification	Designation
Board of Certification in Professional Ergonomics	Certified Professional Ergonomist	CPE
	Certified Human Factors Professional	CHFP
	Certified User Experience Professional	CUXP
	Associate Ergonomics Professional	AEP
	Associate Human Factors Professional	AHFP
	Associate User Experience Professional	AUXP
	Certified Ergonomics Associate	CEA
Back School of Atlanta	Certified Ergonomic Assessment Specialist	CEAS
Columbia Southern University	Certified Ergonomic Compliance Director	CECD
E.K. Gillin & Associates Inc.	Certified Ergonomics Specialist	CES
Ergonauts	Certified Ergonomic Manager	CEM
	Certified Lean Ergonomist	CLE
The Ergonomics Center — of North Carolina	Accredited Office Ergonomics Evaluator	AOEE
ErgoRehab Inc.	Certifed Specialist in Health Ergonomics	CSHE
Ergoworks	Certified Professional Ergonomic Evaluator	CPEE
Human Factors International	Certified Usability Analyst	CUA
IIE/SME	Certified Engineering Manager	CEM
ISR Institute	Certified Behavioral Based Ergonomic Specialist	CBES
OccuCare Systems & Solutions	Certified Ergonomic Evaluator	CEE
Oxford Research Institute (ORI)	Certified Industrial Ergonomist	CIE
	Certified Human Factors Engineering Prof.	CHFP
	Certified Associate Ergonomist	CAE
Roy Matheson and Associates	Certified Ergonomic Evaluator Specialist	CEES
University of Washington Human Centered Design and Engineering	User-Centered Design Certificate	
	Technical Writing and Editing Certificate	

FIGURE 2.3

Certifications.

Salaries

Once you decide to hire someone and make an offer the question then turns to the offer itself. It may be made up of a variety of factors including salary, projected bonus, stock or stock options, other benefits, and subsidized moving costs. The offer is usually developed in collaboration with your corporate recruiter or someone from HR and is influenced by where you believe the candidate fits within the career ladder and what it will take to hire them. The recruiter has attempted to find out what the person wants, what they are currently earning (and their cost of living), and their relevant background for positioning them on the ladder. The recruiter may want to save the company as much money as possible by offering a low salary (although they are often also given incentives to make successful hires). But as a manager you know what you want them to do, and where you think they will fit on the ladder. You want them on your team.

You are now convinced you want this person and want to do what you can to attract him to the job. Still, you do not want to hurt the applicant by paying him too much at the start. Unless the new hire turns out to be an absolute superstar, if you pay them too much only small raises will be given until he is more in line with the existing employee salary structure and they will, as a result, be unhappy. You also do not want to get a reputation with your existing team for giving new people higher salaries than those who have been at the company for a while (this can happen if the company has been holding costs down or focusing on rewarding only the very top employees).

Your best bet is to pay on the low side (not so low that it is hard to get them up to the average over time), and offer larger raises than expected in the early days as the applicant settles into his job and shows his value. The raises will make him happier and bond with the team. It also gives you more tools to reward the right behavior and, if needed, to hold back if things are not going well.

Overlaid on this dialog are the corporate targets. At several of the companies I have worked at there has been a philosophy of not paying top dollar, but rather being competitive by paying at around say the 75th percentile when hiring, and then differentiating the salaries of high and low performers over time. These companies intend to attract and differentiate by the supplemental benefit packages they offer, as well as the work environment and the job itself.

It is worth imagining what candidates may be thinking as you or the recruiter are negotiating with them. When I was exploring one job, I had excellent discussions with a colleague who had been the head of HR for a previous company we had been at and who had been laid off himself. I asked him about the salary negotiation process and his advice was to not focus so much on a specific number being offered but to think through what I thought I needed and wanted in order to make the new position worth taking. I was then able to express my desires for a specific salary, but also to share my major pain point. At the time the pain point was the prospect of carrying a mortgage on a house that was not likely to sell soon while having to buy a second house for the new job. The company was then able to come back with an offer that was not quite at the salary I wanted, but they were able to pay for a longer stay in interim lodging than normal, and they offered an extra-large signing bonus. With that larger signing bonus, they arranged with a mortgage company to help me get a loan and buy down the points to a very low starting level. When working with the recruiter think creatively. Explore all the tools you have available for attracting the candidate and keeping them happy as they get started in the job.

If you are the first UX person in a company and are starting the program there, you may have to drive change in the HR area. The companies where I have worked have tended to be engineering companies. At some of these companies engineers with qualifications and responsibilities equivalent to UX people have been paid more. This is often explained in terms of supply and demand. There clearly have been points where there were a lot of UX people on the market relative to the number of potential openings, and there has been a shortage of engineers. But the inequality in salaries has a way of impacting a variety of downstream processes such as attracting talent, building a compelling environment, career development, and performance reviews.

One path is to try to drive the HR team to conduct a salary survey, and then to shape the survey so it evaluates UX salaries more fairly. The team doing the survey often benefits from an education about what UX roles involve, the typical backgrounds, and where the competition is for those you are trying to hire. Another source for potentially useful information can be salary surveys conducted by professional societies. The American Institute of Graphic Arts (AIGA) and HFES, for example, both regularly conduct salary surveys. It may take effort to draw the line between how the society categorizes respondents and the particular classification used for UX people within your team. A key argument is that you want your UX professionals working at a given level to have the same kind of business impact as other engineers at the same level, so both should be paid roughly the same.

INHERITING

Another way you acquire people is by inheriting them. You might have been made a manager over an existing team, or one or more people might be moved into your team. At one point an organization was combined with the one I was in, and the UX team within it was added to my team. While I personally have issues with many of his policies, Donald Rumsfeld's comment that "you don't fight a war with the army you want, you fight it with the army you have" seems apropos here. When you inherit people you inherit strengths and growth areas, neither of which is necessarily of your choosing. You may inherit history and issues that have to be dealt with. You are adding people who might not naturally "fit" your vision of the culture and feel of the team you are building, and who you might not have hired if you had had the choice. But you still need to fight the war. You still need to get the work done. As important, inheriting people can shake your team out of unexamined habits and add diversity, and you can grow through the process as well. I have found leveraging and growing the people I have inherited is where my skills as a manager have been tested the most.

When you hire applicants, the goal is to have an initial understanding of them that you can leverage as you start to incorporate them into your team. When you inherit team members, the first step is to find that understanding. Spend time talking with them and exploring many of the questions you might use with a job candidate, but change the focus to understanding what they bring to the table. You want to know the strengths you can take advantage of, and where you need to work. Since the new members are internal, you should be able to explore a little of the history through past review documentation and from the comments from current and past managers as well as people who have worked with them. As with job candidates, interpret what you hear within the context in which the feedback is given and in which the person was operating.

Leverage your general coaching tactics and learn what the new members of the team want from you, what motivates and excites them, and learn about their aspirations. The goal is to get them matched to work that fits their passions. The fact that they know how the company operates is an advantage, but it can make it easy to forget that what they really want to know is how you operate and the rules of the game within your team. Take extra care in helping the new team members understand your philosophy and how to fit in. While a peer mentor can be important in helping a new employee learn where the printer is, for someone transferring into the team peer mentoring may be more about getting them plugged into lunch groups.

In Chapter 6 there will be a discussion of how teams evolve. Adding new people that you inherit to your team often restarts the team formation process. It is not always about the new person adapting to the existing team. Everyone has to adapt, and the more people you are adding the more significant the change. Your best bet is to be intentional in driving that evolution. Be on the lookout for signs of difficulty and address them quickly, transparently, and directly. Refresh everyone's understanding of where you are heading, your vision and mission, and your values, but embrace the questions and fresh perspectives. Find opportunities to help the new people get their fingerprints on the plan and to feel enrolled, and help the existing team discover the value the new people are bringing to the table.

When a team that is combined with yours has a manager who is still in the team, you can be faced with a unique challenge. Chances are he wanted your job or feels like he is at least as qualified to run the team as you are. In the worst case the ex-manager will be working to undermine your authority. In the best case he will be your bench; the person you are training for future leadership.

Your task is to bring this person to the point where he wants to help you succeed because it will help him succeed. Early on I try to get to the point where we both can have a candid conversation about the situation. You want to get any steam out, and he should know you understand and can empathize with his feelings even if you do not necessarily agree with them. You want to understand what he want from a great manager, what motivates him, and his aspirations. Then you want to leverage that knowledge to get him to hear and embrace your commitment to leverage their experience, skills, wisdom, and insights to help him grow his career as he help you shape and implement your strategic goals. You want to be especially explicit about your expectations, and diligent in rewarding alignment. Be clear when misalignment is not acceptable.

On the one hand you are trying to leverage this persons leadership skills to help you deliver. On the other hand, this person needs to understand that if he do not like where you are heading and cannot accept it, then he probably should explore other opportunities where there might be a better fit. The review process discussed in Chapter 7 is one of the tools used to help this person reach the right decision early in the process. You do not want someone hanging on who is going to poison the well and work against you. Finally, if the situation is heading in a difficult direction seek advice from your HR contact and your boss. They can help provide a reality check on your approach. Enrolling them also provides a little inoculation against things someone who is really out to get you might try. It is sad to have to think about the downside, but it does happen. On the other hand, the upside of having an experienced collaborator can be great.

FIRING

I admit it. I am not particularly good at this. I have colleagues who take pride in the people they have managed out, and it can be necessary and good for the business. I have on occasion asked myself whether I could hire someone better if I did not have a particular person on my team. However, I have known few managers with sufficient power that they can actually fire someone at will and make it stick. People higher in the corporate structure are known for this, but for many in large companies it is very difficult to do. In one instance, I had a colleague who had identified someone who clearly fell into the category of needing to be "managed out" and HR immediately started questioning the competency of the manager.

Part of my problem is that I have never felt I had anyone working for me who was worth writing off. Each person who has worked for me has felt pride in what he or she has done, each has worked very hard, and even my lowest rated people have had significant accomplishments. I have learned from each person who has worked for me, and whether it is a weakness or a skill, I really care about the people on my teams and am firmly convinced I can help them be great if they will only let me. I also am a believer in redemption, the idea that each person can change if they want to change and should have a chance to grow. I have seen people get tough messages, take them to heart, and make progress in moving forward again. I also have seen people whose skills, interests, and attitude are such that I cannot put them on just any project. Even in those cases there is usually some project I can find that is a fit. Early in my career I had one person at the bottom of my team who, when I got them on the right team and the right project, was viewed as a superstar. In this job the project set that creates the match where people can make a difference is smaller than usual, but it is usually there. This kind of message can be tricky and twice when I have tried to help people find a better fit for their careers and personal goals they have taken it more as a message that I was trying to get rid of them rather than the intended message that I was trying to help them. In each of these cases a wave of layoffs took control of the process.

There have been times when I have had people who — when I sat back, poured myself another glass of wine (they usually were the source of many glasses of wine), and honestly looked into my own heart — I had to admit that if I got rid of them I would be able to replace them with someone better. As a manager, as a steward of the business, I know this is part of the decision process I have to go through. Warning signs for me are when employees become labeled high maintenance and the range of roles I can put them in where they would be successful are very limited and they take a lot of effort to manage. Typically, as a result, they are not performing at their targeted level in their career ladder. Worse, they often serve as a drag on the team in general and potentially as they work with clients. They may leave a wake of bad feelings as they move through projects, they may simply be harming the general work climate, or they may actively be hurting others as they attempt to excel in their own jobs.

These employees typically see themselves as brilliant, performing at a level far above their peers, as being beloved by those that matter, and without real flaws. Any weaknesses that are presented (even with evidence) are dismissed as a plot of someone who is working against them or otherwise rationalized away. Even if a growth area is accepted, at best it is addressed by taking a course to prove that it was dealt with on the checklist they are measuring themselves against. There is little evidence of an attempt to really make progress in addressing the growth area.

I had one person who was a brilliant engineer. He could come up with innovative ideas but would not work on anything he was not interested in. He would fight tooth and nail against feedback that sounded like his ideas were being questioned. He honestly believed — based on what he told me in one of our conversations — that the CEO was personally taking steps specifically to ruin his career. This was a CEO who did care about individuals within the company (e.g., I would get books from him with notes like "I thought you would be interested in this."), but I am confident he did not even know this particular engineer existed. He would actively move through the group talking about how lousy the company was and finding the worst aspects of every bit of good news. It was very hard to build group energy for doing something important when this engineer was pulling back at every point. I tried to work with this person, but I also had open conversations with him about the environment and about where he would be happiest. He eventually agreed and moved on to his next role.

Note that these issues, while important for every manager, are particularly critical for a UX team, especially a team or a program that is just being built. Unless you have a very large team, every person's activity has an impact on everyone. You are dealing with the work as it shows up on your door and as you develop strategically important projects. You need to be able to count on the excellence of the skills your people have. You need people who will be the brand of your group. If they are causing hard feelings as they do their work, it not only reflects on them, but it reflects on you. One person like this can eliminate entire groups of potential partners for an extended period of time. It is hard (although not necessarily impossible) for a team to advance beyond the attitude and morale of its weakest person.

For most large companies firing is not as easy as most people think. Companies are understandably concerned about lawsuits. The first thing to do when you think you have someone who should no longer be on the team or who is trending in that direction is to get together with the HR person supporting your organization and have a heart-to-heart discussion. He probably will start documenting your conversations. If the HR professional is good at his job, he will press you to make sure you are doing everything you can to help the person grow and address any issues. It will also be recommended that you be very concrete about your expectations with the person, the goals he is to achieve, and how you will measure success or failure. It will probably be recommended that you document each conversation. For example, if you have a one-on-one with the person, you would follow up with an e-mail that says something like "These are the points we discussed, this is what you agreed to do, and this is when you will do it. Is that right?" Save their responses as well. At one company this was called "putting the person on a plan." In that company the employee was given a number of months to reach a target level of performance or he would be let go. In other companies, they just build the documentation until the decision is made.

Be aware that as you move into this stage, the person in question might reach out to HR and selectively send your e-mails and other documentation they have saved to HR to support their case. You should refrain from overly candid e-mails that might be misinterpreted when taken out of context. Stick to the facts. As mentioned previously, encouraging people to consider looking for a job that better matches their skills has to be handled carefully in this situation, since these are the kinds of e-mails that can be misused and presented as a hostile work environment. It is a shame, because these types of long-term career discussions should be going on with everyone, yet the person that it applies most to may not react well to the conversation. After the proper amount of performance documentation, there will come a time when you, your boss, and HR will decide it is time to terminate. HR will give you the formal process to go through. Many companies are employment-at-will companies, so when the decision is made it can be acted on within the laws of the state.

LAYOFFS

When I was interviewing at AT&T Bell Labs, Max Schoeffler (who later became my first boss) told me that Bell Labs was wonderful. If you did your job well and worked hard you would have a job for life. It was like tenure, only better because you could concentrate on your research and not have any teaching responsibilities. Not only that but you were going to get paid more than in academia. By the late 1990s when a wave of downsizing, rightsizing, and other names for layoffs were sweeping through the industry, it was clear that the concept of lifetime employment was becoming extinct. At one company in the industry being laid off was such a blow to some employees that a manager was shot and someone else was caught trying to smuggle a bomb into the building. Since then I suspect there is no one who thinks of any place they are working as lifetime employment. Still, each time you have to lay people off or it happens to you it comes as a shock.

The rationale for layoffs usually is that the business has concluded that the economic climate is such that the company needs to reduce its workforce or that an area of the business is not worth pursuing any longer and needs to be pruned from the portfolio. At any given large company it is possible that a specific area of the business may be shut down and the employees will either need to find new roles inside the company or they will be laid off. As a manager you are charged with executing corporate directives. Having shaped your team, you also know you are letting people go who you may have hired and thought were doing well. Given that you probably feel that UX is understaffed anyway, and can see the business benefit of hiring even more UX people, laying them off seems like moving in the opposite direction of what the business really needs. There is some comfort in the data that companies who lay off employees regularly cite that years after the layoff most people are more satisfied with their lives than they were before the layoffs. If the company has made the top-down decision, you act as corporate steward and the process becomes about representing the company, protecting the company legally, respecting the individuals through the process, and then motivating your team to move forward.

At this point, the personal contract I have with each person on my team is that as long as we are working together we will give each other our best as we fulfill our mission and achieve our shared vision with the company. I commit to help each person grow their skills. Over time they become more valuable and desirable to more companies and teams; as a result their careers will grow. I commit to create the best working environment I can that competes well against the alternatives they have so they will stick with me. If at some point they feel there is a better alternative I will not hold them back. On the other hand, as long as they are working for me I ask that they give their best as well and I will reward them for it. When the time comes to part, I want us to part as friends and colleagues. I want to be confident they will have no problem referring great people to my team if I have openings in the future. If they are available and I have an opening, I want them to consider working for me again. I want them to be a representative of what they have learned on my team wherever they are. I want to be confident that I would be honored to work for them some day. This mutual commitment works for both the natural attrition that happens as team charters and individual careers evolve and when layoffs are necessary.

Your HR department and consultants supporting them define the layoff process you follow, but let me share the best designed process I have gone through. The process was designed for Ameritech by a company it had engaged to take it through its first layoff. It was the final step in a cost savings initiative driven by the new CEO, Dick Notebaert. He had first announced that as an organization he believed we could be more efficient. He argued that over time all kinds of inefficiencies had likely been incorporated into our daily work and that at least some projects had been taken on for the wrong reasons. He required that each manager identify the bottom 10% of the work their team was doing based on its value to the company. He said that was not to say that the work should not be done, but that every manager should be able to describe the priorities of the work on their team clearly. This made sense and it was hard to argue against. Everyone should be able to speak to the priorities to make effective trade-offs with incoming work. He told us that each of us would be interviewed by a task force and we could make the case for the importance of the work. The task force would then take the bottom 10% of the tasks we identified and all of our input and then prioritize it across the organization. They would identify a line below which everything would be cut. At a subsequent management meeting, he went through this list and shared what we would stop doing (something like 8% of the organization's work). He also announced that he had told the CEO that his budget could be cut by that amount, and that now we needed to get expenses in line with the budget. It quickly became clear that that meant layoffs.

To do the layoffs, Notebaert said HR would first rank order all of our employees. He did it not by looking at ratings, since he said the performance review process was biased toward giving higher ratings than were probably appropriate. He had noticed that people never want to give bad news in reviews, so people tended to give high ratings. He argued that the real metric should be raises. Organizations would put their money where they really believed they should invest (since it was a zero sum game each year). He also argued that one year could be an aberration, so they would look at a multi-year trend in raises and then rank order people. The next step would be to identify the bottom 10% of the rank order.

He shared his vision of the future of the business. The managers in each organization met and we were to go through the people on our teams who were on the list and discuss them one by one. He recognized that people might be on the list because they were causing trouble for good reasons. They might be real innovators. If we felt anyone was on the list because they represented the skills we wanted to move Ameritech into the future we could remove them. If they were on the list and had skills that were unique and necessary, and hard or impossible to replace we could remove them. That left a pool of about 5% of the company.

Each of us then was trained to perform the layoff process in the most compassionate way possible, and to do real-time diagnostics of how people were feeling. We were put into pairs, with one of us being the "bad cop" and giving the news, and the other person working with the person to walk them through the benefits package. Either of us could take appropriate actions to get people to the right support as needed.

We were to give the news in a neutral room. The room was to have plenty of tissue, but no hot water (since they didn't want anything there that could be thrown on the people giving the news). After sharing the benefits, the person being laid off would either be taken to an outplacement service, a counselor, or security. They had arranged for a database with more jobs than people being laid off. Most people ended up going to the database to find the next job. There were counselors in the building, and if people were just having an extraordinary level of difficulty in dealing with the layoffs emotionally they could be taken there for professional support. If, heaven forbid, there was a potential risk of violence, extra security was available and could be brought into the situation. Those laid off were given a benefits package that included access to the database of jobs, a temporary office environment where they could project a professional image as they looked for work, and support in creating an effective resume, refreshing their interviewing skills, and searching for work. As managers we were allowed to write personal letters of recommendation, although we were not allowed to represent our recommendations as being Ameritech's recommendations.

The most important thing to keep in mind is that the person being laid off is to be treated with respect and compassion. There is no way around it, the layoff process is difficult for everyone, but it is ultimately about the person and not about the manager. For that reason it is better for you as a manager to give the layoff message than for a stranger to do it. The message should be carefully crafted and approved by HR, and practiced so that you can concentrate on giving it sincerely. The message is typically focused on the facts, the situation that has led to the layoff, that the person is one of the people selected, and what the next steps will be. In each of the various layoffs I have been through, one person gives the message and then another person goes through the details of the benefits package and the next steps. The person is invited to ask questions, but most of the questions have been anticipated and the answers memorized in advance so the answers do not wander. The one question typically asked is "Why?" That is the one question where your answer has to be carefully vetted in advance. You are advised to own the process as a manager representing the company and not distance yourself from it.

I can say that when I can get the approval from HR I do what I can to help people find their next role. I will write honest letters of recommendation and stand behind them. I will reach out to hiring managers with roles that I believe will be a good fit for the person. I make myself available for coaching through the process as others have done for me when I was laid off. While I have lost some people in layoffs who had some challenges, I have also lost some of my very best people in the process. In most of the layoffs I was never told why people were chosen and, unlike Ameritech, most companies have not involved me in the selection. The rationale has been that they do not want to introduce bias into the process and they presumably have not shared the process for liability reasons.

After the layoffs have happened, the alcohol is consumed, and the commiseration is over, the next step is to gather up the team that remains, understand the new context, and begin moving forward again. After layoffs there is a lot of work that needs to be done with less people to do it. Work needs to be explicitly removed from people's plates so the higher priority work can be placed on those plates. This transition requires an extra effort from everyone. The team also needs help in working through survivor's guilt. There may be a sense that an implied contract with the company has been broken and that impacts the work climate. This can be a challenge when those who were laid off have left friends behind, and when they may be reaching back into the organization with updates as they search for work. You should be genuine and compassionate. You should be as transparent as you can. You can recognize the difficult time to the extent that you can help the team understand the business need. But you also need to update the vision of your team and re-enroll your team in moving toward the new vision.

2.1 BUILDING A GREAT TEAM

By Barry L. Lively, Manager of the User Interface Design Group (retired), Lucent Technologies Consumer Products

Hire the Best People You Can Find

From the outset it was my intention to hire people I thought were as good or better than I was at human factors engineering. There is almost always far more user interface design work that needs to be done than can be accomplished in the development schedule. First rate people make a big difference. They know how to pick and choose what needs to be done and they do it well.

There is another side to this too. Your people will sometimes come up with findings that go against what, at the moment, is perceived to be the best interest of the company. For example, we were testing a new model handset intended for business use. It was angular and, unfortunately, short; in those days the microphone needed to be nearer the mouth to avoid the effects of extraneous noise.[1] Initial testing showed that it was grossly inferior to what was the standard handset of the day. No one argued with replacing that standard, but whatever the new one would be, it had to be as good as the old one. The one the industrial designers loved was not going to make it; it was too sensitive to extraneous noise. Development was far enough down the path that any change would be serious. This is the point where things can pivot on purely political considerations. If there was any doubt that our testing was not up to snuff, we would have been politely thanked for our contribution and sent on our way. But the testing was first rate and our MTS on the job was the same guy who didn't have a phone in his home. Iterative testing went on for a couple of months and a major part of the development of that system shifted in light of the findings. Our people came out shining.

Over time, almost all of the MTSs in my group became Distinguished Members of Technical Staff. This usually happened after they had left the group and moved on to another part of the company; politically, it wouldn't work for all of the members of one group (at a small location) to be named DMTSs. This was the alternative to going into management for people who were very accomplished in their field. It was not given lightly and I would guess no more than 10 to 15% of the population (if that many) became DMTSs. These were indeed good people.

People Will Surprise You With What They Are Able to Do So Give Them Room to Do It

A lab assistant found a very good way of testing by just trying to be more accommodating to the subjects in the testing. One of our lab assistants was testing the draft of a new manual down at the Home Lab. People were tested there in environments that looked very much like an ordinary home. Two or three people would come in at the same time and would be tested in another room one at a time. The testing was often done in the early evening and subjects would get impatient to be done with it so the assistant started testing them in pairs to move them through more quickly. This had a very interesting effect. When tested individually people would not admit where they were having problems, but when working in pairs they would ask one another about difficult-to-understand concepts. The experimenter essentially disappeared from their consciousness and she was the proverbial fly on the wall. It only occurs to me now, 25 years later, but this assistant had majored in business education in college and could take shorthand. That came in very handy here. We worked on the technique and added audio and video recording, which relieved the need for shorthand. We used that technique to great effect from then on. If I had been keeping tight rein on this assistant, this would never have happened.

---

[1] The closer to the mouth, the less the signal needs to be amplified. You may not be aware of it, but there is what is called a sidetone path from the microphone to the speaker in the handset. You can see what sidetone does by picking up a handset and putting your finger on the switch hook (the button under the handset) and blowing into the microphone. Now release the switch hook and blow again. That is sidetone and it contributes to the "liveness" on your side of the conversation, you hear yourself through the path. Too much amplification leads to a sidetone that is too hot. The result is that extraneous noise is amplified and it interferes with intelligibility. This was before active noise cancellation was practical. Active noise cancellation, or something like it, is what you have today in small cell phones. That there isn't a lot of interference on the sidetone path with these phones seems like magic to me.

2.2 INTERVIEWING AND CANDIDACY

By Gavin S. Lew, Managing Director, User Centric, Inc., Chicago, IL

The tricky thing about interviewing candidates is that in a 60-minute interview, you can really learn very little about a person other than basics of their work experience and personality. Over the past ten years we've tried numerous different interviewing techniques to better determine whether a person is a good fit for our organization. We've tried full-day sessions with six different interviews and lunch. We've tried having different interviewers each discuss a different topic with the candidate. But none of these really gave us the insight we needed to make decisions that would impact the team for months to come.

We must all recognize that this is an imperfect process that is difficult for the interviewee and the interviewers. Let's face it, unless you have direct experience with a candidate, the predicted outcome from the interview process is often less predictable than one believes. Sometimes you feel that the individual is perfect and then the reality sets in and your assessment is dead wrong. Other times you find yourself in disagreement with consensus and the individual is indeed exemplary. So, what are we left to do?

Honestly, we are more concerned with how someone thinks than with what their resume says. But, how do you tap into how a person thinks? For one, we tried "job talks," where we would ask the candidate to talk for 15 to 30 minutes about something they did or thought about, or some aspect of a project they worked on. While this worked better than just asking standard questions, we still found it wasn't completely successful because some candidates will come in and talk about themselves rather than the project. Others will do a great job because they have an extroverted personality, but that's really just showcasing a social skill, not necessarily telling us what we need to know about the individual. We're user researchers, not performers; sometimes less gregarious individuals end up being outstanding researchers. So while we fared better with job talks than with question asking, we still weren't getting at everything we were hoping to learn.

We decided a different approach was in order, and came up with the idea of giving the candidate a challenge, often a hypothetical example of something we're actually wrestling with, and asking how they'd approach it. The key wrinkle is that we don't care so much about the answer, but we want to listen to how they articulate their thought process. With this technique we can get an idea of how creatively they think, how they might work through a list of possible solutions, how they reason, what issues they come up with, and how they finally determine to check options off the list. Since all these are processes we go through in our work every day, we find this exercise can give us a fairly strong indicator of someone's suitability to do our work.

What else will we look for in a candidate? For one, we'd like a degree (preferably a master's degree or above in a related area). Why master's degrees? First of all, there are things that can't be taught in the workplace. No matter how intelligent and trainable someone is, job experience can't make up for the years spent in graduate school (and in part undergrad) where someone is considering experimental design. It takes a long time to pick up on the nuances of user research. The years thinking in an academic environment lay irreplaceable groundwork for the work they'll do in the future.

Second, successfully completing a master's degree program is a rigorous process. It requires a commitment to doing something challenging. You can't teach the kind of ethic and attention to detail that someone gains through that kind of experience. For those who have completed a thesis or dissertation, remember when it was turned in to your advisor in draft form? There was a lot of time and thought spent before submission. Yes, it was called a draft, but knowing that the professor would attack it with red ink, you spent a lot of time on the details and even grammar. The last thing you wanted to do was to turn in something with grammatical mistakes. All too often, this lesson is not effectively taught outside of the world of the academic red pen. So for me, a graduate degree with a written thesis or dissertation gives some assurance that an individual is willing and able to perform with the kind of rigor and robustness that the best user experience studies require. Some graduate programs have terminal master's degrees and there is no formal thesis, but a CAPSTONE individual project. These are different because they are turned-in assignments at the end of the term. The process of a thesis involves an assessment of self-worth that continues during each review and is a lesson that differs from an assignment.

To this end, if you consider writing ability and attention to detail important aspects for your employees then you will want to review their past work. The first rule is that the sample must be well sanitized. If you as a reader can find proprietary information that is not disclosed as non-confidential then this employee would use this same technique when it is time to move on from your job. This is a "red light" for us and the rejection letter starts.

Moreover, when considering candidate samples, weigh group projects differently than individual work. Ask questions as to involvement and role. If the candidate states a large role in the effort, then ask detailed questions. It will be very easy to learn the role if details are vague.

We also look for people with positive energy. If hired, they will become part of a creative, dynamic team. We can't have someone who will drain the vitality of the group. Not everyone is exuberant, but we need people who have at least neutral to positive energy who will work well as a team member.

We want smart people who ask good questions and have thoughtful things to say. They should also be excited about technology. We work in a highly technical environment, and the best people are going to be the ones who think it's really cool that they're doing this research, and care about the project as much as the client cares about it.

Finally, I try to get a sense from an interview whether someone can work well as part of a team. We want independent thinkers, not robots, but we still need someone who will row the oars in the same direction. Do I get the sense they are dependable? Can they think through a situation and make a good judgment call about what's going on? You can't always tell these things about someone at first meeting, but results keep getting better as we assess what about the interview process works and what doesn't, and as we continually seek ways to more effectively assess someone's suitability for user research.

2.3 MERGER AND ACQUISITION: IMPACT ON UX MANAGEMENT

By Janaki Kumar, Director, User Experience, SAP Labs LLC, Palo Alto, CA

Mergers and acquisitions (M&A) are a recent trend in the enterprise software world. To name a few, Oracle acquired PeopleSoft, Siebel Systems, and Sun Microsystems; SAP[2] acquired Virsa Systems, Business Objects, and Sybase; CA acquired Netegrity, NetQos, and Cassatt. While this is a business expansion strategy for the acquiring company, it presents several challenges for user experience (UX) professionals. This is especially true for UX management whose responsibility it is to lead their UX teams through such a transition, while designing the look and feel of the products of the newly combined business entities.

To explore these challenges and to build a body of best practices for UX leaders to effectively manage their UX organizations following such M&A activities, a group of us organized a Special Interest Group at CHI 2010. We shared our experiences and engaged in a discussion with the UX community on this topic. Our panel consisted of participants from both the acquired and acquiring companies. They were Dan Rosenberg (SAP), Michael Arent (SAP Business Objects), Anna Wichansky (Oracle), Madhuri Kolhatkar (PeopleSoft, JD Edwards), Esin Krish (CA), and Bob Hendrich (Cassatt). In addition, the author (Janaki Kumar, SAP) was the moderator and Arnie Lund (Microsoft) was the discussant.

We set out to examine the design, technical, organizational, and cultural challenges facing a UX practitioner from the acquiring as well as acquired companies' perspectives. We discussed design and technical challenges such as multiple UI technologies and platforms, navigation paradigms and menu structures, interaction behaviors, and visual designs, as well as cultural and organizational challenges such as different maturity levels of UX teams, User-Centered Design practices, job titles, talent management, geographical distribution, and other cultural differences.[3]

Our goal was to explore best practice solutions that could help other UX professionals facing similar challenges. A summary of our key insights and recommendations are listed below.

1. Expect a period of uncertainty

   Regardless of whether the acquisition is friendly or hostile, expect a period of uncertainty in the overall organization. There is usually consolidation of management, power shifts, and legal wrangling that happen during this period. Stakeholders on both sides are feeling the uncertainty, so UX management needs to take that into account when engaging with them.

   This uncertainty may also create opportunities. Usually, the acquired companies get a "honeymoon" period, while the acquiring companies determine their course of action. In some cases, teams have been able to seize this opportunity and launch new products.

   During this classic storming period, UX management needs to work toward creating a common culture between the acquiring and acquired companies. Contrary to common belief, the acquired company employees may be often treated better than those of the acquiring company. Regardless of the circumstances and prevailing mood, UX and other related management will want to treat all employees with equitable respect and professionalism.

2. Focus on people first

   While, it may be tempting for UX managers to address the technical and design challenges immediately after the transaction, it is important to focus on people first. If the UX team is distributed, it is advisable to visit these locations to engage with the teams and individuals directly. Taking the time to listen sends a positive message to the newcomers and helps win their trust. This pays dividends later when management will need the engagement of the entire team to solve the ensuing technical and design challenges.

   It isn't unusual for people to move on to other opportunities after a merger or acquisition. In the software business, part of the reason for M&A is talent acquisition. UX organizations are typically understaffed, and any additional talent is, in most cases, welcome. Therefore it is often better to actively retain the acquired talent and manage their distribution and fit in the organization.

   Experienced UX managers make a concerted effort to help new teams feel welcome and establish open lines of communication. Inviting them into the UX community of the acquiring company helps establish a professional bond.

3. Understand relative UX maturity of both companies

   Maturity models can be an indicator of how stakeholders will engage with UX teams. Companies engage with UX teams at either a tactical or strategic level (or at both levels) depending on the level of maturity in which they are used to engaging with UX. When the maturity model is low, the UX team is expected to play a narrow service-oriented tactical role to support the development team and make their UIs look "pretty." In companies with a high maturity model, UX plays a leadership role in a product effort and is a core participant in a company's business and products strategy.

   During the post-acquisition period, UX management will need to assess the relative maturity of both companies. This will determine the UX engagement model for integrating and evolving the newly combined organizations. Some degree of education and level-setting may be appropriate post M&A. Even if both companies are at a similar maturity level, there may be differences in their design processes and methods. It is best to address these early to increase the effectiveness of the overall UX organization.

4. Know the business

   In the end, it is all about the business. It is important to understand the reason for the merger or acquisition. Are the two companies in the same business or in different businesses? Will the product lines from the two companies complement one another or overlap? If there is a great degree of overlap, usually there are tough decisions ahead for the business. UX management that comprehends the business objectives and motives will better understand stakeholder priorities, drivers, cultures, and values.

To conclude, M&As are inevitable in large enterprises today. UX management can provide effective leadership during this period of transition by focusing on people first, understanding the relative UX maturity of both companies, and aligning the UX organizational goals to the success of the business.

[2] Personally, I was part of the UX team involved in integrating the Virsa Systems into SAP to form the Governance Risk and Compliance Suite, and Business Objects to form the Performance Optimization Suite of Applications.
[3] For a transcript of our discussion notes, please visit http://mergers-acquisitions-ux.wikispaces.com/.

2.4 BUILDING AND MANAGING A CONSULTING TEAM

By Robert M. Schumacher, PhD, Managing Director, User Centric, Inc., Oakbrook Terrace, IL

Early in my career, I never would have thought I'd end up running a consulting company. I was very happy doing technical work or leading a team within an organization. The opportunity to join User Centric arose at a good time to move from my current situation. But like many who find they may be accomplished technically, they often find that successful management uses different skills. I really was not equipped to help build and lead one of the largest, most successful user experience consulting firms in the world. As much as anything else, I had to grow into the position I'm in now.

What have I learned that has enabled me to help successfully build and manage a consulting team? I now believe that corporate culture is one of the most important elements of business. We stress getting people on board who have similar passions, attitudes, and work ethics. We wanted people who will put our customers first, even if it occasionally is disadvantageous to the business. We ultimately believe that whatever effort we put into the customers will come back to benefit us. It's important for us to be able to trust our employees, empower them, give them the tools they need to do their work well, then we stand behind them. We let our employees know they're supported if things run afoul, we'll pick them up if they get down, and we try hard to give them opportunities to succeed. But much of this stems back to hiring the right people in the first place. While we don't always get it right, we do our best to assure a mutually good fit with each new hire.

Once we find good researchers or designers, we make every effort to value their contributions as employees and make sure they know their efforts are appreciated. We try to make time to understand what they're doing, know how they're feeling, and get a read on how they're succeeding or struggling. In this sense, a lot of "managing" becomes walking around and just talking to people, *aka* "doing rounds."

Another thing I've learned is that just because I'm the manager doesn't mean I'm smarter, that I don't make mistakes, or that I have all the answers. Being the leader mainly means that there's no one behind me; I'm ultimately responsible for decisions, and the errors I make may have worse consequences than errors others make in the organization. I need to accept that this will happen. But I have also learned to trust the fact that along the way I have made many good decisions, and have benefited from having very good people around me.

In the end, there really is no magic formula for successfully managing a consulting team, but what has worked for User Centric is being very open with our people, being very considerate about goings on within the company, treating people as professionals, and respecting them as skilled, capable researchers. One more thing: We genuinely believe that *what we do matters*. That is our meaning, our purpose. When we conduct a project, it's about the difference that it will make to the users – not just about the 'project.' Each of our team members has a passion for their work, and it is that passion that drives us to do better everyday. We genuinely value the people around us, and try to make sure they know it.

2.5 LETTING PEOPLE GO

By Robert M. Schumacher, PhD, Managing Director, User Centric, Inc., Oakbrook Terrace, IL

In my years managing user experience teams, I've discovered I have a particular competence that I'm not necessarily proud of, but one that's important: letting people go from the business.

In any organization, and in consulting organizations in particular, managers must be aware of and careful about the culture of the team. As a leader, it's my job to make sure the *team* stays healthy. Also, I understand my obligation to the customer — and to everyone else in the organization — to ensure the highest quality of service delivery possible. Accomplishing these objectives sometimes means, unfortunately, releasing certain staff members who are underperforming or otherwise not meeting their responsibilities.

Over the years, we have had several people that, for a variety of reasons, have not worked out. My staff rightly expects me to do my job and exercise leadership when dealing with individuals who are consistently a net negative to the team or to the projects they're working on. So by taking action I'm not only exercising authority over the matter at hand, but I'm also demonstrating to the rest of the team that I take their well-being seriously and will do what must be done to maintain it. The staff know, perhaps even better than the manager, who is doing well and who is not. The worst thing a leader can do is let performance issues fester.

There can be many reasons for making the decision to fire someone. In some cases, the person who must be released is just not a good match — maybe their skills looked great on paper but in reality they didn't perform, or they work well in a large corporate culture but not so well in a fast-paced consulting environment. In these situations, the first step is always to deliberately work with individuals to improve their skills or their fit. Sometimes this takes care of the problem, sometimes not.

In another vein, due to the nature of the consulting business, there are also circumstances where a single event might cause the summary firing of an individual. These situations would typically happen when a team member has done something deliberate or incredibly stupid that put the business, the team, or a major client's project at risk. Most of these matters are beyond common sense. Some are egregious. As a matter of principle, the staff understands the corporate implications of their actions, which ideally should prevent major missteps from occurring. But in the event they happen, I have a responsibility to the team to rectify the situation and remove the culpable individual from it.

Finally, there may be times when a staff member must be let go simply due to the economics of the business. The appropriate number of staff and the makeup of the team must fall into balance with the needs of the company. As work demands change, you have to create the team at the right level. If the needs of the business get out of sync with the skills or maturity level of the team, managers must take action to re-balance the team. To not do so, puts those that remain at risk.

Whatever the circumstance, the process of letting someone go must be handled deliberately and delicately. From the employer's standpoint, it's important to be sure all legal matters are in order and project implications are considered before meeting with the employee. Once the person is brought in face to face, get straight to the point. Make it very clear that their attitude or skills or goals are inconsistent with those of the organization, and therefore a separation is required. Dancing around this fact or hemming and hawing or failing to come to the discussion early in the meeting can make things more painful. It is essential to leave the person's dignity intact, and keep the discussion focused on performance and behavior. I try to assure each person that this decision is based solely on their inability to perform according to the needs of the organization, not on who they are as an individual.

While this conversation is never fun, oddly, often the individual being released is relieved. He or she realizes things have not been going well, and has been under a great deal of stress. The employee is usually well aware that he or she has been underperforming. Only once have I had someone be surprised about being let go.

Firing someone is one of the most unpleasant, but *necessary* responsibilities of a manager. When viewed as part of an overall regime for keeping organizations strong, and carried out in an everyday culture of open communication and clear expectations, the process becomes much more straightforward and less fraught with emotion and uncertainty. Over time, your organization will be increasingly stronger for the fact that you carefully manage the makeup of your team. Never underestimate the fact that the rest of the team counts on the manager to do her or his job to maintain the team at the highest level of performance — they look to management to make sure the right decisions are made at the right times.

Creating Your Team

3

> Coming together is a beginning; keeping together is progress; working together is success.
>
> **Henry Ford**

A FIRST DAY EXPERIENCE

Because it was a fairly new organization, when I was hired at Ameritech things were not as well organized as when I started at Bell Labs. The vice president who had made the offer had a few of his other managers already on board and they in turn had just started hiring. The overall organization, however, was still small. My acceptance letter gave me a day to show up and an address, but not a time. It turns out on that day they were being moved from one building to a small remote building serving as a temporary facility until the new corporate location was completed. Without any guidance I figured 8:00 was a good time to show up. When I arrived all the doors were locked with security interfaces. There was no lobby or receptionist that I could find. I wandered around until I noticed movers arrive, and as they started rolling equipment into the building I crept in behind them. There was something telling about needing to sneak into your first day of work. Once inside the building I checked out the largely empty halls with that fresh paint smell, paper on the floors, and movers moving boxes, tables, and chairs around. Eventually someone asked "Can I help you?" I responded with something like, "This is my first day of work. I probably need to talk to someone and find a place to sit." They took me, as I recall, to Jim Bradley, a Senior Director who was going to be one of my peers. He in turn introduced me to a few people, connected me up briefly with my boss, Joel Engel, and found the sheet that listed where my office was going to be. He led me to the office, and someone pointed out that I could have a plant if I wanted it. It sounded great, so in the big office with the windows looking out on the hall, there was a desk, a chair, and a bushy plant. There was no computer at that point. There was no UX team. There was nothing to do. There nothing to read. So I remember leaning back in the chair, looking off into the future, and asking myself "Now what?"

I have been an individual contributor and made a manager over people who a moment before were peers. I have been hired to start something new, as at Ameritech, or at my most recent job within Microsoft IT. I have been hired to take teams that had a vacancy for a manager, and teams in some cases that had acting managers who probably felt like they should get the job. I have had a team and absorbed another team and had to organize them into something new. I know of people who were managing engineers and were suddenly told that they were now going to have UX people reporting to them. Early on in each of these cases there is virtually always a "Now what?" moment.

It would be nice to say that the first thing to do is to create a vision and define a strategy. When you are new to a team, practically speaking, the first steps are often more basic. Make friends with the administrative assistant(s). It is amazing how important they are both in removing the on-boarding friction and facilitating innovative solutions to projects that will later be undertaken and problems that will be faced. They can help find out how to get a computer and get set up, they can introduce you to everyone within the organization, they can get you furniture, and they help you get the stuff you need to do everything else. Time and again lab space I have found or design studios I have created happened because I had a sympathetic administrative assistant helping me. They knew someone who knew the space planner and could put in a good word. Administrative assistants can also get you time on a busy boss' calendar. Making friends with the administrative assistant(s) is clearly a key place to start. Being polite, being profusely thankful, and finding ways to connect personally with the administrators are some of those soft skills that should be explicitly developed, but, unfortunately, are rarely covered in management training.

Once you have a place to sit, a phone, and a computer, the next step is to understand the players and the rules of the game. In Chapter 8 there will be a discussion about how consultants work their way into companies. This involves finding a coach who can tell you who the influencers are and who the deciders are, and what the known problems are that need solving. Getting started in a job is similar to getting started on a new project. Find out who is doing what and why. Get to know your existing team, clients, and peers. Understand what each person on your team is doing, their existing commitments and their blockers, and what they are proud of and the things that excite them. Mine their wisdom and insights about where things should be heading and why. Leverage your team and those in the organization to build out an annotated organization chart around the work your team will be supporting, annotating both the formal roles and responsibilities but also including the sensitivities, goals, personalities, and any other information you can get about the people with whom you will be working. Immerse yourself in the systems and processes that shape the context of the work, which may include going through the same formal training that the users go through. This most likely involves getting demos and quizzing people on the users and the scenarios. You will be spending a lot of time in your office (perhaps with your plant) reading Web sites and other documentation about the area. New executives often call these listening tours. They provide needed information, buy time to formulate a point of view and hold off those demanding a still unformed opinion, and begin the process of enrolling the existing stakeholders as people realize their voices will be heard as you shape your opinion. If they are part of the process they are more likely to follow the direction you provide.

Look for the big problems that need to be solved, and the strategic goals of the organization and how they are being approached. Figure out the rules of how the game is played in your organization. This part of the process will be discussed later in Chapter 8 in the section on ROI and involves identifying the needs and desires that your work will be positioned to deliver. This search is also a chance to educate the organization about your point of view, what you feel user experience is about, and how it should work within the organization. When you are the first UX person in an organization that has not employed this discipline before, you are in a great position to define how people should think about UX. Once people start to form their own opinions based on what they observe and their experience, those opinions are hard to change; so use the opportunity wisely. Think about your message ahead of time and stick with it through the process.

SIZING THE TEAM

> The basic unit is [a group] which varies from three to twelve or fifteen in number, and perhaps optimizes somewhere around ten; that this group is bound together by a common objective, and that the bond of trust and loyalty thus formed can become an extremely powerful uniting force; that the group needs to decide on (or at least take part in deciding on) its own objective, and to work out for itself how that objective shall be achieved . . .
>
> **Antony Jay**

One of the most frequent questions asked by new managers is "How big should a UX team be?" It usually arises around the annual funding process and is especially relevant once you have gotten past that first flush of excitement from having anyone to manage. It may even have come up in the course of interviewing. Experienced senior managers bringing in a manager to start a new program often ask about the person's vision for the organization during the interview process.

As you lay out a strategy it can also be helpful to have an idea of what the end goal might be like. It can help you as you explore where the team might fit and the mix of skills you want to hire for the team. While some hiring is opportunistic (e.g., discovering your boss has five vacancies that have not been distributed and then going after them), often it is because you have built up a case over time for a particular need and then seize the moment during the funding process to make the case to act on the need that everyone has already accepted is there.

When you estimate the staffing for a project begin by defining what needs to be done (e.g., the number of screens to be designed, the number of usability studies to be run and at what size) and estimate what it will take to deliver. When you extend this to a team providing support across projects, look at the size of the team over time and what you have been able to do (if you have a history to draw on), and try to get a sense of how needs and resources will change over time. Look at the variability in demand as you will want to provide stability for your full-time staff, and probably supplement with contractors and vendors to respond to spikes or dips in demand. The challenge with this bottom-up approach is that you may end up barely having enough resources to respond to the immediate demand. It can be hard to drive the kind of strategic activity that returns the biggest value over time unless you are able to fund and staff it directly as a project. An alternative method is the top-down approach.

In the 1990s I did two small studies to see if there was a relationship between the size of a corporation and the number of human factors employees within the company (Lund, 1994b). The rationale was that companies that have had human factors departments for a period of time would have grown teams to the level where they were getting enough business value to justify the size of the team, and that further investment would be outweighed by other places where the company might invest. The curve interestingly was a positively accelerating curve, which suggested that very large companies could justify a much larger percentage of their budgets for human factors projects. In these very large companies it was found that once human factors groups were created to support enough of the most critical products, they were able to justify human factors efforts that were more strategic, more research oriented, and/or focused more on common requirements and best practices. There was also a suggestion in the data and reviews of these companies that a department of around 18 (typically about three groups) was one level of critical mass. Overall, however, investment in human factors represented well under 1% of the overall corporate size of the companies studied at the time. I have attempted to model how investing in user experience resources for the most important projects (where full support provides the most value) interacts with investing in activities that benefit all projects. What I find is that while the curves vary based on the set of projects considered, there is typically a trade-off where the greatest overall value comes from supporting a few key projects. Then as your team grows, there is more value in investing in more cross-projects, more strategic activity.

A more recent study of 40 clients by Usability by Design in 2002 found that the average development budget spent on usability-related activities was only about 2.2%. Nielsen (1994) reported some evidence that the proportion of budgets going to design and usability is growing. He noted that in 1971 Shackel estimated that the budget for non-military systems for usability work was about 3%. By 1989 he noted that Wasserman found that several companies were budgeting about 4 to 6% of their research and development staff for design and usability work. Nielsen also reported that in 1993 his survey of 31 development projects revealed that the median share of their budgets devoted to usability work was about 6%.

Much has changed since those studies; most notably, the growth of the Internet as well as the explosion of consumer electronics in general. This has placed a premium on effective user experiences for corporate success. Another approach, therefore, is to focus on the percentage of the corporate budget that should be invested in user experience work. Nielsen in his January 22, 2008, Alertbox (Nielsen, 2008) stated ". . . the share of project resources allocated to usability has held steady at around 10% in those enlightened companies that include usability in their design lifecycle." This 10% figure has floated around the discipline for years as a common rule of thumb. In Nielsen's Alertbox he discussed the business benefit that comes from such an investment.

Another way to look at the problem is to look at staffing ratios. These vary depending on the nature of the work in an organization. In a UX-intensive area that is more consumer oriented or that represents a new product, more designers and researchers are likely to be needed than in an area where incremental improvements are made to systems that are improved release after release and the users are already reasonably well understood. In some of the system software areas a ratio of 1 UX person to 10 developers or 1 UX person to 3 or 4 feature owners (project managers) is fairly common. UX people tend to work closely with developers on software teams as designs are shaped and implemented, but often it is the feature owners that drive the demand for UX support. For projects that are more design intensive such as consumer products, the ratios might be more like 1 UX person for 1 or 2 project managers and 1 UX person to 4 or 5 developers. In these ratios the UX people we are focusing on are assumed to be in the design (e.g., interaction or visual design, graphic design, and information architecture) and research (e.g., usability and ethnography) disciplines.

In companies where there are also user assistance specialists (who design the embedded and other user assistance that brings discoverability expertise to the design process), these teams can be nearly as large as the team of designers and researchers. In the UX team, a good ratio is 1 researcher for every 1 or 2 designers. There may be specialist roles such as UX project managers or producers, developers that specialize in the interface, content managers, and so forth. On many teams, the full-time UX work is often supplemented by contractors brought in as demand for varying skills spikes at different stages of the development process. When added up the user experience budget often does float around the 10% figure that Nielsen reported (with 50 to 75% of it going to the full-time staffing of the design team).

Small, Medium, and Large Teams

Think about sizing more locally. The basic unit of stability I have seen is the group. A group is made up of four or five designers and/or researchers and a UX manager. This group size has several advantages. UX managers can look across the team and ensure reviews are fair, and they can provide senior level coaching. The existence of a manager provides a career goal for some members of the group who might aspire to the UX manager position. A UX manager can serve as the face of the team and, being at least one level up in the hierarchy, can influence across the organization at the management level to advance the UX agenda and be an advocate for the members of the team. Members of a UX team share a similar orientation toward design and commitment to users as well as common approaches to their work. As a result, they enjoy being together, and diverse design and research perspectives help each member of the team produce better work through critiques and collaboration. Having several UX people on a team also gives the manager and the group flexibility when handling the demand for work that might rise or fall over time, and typically gives the manager flexibility to drive initiatives that can provide benefits across projects and releases (e.g., around design guidelines and patterns).

Individual UX people (or two or three people) reporting to a non-UX manager tend to be more unstable (Schwartz & Riley, 1988). The work climate is not as satisfying, and team members often have trouble getting their work valued by those who do not understand it, and they are frequently pressed into non-UX jobs when local engineering needs have to be met (and in performing them they may not be as effective as others within the organization and that puts them at a career disadvantage). Many have noticed a cycle where a champion may start building a UX team. As several people are hired and a group forms, more and more teams around the hiring organization see value and come for services. As the demand for services grows, stakeholders outside the funding organization start to get frustrated when their issues are not always the highest priority and they may pressure management to distribute the team. If the team is broken up and distributed some individuals will find themselves in fertile ground, have early success, and start to hire (and potentially become leads or managers). Others will find themselves the lone voices in teams who do not understand what they do and will become increasingly frustrated and either leave or move to other disciplines.

I have regularly found when managing individual teams that when I am managing up to five or six people I feel most intimately involved with the work. I also can lead complementary activities personally. Beyond five or six people the balance shifts to being more administrative and distant, and I hear, sadly, more people complaining about not having enough of my time. This is really frustrating since I can understand their needs and see some of what I can do, but the administration and the meetings to support them just take too much time. As the team gets up around ten direct reports, then the frustration about time can sometimes move from mild to severe. That definitely is not a good situation, and well before that is when I try to set up other structures to help each person feel as much support as possible even if the formal rules of the company do not allow for a new layer of management (e.g., because of requirements for a specific number of directs). In many engineering organizations an acceptable span of control seems to be larger than for the ideal design team. This may be because of differences in the fundamental nature of design versus engineering work.

The next level of stability I have seen is the department, or group of groups. From earlier research, and in practice, this starts around 16 to 20 people. In general, the more UX people in an organization, the better the climate seems to be for the team.

There is a sense that there are more growth opportunities (there are now first level manager positions and a second level manager position). A department typically supports a wider range of experience with a range from senior people to early career people who can be mentored by the senior people. New graduates entering a team face a wide variety of challenges, but when they enter a department there are many more resources available to support them as they rapidly get traction in becoming productive and growing their careers. There are typically more opportunities for internships. Performance reviews with forced curves tend to be fairer. The senior level voice can represent the UX vision at higher levels in the organization and the individual designer or researcher is typically seen as having more clout behind them. A department can often support specialized talents such as a lab manager, technical writers, and accessibility experts. A department can also invest in work that benefits all the projects and that provides benefits across releases. The department usually has the ability to apply for more substantial budgets and can advance particularly innovative programs and efforts (e.g., large user panels or major field studies, or perhaps the creation of a design studio). With its range of talent, the department also is often able to generate more of the "glue" that creates culture within a UX community, a branded Web site, communications vehicles, team events and shared experiences, and so on. Beyond the department, some larger companies have found collecting the departments into a design center can drive design thinking through the entire business.

At the department and design center level of organization there is often some heterogeneity in the structure based on the needs of the organization, span of control and management depth restrictions, seniority, and so on. At several companies with sizable UX communities, a given UX middle manager or executive might have groups of various sizes focused on specific projects or functions (e.g., prototyping and branding), senior individuals, specialists (e.g., accessibility), administrative support, and others reporting to them. The larger the organizational unit the richer the view of how to best deliver the corporate goals through exceptional user experiences can be reflected in the skills available and how they are structured.

DEFINING THE MIX OF SKILLS

Jon Innes (2007) of Intuit wrote an article titled "Defining the User Experience Function: Innovation through Organizational Design." He points out that most experts in our field recognize that to create great experiences and products requires highly collaborative multidisciplinary teams. He cites a quote from IDEO's Tom Kelly (2005) stating that ". . . you don't need every person on every project, and certainly not at every moment . . . you seldom need all the tools at once, but the perfect kit of tools is a set where you use all of them pretty frequently." One of the tools Innes provides to the manager is the use of a spider diagram to articulate the mix of skills you are trying to assemble. He lists six dimensions or skill types that can be thought of as candidates for an effective team. In his diagram he includes field studies, interaction design, usability testing, concept prototyping, information architecture, and what I suspect was intended to be visual design. For other application domains, it is easy to imagine variations in the set of candidates. His diagram shows levels for each, presumably representing the needs of the organization. He uses the metaphor of the nervous system to capture the notion of how skills work together and how they can be trained to grow stronger and better satisfy the needs of the organization. He cites several sources suggesting that the role of the leader of the UX team is like a movie director, casting the right actors and getting them to work together to produce great experiences.

I agree with Innes. I have found that each time I have an opening, the person I am looking for is heavily influenced by the mix of skills, passions, and experiences I already have on the team. When a person moves on and leaves a vacancy, I often do not fill the vacancy with a person exactly like the one who left; instead I look for how I can advance the overall quality of the team. It is a little like playing cards, where at each point in the game you are trying to improve your hand. Some of the skills you may be looking for are illustrated in Figure 3.1.

Potential Team Skills

- Interaction Design (incl. HCI, and human factors)
- Information Architecture
- Visual Design, Product Design
- Branding
- Graphic Design
- Media Design
- Organizational Design
- Field Research (e.g., ethnography, contextual inquiry)
- Usability Research (incl. traditional, experimental, and quantitative)
- Market Research
- Statistician
- Process Analyst
- Experience Architecture
- Content Management
- Technical Writing
- Editing
- UI Development (incl. SDK code samples, tools, etc.)
- Prototyping
- UX Project Management, Production
- Design or Art Direction
- Localization
- Accessibility
- Lab and Tools Support
- Recruiting Coordinator

FIGURE 3.1

Potential team skills.

executive arrived. If you could show up on the company's doorstep and explain how UX could be their salvation in a compelling way, the executives could often turn into supporters and advocates who in turn could open doors for UX to have an incredible impact. In one case after such a presentation I was given a standing invitation to participate in the vice president's staff meetings to represent user experience at the general manager level of that area of the business. In another case, such a presentation resulted in an effort to define and drive design pattern standards across an entire vice presidential level organization.

One ongoing debate is whether there should be a vice president of UX. Those who argue for it seem to feel that a vice president of UX will fix all of our problems and will be able to force the rest of the company (largely engineering based) to "do the right thing." Doing the right thing is of course doing things the UX way. Those who argue against it make the point that waiting for a champion from above is just giving up personal responsibility to make a difference, and if we keep moving forward eventually one of us will be promoted to that level if we are producing real value. I have to confess my personal bias. Based on what I have seen in companies for which I have worked and in companies where I have seen vice presidential level UX people, a senior officer with a UX background can have a tremendous impact on accelerating the growth of UX and driving a user-centered design culture. When they are absent it is just too easy for UX to be relegated to the niche role of staff augmentation to development and testing (quality). That does not remove the responsibility for those at the working level to continue to take ownership for advancing the UX agenda, but it can amplify the impact of UX people working in the frontline and can materially drive broader UX impact at the strategic level of the business. One of the changes over the last decade has been the explosion in the number of vice president of UX positions opening up across the industry. The opportunity to influence from the executive ranks is unprecedented.

At Sapient there was a Chief Experience Officer (Rick Robinson) and a Chief Creative Officer (Clement Mok). Sapient had largely been a middleware company before E-Lab and Studio Archetype were acquired, and having these important voices at the very top of the company inserted UX language into the corporate strategy discussions. This in turn drove culture change throughout the company. Neither appeared to be inserting themselves in daily decisions at the working level but their voices — and their voices as heard through the voices of the CEOs — made it clear through the company what the values of Sapient were. They clearly brought inspiration to all of us and provided a validation for the work we were doing and the points of view we were expressing.

The most senior level UX people should influence those executives across the business like a vice president of UX might. Some clearly are doing this and are visible at the very highest levels of the company. Even those at a somewhat lower level have many opportunities. I have been fortunate to be on projects where I was part of periodic reviews to the CEO, had a chance to share what the user experience community could and was doing, and have had several one-on-ones with the CIO and CTO talking about the vision for user experience.

At each level of the management chain there are decisions being made that would be made more effective if UX expertise was inserted into the conversation. In other words, there should be UX people at each level of the business from top to bottom bringing a UX perspective to the table. At each level of the management chain the skills needed are going to be different. It may also be that very few UX people are prepared yet to speak the language of higher level executives and with the appropriate business authority, to do it with a rich background of UX experience and insight, and to swear and yell with the best of them that this is where UX should be. It will be interesting to see how the field evolves, however, as more and more people grow to these higher levels, and whether academic programs begin to form hybrids between human-computer interaction (HCI) and other departments, and business schools grow these kinds of senior level people. When there is a specialist MBA for executive level UX people at the University of Chicago, Harvard, or Northwestern Business Schools, a milestone will have been reached.

Distribute the Team or Centralize It

One continuing debate is whether to centralize UX or to distribute it. At one extreme is the single UX department that supports the company or a major product area. At the other extreme are individuals embedded in the teams they support. Most UX people want to be in a centralized team. We have discussed many of the advantages of a centralized group. A few professionals prefer to be the lone UX fish in an engineering pond, because they can define their own ideal role and are rewarded for it, or because they are in a position to grow their own team in the future. In practice, as noted previously, in large companies or large organizations there is a pendulum that tends to swing over time driven by the fact that there are advantages for each. Furthermore, in many large companies there will be variations along the pendulum's swing in organizations across a given company. From a corporate perspective, the pros and cons are probably more evenly weighted resulting in the pendulum.

Rosson and Carroll (2002) noted that integrating usability professionals into project teams increases the likelihood that the questions that need to be raised are raised at the right time, and that the issues are dealt with directly during the development life cycle. The usability people have skin in the game and are immersed in the domain of the problems. They can both see issues that might not otherwise be noticed and recommend solutions that are more likely to make a difference. On the other hand, there usually are not enough usability people for every project and when they are focused on the local priorities they often miss the issues that cross project silos.

My current organization is a concrete example of whether to centralize or distribute UX. After the recent changes in the organization, there are seven designers, one researcher, and one product planner (similar to a market researcher, and coordinating across business groups). The team is responsible for Microsoft.com design work, including sites for Microsoft's partners and small and mid-sized customers (among other projects). There is also a sibling team of designers and researchers in the organization that supports HR applications, applications for legal and finance, and similar internally focused applications that sit under a different general manager. Both are under the same vice president. A third general manager under the vice president has a single UX person, and there are a few other individual UX people scattered under other vice presidents in the IT organization. The general managers under the vice president are naturally quite competitive, and for much of the time over the last few years have each wanted their own UX people as part of their teams' core competencies.

The manager of the other UX team and I have talked about combining so we can have the advantages of a centralized team, and we have talked about where it would then make sense to position us as a team. The general managers each have enough work and funding for their own teams. One result, however, is that each team is driven by local priorities and does not have the support to work on larger IT priorities where UX might have a larger impact. It is unlikely that either general manager will agree to let the other control the UX resources that support their own team. One general manager remembers being supported by a centralized team and he feels it did not work. He argues that because of the problems it was broken up and distributed, and he remembers that as the preferred model. Interestingly, the distributed model has not been working in his old organization and so now they are centralizing again.

One option is to combine the teams and have the centralized team report to a general manager who owns common process and tools efforts for Engineering and IT. Another option is to report into the CTO under the CIO. That would place UX very high in the organization and link it more tightly to where many of the strategic decisions are being made. Another option is to report to someone who has major projects (e.g., quality, the intranet, etc.) that benefit all of IT. Still another is to move it to an organization that works much earlier in the development process, at the point where early envisioning and user research takes place and requirements are written. Complicating the discussions are a wave of reorganizations taking place that are designed to provide more engineering focus on key problem areas.

Janice Rohn (2007) argued for the centralized model as well, arguing that "centralized UX teams produce higher-quality work more efficiently and attract and retain top talent." The reasons she made this argument include the ability to support a broader range of priorities across the business: improved training and support; better development and career growth; and superior quality, consistency, and efficiency. She also cited other sources supporting centralization as a best practice such as Bodine (2006) and Rosenbaum, Rohn, and Humburg (2000).

Figure 3.3 illustrates the dimension of centralization versus distribution. The key value in distributing UX is driving impact by focusing individuals and small groups on the priorities of the teams in which they sit. They own the problems with which they are tasked and impact through that ownership. The key value of centralizing is that when massing the UX resources you can address priorities for broader areas of the business, apply a richer set of skills and resources to them, and have more impact in part by having more visibility and presence within the larger organization.

Figure 3.3 also illustrates two models of organization — by project or by discipline. When I started at Microsoft the server UX department I was in was organized

FIGURE 3.3

Centralizing versus decentralizing.

by discipline (research and design). The disciplines had a great deal of rivalry, and the products we supported did not feel they had their fair share of support. As a result, I restructured the department into multidisciplinary teams focused on individual projects. Part of the goal was to get the benefits of centralization, but also to have the projects receive the equivalent benefits of decentralization.

As a different example I organized my Tablet and notebook computer UX team into a design team, a research team, a content publishing and user assistance team, and a team creating a software development kit (SDK) that helped partner companies create more usable applications consistent with the work my other three teams were doing. This worked because the entire team was supporting a fairly homogenous area, Tablet and mobility. At times members of each of the teams were collaborating on some of the same features and at the same point in the development cycle; at other times each team was driving initiatives either in different areas of the business or different times in the cycle. For example, the research team had a major effort around identifying needs for the next-generation mobile device, while the design team was still focused on fit and finish for the last version of Windows Tablet software. The content publishing team was leading an effort to shift the support paradigm to an online Web site rather than depending so much on help files. Because I had specialists in each area leading each team, they were able to raise the level of excellence for each type of work.

The closest I have been to the distributed product orientation cell in Figure 3.3 is when I was at Sapient. At that time people were hired into disciplines such as information architecture, visual design, content management, and experience modeling. When you were assigned to a project, you would report to a project manager for the duration of the project. To grow skills across projects there were discipline leads, and senior people within each discipline had dotted line oversight for individuals within the discipline. I was responsible for supporting people across projects along the west coast, and participated in projects to grow the information architecture discipline. The lead drove discipline-wide activities (e.g., the creation of best practices and training and ensuring quality control in hiring), but in essence each individual was matrixed both through their discipline and to the projects they supported. A senior person within the discipline conducted career coaching and performance reviews, and the primary performance evaluation came from the project manager to whom the person was reporting.

To get some of the benefits of centralization in a distributed environment there needs to be a person or organization that attempts to create a virtually centralized organization or community. In my current job, for example, one of my roles is UX Community Lead. In large companies I have been in there are leadership teams for the discipline that attempt to build community and to work issues that apply to the virtual organization. Other companies use teams high in the organizational structure to drive common practices. Often these structures operate without authority, however, and compliance requires teams throughout the company to buy into the effort.

Positioning Within the Company

The productivity of a work group seems to depend on how the group members see their own goals in relation to the goals of the organization.

Ken Blanchard

UX teams have been positioned in a variety of places across companies, and are most frequently placed in engineering teams close to where UX work is turned into product (probably since they are taking on design tasks that would otherwise be performed by developers and usability appears to be similar to other quality assurance activities). However, UX teams are also placed earlier in the development process closer to where they can have the biggest impact on what matters to users or higher in the organizational structure where they can influence strategy. At Bell Labs there were UX teams in corporate, in systems engineering, and in development, and as projects moved through their life cycle the experience was handed from team to team. At another company I worked at, we were positioned in a user assistance team (a very large one) supporting several product areas. My current UX team was positioned in an architecture team for a while and then was moved into an organization responsible for "common services" across all of the engineering teams. These services included supporting the software builds and deployment, release management, tools, and the quality initiative.

Another place where you find UX teams is closer to the strategy area, and when positioned there they tend to drive more common guidelines and processes. In the Tablet organization, UX reported to the general manager in a functionally organized team along with the project managers, development, and test; UX was treated as one of the core competencies needed to deliver the operating system. UX may also be positioned in the product management area to shape and drive the vision of the experience downstream through development. The design work for the core project on which my team is working is currently owned by two teams — one is my team and the other is a design team inside corporate marketing and near the team working on branding. Marketing is a common place for UX teams as they work with customers to drive the vision of the experiences that will be developed. When teams are organized by discipline some companies and organizations place design in one part of the organization and usability in another part of the organization with the former treated as a type of development and the latter as a subdiscipline of test.

If you have a choice, being positioned in an organization at the point where the requirements are defined is a good compromise. This might be in marketing or in the systems engineering area. The heart of what UX does is to design and deliver user experiences that people find useful and compelling, but the biggest barrier to that is when the design does not quite make it into what is being built. The more organizationally and physically removed from development the more effort you need to build how you operate to make it feel to like you are part of their team. It is usually a little easier to work across organizational boundaries to partner with the business when generating the requirements. Often the business will see UX as their insider connection to engineering. The key is to build relationships with them, negotiating to get the intent implemented, and collaborating on finding the design alternative that can be built efficiently and effectively and supported. The further away you are from marketing and strategy and with the business itself, the more you have to build similar relationships with that organization to have an impact on the most fundamental aspects of the user experience that impact the business.

Being in the marketing organization or the strategy group has the advantage of placing UX up front where it can shape the vision of what is being built, and where one typically can spend the most time with the users to generate the best insights into what should be built. Often there is a big gulf between that visioning work and what comes out the back end, and many great visions stop at the point where the business requirements get picked up by engineering and turned into what the developers believe they can actually build.

Because UX shares a common commitment to a deep understanding of users with market research and strategy, it turns out that it is often easier to build bridges to those organizations from engineering than it is to build the bridges to engineering from marketing and strategy. Indeed, being in engineering often means UX is viewed as the translator with marketing, and this translation function is an additional value that UX can provide.

Architecture is a powerful place for user experience to be located, because shaping the very structure of the products enables the most effective experiences to be created. Furthermore, architecture gets involved very early in the engineering process. Unfortunately, in many teams architecture may be positioned outside of the heart of the organization so their guidance may not always be followed. Architects often are pretty hard-core engineers and may have trouble reaching across the cultural differences between a design team and an engineering team. In other words, they often do not "get it," so UX can struggle to have its contributions recognized in such a team if the right people are not running the team.

In a shared services team, the problem is often that the emphasis is clearly on the "services." Because of this there is a tendency for the group to be treated as icon jockeys or a usability-study-on-demand shop rather than as a team that can provide design leadership. Shared services teams are often viewed as overhead, so the pressures are on cost reduction and service levels. This makes it very hard to grow a program and its impact. The way UX is treated and the fragmentation it forces on the team as it delivers the demands of a wide variety of groups can harm the morale of the team and the design environment itself. It also raises the question in some people's minds about the value of having a permanent UX team, and whether or not the same results can be achieved by vendors.

Higher or Lower in the Company

Janice Rohn (2007) argued that

> **The organizational position of UX in the company, both reporting level and department, is one of the most important factors in determining how effective and influential UX will be. This organizational positioning is a truer indicator of how much value the company executives place on user experience than any well-intentioned statements of how important user experience is to the company.**

She noted that marketing and development report to higher levels in organizations (e.g., CEO, president, or top executive), and that when UX does not do the same, it suggests UX does not have the same level of influence. She recommends pushing to arrange for UX to report high in the organization. What functions report higher will vary from company to company, but the principle of identifying where the influence points are and aiming for those is a good one.

Recognizing that in many companies UX does not report to a higher-level person, Rohn believes UX should report to the department with the most power (control and influence) in the organization such as marketing or development. She suggested that the quality assurance or technical writing/user assistance teams typically have less influence and should be avoided as a place to position the UX team. In essence, she recommends assessing whether your team is more marketing driven (where detailed requirements come from) or more development driven (with products and features coming from development) and to push for positioning based on whichever is core.

As you look across various companies where the UX team has been placed high in the organizational structure, they do tend to work broadly across the corporation and can get involved in and even generate projects that address corporate strategic needs. On the other hand, many such teams (and this includes architectural teams) often have serious challenges when it comes to being an influential part of front-line teams and having impact on the ground. Contributing to this challenge is that some people at the general manager level and higher do not want to get involved in operational activities; they just want to work at the higher strategic and business levels. This means they will be less likely to attend to the day-to-day challenges the UX team is facing.

Where Should People Sit

> Great discoveries and improvements invariably involve the cooperation of many minds. I may be given credit for having blazed the trail but when I look at the subsequent developments I feel the credit is due to others rather than to myself.
>
> **Alexander Graham Bell**

Yet another person on my SQL team burst in the door with the complaint "They didn't include us in their morale event! They went to the movies and didn't include us! Make them include us!" This person was not the first or the last with that concern. Instead of the movie it could have been, "I heard the team had a meeting to discuss the new feature and they didn't include us!" or "They decided to change direction [having met in the hall] and they didn't tell us!" or "They won't let us see their designs. They are keeping them hidden in a server and only showing them at their team meeting, and we aren't invited!" One perspective on the problem is that UX is not loved enough. When UX works with teams who really see UX as vital to their success, they will invite your people to the morale events, make sure you are not forgotten when the spontaneous meetings are pulled together, and give you access to the key information. It is often true that everyone has limited budgets, and you may not be inviting other teams to your events, or remembering to engage them in every decision you make with your team. The root cause is often simple and pragmatic. The applicable phrase is "out of sight, out of mind." If your team wants to be there, they need to be there. They need to be reaching out to the teams with whom they are working and getting involved.

One of the questions that comes up time and again is whether the UX team should be physically collocated, or whether the team should be distributed among the teams that are supported. There was a study in the early 1990s at Bellcore that showed the further apart two people are physically the lower their probability of casually meeting. As you separate two people by a hallway, the probability drops about an order of magnitude; by a floor, another order of magnitude; and by a building yet another order of magnitude. That obviously impacts the likelihood that people are going to meet spontaneously, discover things they should get involved in or remember to invite others, share the gossip that serves as the bond that leads to further engagement, and collaborate in other ways.

The argument for embedding with the supported teams is that you want those teams to feel UX is part of their team. You want the UX people to know what is going on and be part of those casual meetings that spring up where decisions are made. You would like project team members to be enrolled in what UX is doing almost in spite of themselves (e.g., because the designs or data are on the walls and in the air). When people see you in the hall they tell you things you might not otherwise learn, as you pass people you overhear things that are relevant, and people see you and a synapse closes and they say things like "Hey, Karen should be in this meeting. I don't think she was invited. I'd better get her there." Spontaneous gatherings of people from across disciplines within the team for lunch or coffee build bonds that serve as the foundation for project collaboration.

Designs get put up on the walls so people know design is happening, they get a taste of the process of user research and design by seeing it around them, and the designers and researchers can pull team members in spontaneously for a "Hey, what do you think of this?" session. Furthermore, for various activities such as fit and finish work the designers spend a lot of hours working side by side with the developers. In situations like that, it clearly makes sense to have a base where the UX people can work closely with the people they collaborating with on a daily basis. Your team will be a lot more efficient in this environment.

On the other hand, if your project portfolio is likely to change it will be hard to move people from location to location with those changes. Space typically does not work that way. Each group holds onto their space very tightly in most companies, and it is usually a battle to get more. One of the reasons for bonding closely with the administrative assistants is they often have an inside track in the process of getting space. The only time things really loosen up is when major moves happen and the amount of space is up for negotiation again. So unless your team is dedicated to a small number of projects with a stable set of project managers, developers, and testers, you probably will not be embedded with the supported teams. In that case, you will almost certainly want to be collocated. One compromise is to try to negotiate satellite offices in the area of the supported teams that your team can use when they need to work locally. You will need to find ways to increase and support face-to-face time with the teams you support. This might include inviting them to participate in your morale and training events.

My current team recently was in a situation that represented several of these challenges. As a team, we were located in a small campus of three buildings in Issaquah, WA. Half of my team was in offices in one building and half were in cubicles in another building. The type of space allocated to each person was determined by seniority. There is a big room that contractors are typically placed in, but since the contractors work so closely with my team members the team chose to have the contractors share their offices and cubicles. Most of our business contacts, however, have their offices up in Redmond (about 30 minutes away), and some of my team work with the development organization that sits in a different part of the Redmond campus. We tried, without success, to get a satellite office that my team could use in the midst of the business contacts; but we were only successful in getting a remote office with the development team.

For usability research we were using the shared testing space in Redmond that is primarily used by the product groups. We did manage to work with the administrative assistants to get access to lobby space we turned into a small design studio and a storeroom that we redesigned to create a team space for design and research activities.

After a year and a half in that arrangement it was announced that all of the general managers were going to be shifted like pieces on a game board. The general manager that I work for moved his entire team (including the development organization) to a building in another part of Redmond. As expected, we were then able to work much more closely with that team. On the other hand, most of my team was moved far away from the other development teams they were supporting which remained in Issaquah. I am now trying to get the administrative assistants handling the space to see if they can grab a satellite office for us. I am also trying to keep control of the former storage space room, so in the worst case we can continue to use that as a satellite office. We discovered an unused user research area that technically belongs to another organization, and have arranged to bring the lab back online, turn another area into a participatory design space and team room, and use another part of the testing lab to house our growing set of contractors. Since we have been distributed this way, we have been using instant messaging and teleconferencing heavily to support our team activities, and I supplement with weekly team meetings and periodic all-day mandatory off-sites to support team bonding.

Personally, I have found the benefits of collocation tend to outweigh the benefits of being distributed and embedded in the diverse teams we support. A key to getting your team to the high performance level is physically having them together. UX people typically enjoy and get energized by being together because they share a similar approach to problems and are stimulated by the creativity in others. Being together improves the quality of what each individual designer or researcher does since they get the benefits of ongoing critiques from their colleagues. They also grow their own skills by airing their own points of view and exploring and debating them with others. Designers and researchers solve problems faster when they can pull in colleagues. It is easier to manage as you stay in touch with what each person is doing and move from person to person. You can communicate more consistently across the team and manage the rumor mill more effectively by being in the middle of it. You can create spaces with labs, studios, and getting the design process on the walls that become a brand for the team. You communicate the weight of the UX effort as others come to the area for meetings, which in turn helps increase influence.

Working Remotely

Collaboration is to the networked organization what leadership is to the hierarchical organization, and we are living in a world where the networked organization is replacing the hierarchical organization because it's more natural, more engaging, and more effective.

Dave Pollard

There are times when at least some of your team may be working remotely. Not long ago I was approached by a member of my team who wanted to explore a telework situation, where at least for one or two days a week he could work at a shared space in another city or work from home. This team member lived far away, the distributed nature of the teams he supported was causing him to travel a lot, and he was concerned about the environment and his own work-life balance. Another person wanted to work extra-long days for four days, and have three days off.

Jean Scholtz organized an excellent panel at CHI in 1997 on telework (Scholtz et al., 1998). The panel had both managers and people working for the managers remotely. Victoria Bellotti was on the panel talking about her research on systems supporting remote colleagues. She distinguished two types of teleworkers: teleporter and telepath. The teleporter is a person who occasionally works from home and takes work home at night or on the weekend. The telepath works more consistently from home or a remote office. She found that teleporters talk about how occasionally getting away enables them to get a lot more done by going heads-down and avoiding meetings and interruptions. I personally recall as a lead disappearing periodically for a day to work on requirements and being able to complete about a week or two's worth of work in a long day; even now, when work starts to pile up it is clearly a blessing of technology to be able to duck out of the office, squat at a table in the corner of my favorite latte shop up in Snoqualmie, WA, with a gorgeous grande latte (and for very difficult tasks, a homemade shortbread cookie), and just crank out results.

Telepaths on the other hand have particular challenges around driving influence, having their influence be recognized, and getting the kind of low-level information that over time becomes critical to having the greatest influence. Scholtz noted that consistently telepaths want technology to help them gain access to people and to interact as informally as if they were sitting near them. We all know how e-mail is much weaker than face-to-face communication in its ability to carry important emotional cues and information shared through the physical interplay that happens in face-to-face situations.

Jenny DeGroot and I were on the panel as one of the manager and remote worker combinations. Jenny is great, and she came to me at one point and told me that her husband was attending school for a while in another part of the country. I did not want to lose her from the team. She was clearly an excellent member of the team bringing energy, accomplishing wonderful things, and helping advance UX within the projects on which she worked. We had already gone through performance reviews where we had had great conversations about her career and it was exciting to watch her grow in the job and anticipate future successes. On the other hand, time and again I have either been in or heard of the conversation where the significant other is going to move and the person quits to be with them. How can you blame them? When she proposed the possibility of working remotely it opened up an entirely different alternative. As we talked about it, it was clear that many of the people she worked with were already in other states, and so from their perspective her move would be transparent. There was no question that she would be able to be successful in delivering her work.

One of the biggest challenges turned out to be more local, more about how the two of us would work together. I wanted to make sure that I was able to coach her effectively, and that I would be able to give her a fair performance evaluation. We realized we needed to make sure we worked much harder and more explicitly at communicating. The fact that we had been working together helped with our communication. We already knew a lot about each other's styles. In addition, we needed to make sure that through that communication we were very clear on what was being done, the deliverables that were being created, and the process of creating them (what was going to be done, how it was going as it progressed, and the results). These same conversations are important even when you are surrounded by your team, but there are more incidental opportunities to stay in touch with the work. When someone is remote you have to work at it explicitly.

The most irritating challenges in some ways were the more subtle ones. Jenny captures it well with her comments. Here is an excerpt that contains her feelings while working remotely.

Some colleagues in other work groups had a frustratingly wrong mental model of my situation. Because I was not physically present, they seemed to think I was on a sort of vacation or leave of absence. For example, they behaved as if I had no access to company information or e-mail. When I visited the main office periodically, they would fill me in on old news such as, "Guess what? Our division has been reorganized!" When I returned to the main office full time, I was sometimes asked, "Are you back at work now?" as if I hadn't been working all along. As a result, I made extra efforts to justify my telework during casual conversations, by mentioning the benefits of working without interruption, or of attending conferences in my area without travel expenses.

When in a telework arrangement formal activities such as status reports are even more efficient than when held face to face because extra effort is usually invested in scheduling and preparation. The informal level of communication that supports creative collaboration and team bonding typically is tied to the existing trust relationship. If a group of people have already bonded as a team, introducing technology may not strengthen the team's effectiveness, but it usually does not hurt it too badly. The bonding persists despite the insertion of the technology. There is some evidence that face-to-face bonding may be required to refresh the relationship. Again, Jenny noted

---

A disappointing surprise was that the friendlier a group is, the harder it is to attend its meetings via speaker phone. For example, our weekly Human Factors group meetings are lively and interesting — for those in the meeting room. But via speaker phone they're frustrating. People talk at the same time, interrupt, crack jokes, rustle cookie bags. The very things that make the meeting fun in person make it difficult to simply hear what people are saying, let alone contribute, over the phone.

When people are separated you have to take extra steps to bring them together. When half my team was moved into another building, with half in offices in one building and the other half in cubicles, we held nearly all our meetings in the building where the people in cubicles were located. We exchanged calendar access so we could easily find each other and find meeting times when everyone could attend. As a team policy we leaned heavily on instant messaging to stay connected electronically. As a manager, management by walking around became even more important.

These issues are pushed to the extreme when working with team members working internationally or working with teams on another continent. All the issues that we have been discussing for remote workers apply, but there are additional issues such as cultural differences, the organizational strategies that have led to the relationship, and practical issues like working across time zones. The organizational strategies are often about having a 24-hour design and development cycle, taking advantage of different cost models in different countries, and taking advantage of unique skill sets and experiences.

Globally Distributed Teams

Many companies are global companies and sell internationally. You want the users of the products to be engaged in the design process, so having a local presence in key international markets helps product quality. Even practically, when I was at Ameritech, one of my team (Bob Schumacher) worked remotely in Europe for a while. Remotely, he had immediate impact of being embedded with the project and there were long-term benefits through the connections he made with the international parts of our business.

A common chronic complaint when managing a team that is spread internationally arises when U.S.-based teams treat remote members as merely staff augmentation and just send them the work on the edges of the project — the work that the people in the home office do not want to do. As a manager, it will be up to you to make sure that the work of your remote employees is as meaningful, challenging, and rewarding as the work the rest of your team is doing. The advice from a recent manager who has worked with many teams on separate continents is that what is important is having clarity in roles and responsibilities as well as deliverables and expectations. There needs to be a crisp and clear decision-making process, and as with other remote work situations you need to maintain frequent communication (he called it "high fidelity, low friction communication").

The obvious implication is that maintaining regular open communication will take extra effort. That means calls and meetings need to be scheduled early or late in the day (which will be early or late for your remote person as well). As the manager, there may be times when you will need to hold a meeting twice, once for each location. When there is budget, you should periodically travel to the remote location to spend extended time going deep with the remote team members and learning about the context of their work, bonding with them face to face, and catching up on the aspects of projects that do not come out in formal meetings.

When I was at Sapient, to help with the bonding and to smooth transitions as work moved through the development cycle and across locations, the company would bring people from one location to spend an extended time at the starting location before the work transitioned between physical locations. Then when the work did transfer, some of the people who had worked on it at the beginning went with the work and spent time at the remote location to help with the transition.

Another thing to keep in mind is the cultural differences that may impact the remote work situation. Today this diversity needs to be something a good manager is aware of even within their own team when they are collocated. You want diverse teams because they bring extra value and improve the quality of and innovation in your work. Be aware of whether the remote person is comfortable expressing bad news or sharing information that might seem more personal, or desires to be more autonomous or to be more a member of the group.

A quick refresher about some of these considerations is available from a book *Kiss, Bow, or Shake Hands* (Morrison, Conaway, & Borden, 1994). You will learn plenty by just be being open with your team members and curious about their culture, talking about their wants and needs, and sharing your own. There are also many other resources online or through available books and articles about cultural differences (e.g., Marcus, 2002). Another newer source is a book that has just come out about conducting international research, which also offers insights about the issues that come with managing across cultures (Schumacher, 2009).

Moving Your Team in the Organization

What if you and your team are reporting into Dilbert's boss, or a jerk, or someone who does not quite get it and probably never will? What if you are positioned in a team that is actually hostile to UX or that does things in a way that will kill UX and clearly will not change, or you are just simply in the wrong place for what you need for success? I have been in each of those situations at various points. I like to think I can work with nearly everyone, and I hate to admit that there is a situation I cannot work through to advance the UX agenda. At times, however, when I think about the cost-benefit trade-off of beating my head against a wall versus taking ownership of a bolder and often riskier move that offers a chance of moving to a positive place, I conclude that the risky move is in fact better than certain failure. That risky move could be to start exploring the possibility of navigating your team to another position in the organization.

When you find yourself in this position, it may be time for what is sometimes known as a career-impacting decision. You hope you are making the right decision for you and the team. One thing is certain in most companies, change is the rule. If you can survive long enough, there is a reasonable chance that your management and perhaps even the organization itself will change. In my latest job, I had 5 managers in 2½ years. That degree of change obviously did not help my career, since career growth in part depends on your reviewer getting to know you, your work, and your impact. It will help if you have in mind where you would like to be when change comes since it is sometimes easier to steer something in the midst of change than when the systems have all settled into place. I have also been in a couple of spots where I felt the position was harming my team and risking future UX impact, and have taken a more aggressive role in altering my team's destiny.

This navigation is delicate at several levels. You cannot talk to your team about it, because the last thing you can afford is rumors starting to fly and taking the decision of your team's fate entirely out of your hands. You cannot appear to your boss like you are disloyal, or cause your boss to think you are not giving your all to the organization's goals (especially if there is a chance that the move will not happen). Indeed, you should be doing your best to simultaneously be as successful for your organization as you can in your current situation, even as you try to navigate to a better one. You might find it useful to find a trusted mentor who can be a sounding board as you develop tactics.

One approach is to talk with the manager you want to work for by trying to create a conversation where he comes up with the thought "Hey, you should report to me!" Another, depending on your current boss' attitude about the team, is to try to engage the targeted manager in developing strategies for increasing the impact of your team on the overall organization, including at least as a thought exercise thinking through organizational alternatives. Like any sales job, that discussion is about trying to get the boss to realize that some goal they have (perhaps a pain point they want to reduce) will be solved if your team moves to another place. You may need to prepare assurances that the manager will continue to receive services that led him to acquire your team in the first place.

The ultimate step might be to go over the manager's head and talk to someone higher in the organization about the issues. If there are champions above, you can leverage them. If you are going to take that step, you had better have your arguments together and be reasonably certain of the outcome. There is probably no going back once that step is taken. I have taken this ultimate step, however, and it did result in a move. I did need to put in the extra effort over the next year to try to heal the relationship and the hard feelings persisted in causing irritation for some time (mostly negative comments during public reviews of my team's work from the former boss, and some payback at performance review time). With time and effort the person became a supporter (at least a mild supporter) as we were able to accomplish things that could not be accomplished if we had stayed where we were.

One final form of escape is personal escape. I had one wise manager tell me (after he was no longer my manager) that I needed to watch out for myself first. He argued that in a new and better place I would inevitably be building a team again and some of my best people would be likely to follow. As I have moved from place to place, I have been fortunate in having some of my best people follow me to new teams. That has been a great help in seeding efforts and rapidly growing to excellence. It is another reason to be absolutely committed as a manager to helping the individuals on your team be the best they can possibly be, and to grow their own careers while they are contributing to your team strategy and to the business goals. In general my moves have been to grow and try something new, or to take a big jump in the impact I can have, but there have been one or two times when it has been at least partially about getting out of a bad situation.

FUNDING THE TEAM

Estimating Your Needs

There are several ways to determine how much funding will be needed for a project. One approach is the top-down approach described in the section Sizing the Team. Here you are basing the estimate on the expected demand from the project managers and the developers (either by size of total budget, or based on staffing ratios). For example, if you are supporting a team with 10 project managers and 30 developers, and you know it takes 1 designer to support the work of 3 or 4 project managers, you can begin to build a staffing plan. Or you might look at the total budget and know that for projects of the type your organization is supporting it should take 6 to 10% of the budget to support the needed design and user research. Another approach is historical. Here you know how much your team was able to produce last year against a projected set of features and the organizations you supported, and you can size up or down based on changes in the forecast for the upcoming year. Then there is the pragmatic approach where your funding may be reduced for a given project, while the project itself may continue with the same level of need. Again, you can reduce what you can produce appropriately and that will force a conversation with the team on what they will need to pick up, and where you can provide leadership that will enable others to take on more of the design under your team's direction. This is similar to the analysis described in the engagement model where you provide more or less support (and will do more or less work) based on the business impact of the project and the importance of the user interface to the project.

There are also various bottom-up methods. If you can be clear about what the required activities are then you can put together an estimate of what will be needed to deliver. I cannot tell you how many times I have had people saunter into my office with a "Hey, can you put some designers on my project? I am in a hurry and need screens designed for Monday." I am always amazed that they think I have a designers and researchers sitting around apparently doing nothing. The size of the project described usually bears no relationship to what it will actually take to do the work, and that is unfortunately due to a lack of understanding of what it takes to create an effective design. A model of the default deliverables through your process and the parameters that impact the effort required to support them can be helpful in putting together a quote for the work.

My team put together a table (see Figure 3.4) that we use to help with the estimation and to set expectations with clients. It shows the major deliverables we produce and the T-shirt sizing for the work. We distinguish new-to-the-world projects from those that focus on major problem areas of an existing application or significant new features, and those from smaller variations on an existing design. We point

Typical SDLC Phase	Activity	Size of Project			Skills	
		Small	Medium	Large	Design	Research
Planning	Field Research	NA	1–3 M	2–3+ M		■
	Vision Prototype	NA	2–4 W	1–3 M	■	■
Requirements	Questionnaire Design	1–5 D	2–4 W	2–4 W	■	■
	Competitive Analysis	2–4 W	1–3 M	1–3 M		■
	Persona Definition (Assumptive)	1–3 W	1–3 M	1–3+ M	■	■
	Scenario Definition	2 4 W	2–4 W	1+3 M	■	■
	Task Analysis	1–5 D	2–4 W	1–3 M	■	■
Design, Build, and Stabilize	Storyboard (wireframe prototype)	1–5 D	2–4 W	1+3 M	■	
	Wireframe Page	1–5 D	1–5 D	1–5 D	■	
	Card Sort or Affinity Diagram	1–5 D	2–4 W	2–4 W	■	
	Information Architecture (incl. research)	2–4 W	1–3 M	3+ M	■	■
	Interaction Design	1.5D	2–4 W	2–3 M	■	■
	Interaction Prototype	1–3 M	3+M	3+ M	■	
	Usability Study	1 M	1 M	1 M		■
	Guidelines Reviews	1–5 D	2–4 W	1+3 M	■	
	Heuristic Review	2–0	1 W	2–4 W	■	
	Icon (If existing)	1.5 D	1–5 D	1–5 D	■	
	Icon (If new, and going through full reviews)	2–4 W	2–4 W	2–4 W	■	
	Production Assets	1–5 D	2–4 W	2+3 W	■	
	Red Lines	2–4 W	1–3 M	3+ M	■	
	UI Style Guide/Specifications	2–4 W	1–2 M	1–3 M	■	
Operate	Baseline Competitive Analysis	2–4 W	1–2 M	1–2 M		■

FIGURE 3.4

Menu of activities for planning.

out that the specific levels of effort will depend on details of the project, that activities can happen in parallel (e.g., you can get an icon reviewed by legal while you are working on other design tasks), and many of the things we do that deliver the greatest value do not lend themselves to being represented in a menu (e.g., participating in a strategic planning task force).

To improve the accuracy of estimates, we are pushing teams toward early rapid, low-fidelity prototyping to rough in a user interface that implements the top priority scenarios and to kick-start user research. For one project, a multidisciplinary team using a rapid prototyping tool was able to convert seven major scenarios into several dozen use cases, then they could wireframe the interaction patterns supporting the use cases in a matter of just a couple of days. They were then able to estimate how many template types would be needed, how many total screens, the number of graphical elements that would be needed, and the key design problems that would take more work. A side benefit is that the prototype became a common language that everyone on the team could use and agree to as a representation of a specific implementation of the scenarios. You need to be careful that this rapid prototype is not the final design, but rather is used as a tool — an initial mound of clay roughed into the general image of the final result — to help in working toward the design. Clearly, it is the designers and researchers who are the key to turning a scoping exercise into a working estimate. They have the best handle on what they can produce and how quickly.

Direct Funding Versus Strategic

In 2007 there was an excellent panel at the ACM SIGCHI conference on incorporating HCI into companies. One of the most interesting parts of the discussion was on how best to fund user experience work. There are basically three approaches: direct funding, shared funding, and a hybrid. The funding might be provided at the beginning of the year and budgeted, or it may be cross-charged in an internal service model (e.g., the expenses for the month are billed back to projects at the end of the month). The recommendation of the CHI session was that the hybrid model made the most sense, and that has been my experience as well.

In direct funding, a project includes the funding for the UX work for the year in its budget and funds it up front. If the UX team is organized within the project team, the UX budget may be treated in the same way as the development, project management, and test budgets. If budgeting is based on feature areas and initiatives within the project, the UX budget may be handled in a similar manner. In either of these cases, your job as manager will be to identify not only the number of people to be covered and the other costs associated with the ongoing UX work (e.g., hardware and software, research costs, etc.), you will also have the opportunity in the process to think about specific initiatives that you want to drive into the budget (e.g., the cost of a major user panel, or an exploratory ethnographic study, or a Web site for providing access to reusable assets).

Another model of direct funding is the cross-charge or chargeback model. In this situation the team is funded much like an internal consulting firm. As work is done the requesting teams are billed for the work. In direct funding, if the UX is not devoted to a single project and embedded there, the UX team is often placed at the highest level that covers the majority of the relevant funding teams, or it is placed in a team that provides support across projects (e.g., a common services team or an architecture team).

In the shared funding model, the UX team is funded like other initiatives within the organization (in essence equivalent to an entire project, and with a similar implicit or explicit business case). Funding is set aside for the team, and the team develops its work program within that budget. Each year appeals for increases in the budget are made based on the major initiatives that are planned. The shared funding model may be implemented as part of a larger funding process where the money is allocated early in the corporate funding process or higher up in the organization, or it may be implemented as a tax on the other programs in the larger organization in which the UX team sits. Shared funding tends to recognize that UX is a core competency and is strategically important for the business. With shared funding, there is often a discussion that UX should be positioned at a place in the organization relatively high up so that the "view" of UX covers a broad area of the organization, often at the executive level. This can have a side benefit of providing a UX voice at the executive levels.

The pros and cons of the two models based on my experience are shown in Figure 3.5. The shared funding model gives the most flexibility in responding to the needs of the organization. It lets you respond quickly to emerging and strategically important needs, to invest in key projects that need UX support, and it lets you initiate projects that are beneficial across projects and during the release of projects. The downside is if teams are taxed and they feel slighted, it can build resentment. In shared funding, people are likely to assume that your services are unlimited and free, so they feel they can walk in and demand those services. The value placed on your services may be lower, since they are likely to walk in for specific needs rather than strategic end-to-end involvement, and people tend to value what they actually pay for and to the extent they pay for it. If they view services as free and if they do not like what you recommend or produce, there is little incentive for them to go ahead and use it. Finally, any shared service in an organization has another word often applied to it besides core competency and that is "overhead." When budgets get tight, teams not seen as directly integrated into the value engine of the business (and sized based on the value they produce) are among the first to be squeezed.

The direct model has the advantage of being need and value driven. When you are providing value, people want more user experience. Under the best circumstances it is almost like they become addicted to the value they receive and are hungry for more. It is a straightforward argument that if a team wants more support, the team should pay for more support and as a result your team will grow. Accountability is clear because the team funding you is defining the priorities and since they are paying for what they get, they are motivated to value and use it. Unfortunately, it also can mean the work gets locally optimized and may not be the most strategic application of UX resources for the overall business. Your team will spend time on the needs of the team but not necessarily on the things that will produce the most value. Since projects go through busy times and slower times, demand may wane and you may not have funding for some of your team (at least in the chargeback model). I also find that other teams can bond to specific people on your team and only want those people. That can restrict your flexibility in making staffing decisions that are smart for the business, and it can make it hard for you to help people develop their careers if their goals are to move into different kinds of work. There is also very little motivation for teams to support cross-project work like reusable assets or standards. If they sense that some of the cycles of "their" people are going into these kinds of things, their pushback may be to suggest that perhaps the people should just be moved directly into their teams.

I have found the hybrid model works the best. If I can get shared funding I can use it for "business development." It lets me respond to the most critical needs of the larger organization. It also lets me make smart investments if I see a corporately strategic project that does not have UX but should, or when I see an emerging project that is likely to become a more strategic project and that clearly is at the right place in its life cycle to take in user experience. I use the shared funding for some of those common activities that make the team more effective and efficient over time.

Type of Funding	Pros	Cons
Direct	• Need driven • Makes accountability clear • Engages funder in results • Enables growth in response to results	• Often low budget priority and underfunding risk • Viewed as "owned" • Priorities locally optimized • Little room for cross-project work • Variable demand
Shared	• Enables flexibility in supporting organizational priorities • Enables investment in emerging areas • Enables cross-project priorities • Relatively stable funding	• Frustration from teams under-supported (and possibly paying "tax") • Being seen as a "service" organization • Being viewed as an unlimited resource • Viewed as overhead

FIGURE 3.5

Types of funding.

These activities include standards and best practices, reusable assets, and projects like Web sites to serve the assets to those who will consume them. It was this kind of funding that let us invest in the work on understanding what makes products successful and to develop the USE questionnaire (Lund, 2001) as a way of doing a better job of creating successful products. It also is the kind of funding that lets us support our lab environment and create some of the branding assets that help promote the team and grow direct funding. The shared funding also supports a stable staffing model when direct funding varies.

The growth in the team often comes from direct funding. Projects were first supported by people who had been hired using the shared funding and our initial support might have been in that strategic investment category. The projects we support directly often have their favorite people largely dedicated to them, and as more and more value is provided they begin funding people directly, and as they fund more I hire more. Critical to the success of this model is that they feel the people I have supporting them are virtually on their team. I build into my climate assessments and 360-degree feedback process metrics to ensure we deliver the most value and are collaborating effectively. If at some point I conclude that someone should be on a different project (e.g., because their career aspirations have changed or the project needs are shifting), then I manage it with the team. There can be some resentment, but I have found that they usually come to love the new person just as much as the previous one who had been working on the project.

This can be illustrated with a recent example. When I joined the organization three years ago I came in as an Experience Architect to define and build a UX program that would change the way our customers deal with us through their life cycle of product experiences, and to serve as a UX Community Lead and grow the UX people and teams already present, unite them as a community, and evangelize continuing investment in UX. I reported to the senior general manager of the organization and worked closely with him and with the vice president on developing and implementing a strategy. I was funded directly by the general manager out of his budget. Even before I showed up, one of my previous designers (Pam) from another organization had joined and I suddenly had a team. As I laid out the plan I had in mind, the general manager announced in his staff meeting that he was pulling funding from each of his direct reports to fund the growth of UX within his organization. While I suspect I did not win a lot of friends in that staff meeting, he was receiving clear direction from the VP at the time (a champion) and saw user experience as a core competency that he wanted to build to deliver the vision he had for the larger organization.

I initially focused the team primarily on the general manager's top priority — developing a relationship experience through the self-service interfaces customers have with us. We were at the incubation and planning stage at this point, and I was also working on the experience architecture needed to support it. To enable these activities, my team was moved to the architecture team (which, as it happened, was also where the incubations were taking place). We became a center of gravity for UX and additional UX people, and those who wanted to work in the UX area were moved into my team. We grew the work plan to support teams who sent their people to us, as well as initiating projects to leverage the skills of the senior people who joined the team (e.g., working on user-centered process innovation). I was also able to invest effort in community building across the IT organization. There were important projects that came through the door that I was able to support (e.g., designing a prototype of a profile center to address regulatory requirements and launching a major international ethnographic study to understand what self-service and relationship meant to small and mid-sized business customers).

By the second year, we were sufficiently successful that funding was doubled. We hired a range of excellent and diverse designers and researchers. We were still funded primarily through the tax. The general manager and I agreed that we should focus on the project priorities within the organization where the UX work would have the greatest impact, and I argued that we wanted to take full ownership of the excellence of the experience. That meant I focused my team to put a critical mass of people on the projects we were working end to end. With that concentration and visibility of work there was a side benefit of opening the doors for direct funding as well for special projects requiring unique skills (e.g., information architecture). We hired contractors and vendors for those projects, and cross-charged the contractors and vendors to the requesting teams. I used managing the contractors and vendors as an opportunity to grow leadership skills within my team. As the rhythm of the projects varied over the course of the year we were able to shift people among the projects as needed. Organizationally we were moved to a team that provided other services across the organization such as release management, various tools, and software build engineering support.

I did get people walking in my door, however, wanting to know where the UX people were that they were paying for with their tax. They were not happy when I explained how the model was working. Others had just heard we had a UX team and wanted to know how they could get help. They also were not always happy with the answer they received. They would often walk in Friday wanting a design delivered by Monday. But the master plan was that with a focus on excellence we would be in a position to harvest best practices and reusable design ideas that could be applied elsewhere to help bring broader benefits. We also started what we called Office Hours. Office Hours were a series of sessions where any team could request support through a member of my team (Sindhia, who was a new graduate from Indiana we had recently hired), and subsets of my team would come together to provide a concentrated design or research critique. Finally, we were actively a part of a larger quality initiative where we would work closely with teams to build user-centeredness (through scenarios) throughout the development process.

Entering the third year we were reorganized yet again. My new boss wanted to deal with the ambiguity that came from the taxing model. He wanted the certainty of people paying for what they get and getting what they pay for. As a result we moved to the direct funding model and more of a service orientation. Each member of my team (with one or two exceptions) was funded by one of the teams under my general manager. This meant that we could not assemble a critical mass of effort for any project. Instead, we had to come up with a way of scaling the impact of the team by more actively educating the project managers, developers, and testers on projects to take on user experience tasks under our design direction and cranking up the efforts to grow the library of reusable design patterns another notch.

In this situation there was clarity, because as new projects came in requesting work we could point to the existing model and say that they had to have funding, and when they did, we would bring on contractors. Our hope was that when we reached the next funding season, we would be able to get a commitment up front from those teams so we could hire more permanent staff. To the extent that funding is a sign of success, at our height during the year we had tripled our funding. It dropped a bit by the end of the year to just doubling the funding with which we began the year. Unfortunately hiring was capped across the entire IT organization and so no new vacancies for full-time employees have appeared.

We keep running across project needs and not having the people to address them (and the teams do not have the flexibility in their budgets to let us hire). Where we have someone with the appropriate skills and where there is funding, we potentially can find a way to move money from one budget into another as we move people around. It does feel a little like a shell game at times, and there is a lot of overhead in keeping track of the budget and managing the hiring of contractors. This arrangement has also restricted our ability to address the biggest issues on the projects that will return the greatest value. Alas I am reasonably confident that when user interface issues arise in the customer feedback, my team will get the blame even when we are not involved in the design of the interface. This is obviously a concern. Still, we are doing what the organization currently is looking for — setting up a system of predictability in the funding process.

Perhaps even worse, the work climate has taken a major hit. People no longer feel like they are part of a team since they are each working on separate projects and often are scattered geographically around the Redmond area. They do not get to interact spontaneously with each other to improve their designs. The contract researchers take the intellectual capital that would otherwise accumulate across projects with them when they move on to other jobs. Teams are motivated to treat even the full time people like contractors and to leave them out of planning meetings, to push the least desirable work to them, and make impossible demands on delivery. This model definitely does not work well from the perspective of building the vision for the team.

We are in the process of again rethinking the approach. I have defined a new charter for the team that will allow the majority of the full-time staff to focus on one shared goal, even as they support individual projects. Nearly everyone on the team will be working on re-envisioning our corporate site and driving that vision across the sub-sites they are supporting. I will be pooling the funding from each and have the general manager's support of a charter where some of each person's role will be to drive themes across all the projects (e.g., a common brand framework), and where each person's top priority will be to drive a scenario-based vision into their projects. I am hiring a vendor who will provide a program management office function to handle the overhead of budget details and management of the temporary staff. Our hope is that the staff augmentation will allow us to grow and shrink as needed. We are also creating a design center where project themes will have team areas, the UX team as a whole will be able to meet, where our research will take place, where participatory design will be supported, and where we will collocate our team offices and cubicles for the contractors. Finally, we have obtained limited but stable shared funding that we intend to grow over time for more generic work whose value will be felt across projects.

An Engagement Model

Put all your eggs in the one basket and watch that basket.

Mark Twain

Given the challenge of both the shared and direct funding models, it has been important to have a standard response that can be used to answer the question: "How can we get UX support?" The place to start is to begin by scoping the business benefit and determining the level of effort needed to achieve the benefit, rather than just estimating the effort needed in the abstract. For any given project, you can provide more support or less, and for any level you have a variety of tools at your fingertips that can be applied given a specific set of constraints. A tool to help in the discussion is shown in Figure 3.6.

One dimension in Figure 3.6 is "How strategic is the project for the larger organization?" It is described in more detail in Figure 3.7. In most companies where I have worked, projects are assigned a priority when they first enter the queue as candidates for funding at the senior executive level. A subset of those projects are selected by senior management as among those they will focus on during the year since their potential business impact is considered to be so great. Senior management tracks

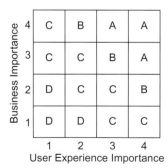

FIGURE 3.6

Assessing engagement level.

metrics on them, gets regular reports, and engages to drive progress. The big bet projects end up being in senior managers' commitments, which in turn ensures that they get the needed focus and support. There are many benefits that come from UX playing a critical role on projects that are in a senior management's sights as well as being seen as responsible for part of the business value the projects will deliver. At the low end of the dimension might be projects that are internal tools that teams are creating for themselves, and in the middle might be projects that are important for divisions within IT but that do not merit IT-wide attention.

Not every project, even strategically important ones, should have UX support. An additional question to ask, therefore, is "How important is the user experience to the success of the project?" This metric is illustrated in Figure 3.8. Projects that have many users or where the users are making decisions that have high business importance are good candidates for a high rating. New–to-the-world user interfaces or projects with major user interface design challenges are candidates for a high rating. Our project to create a business center for millions of small and mid-sized business customers that would leverage the latest social networking technologies fell into this category.

At the low end of the dimension might be incremental improvements in an existing interface or where there are only a handful of users (e.g., administrators). For such incremental improvements, the rest of the user interface becomes a model of how to design an improvement. As an example, another tab might be added or a modification of a menu is needed and a couple of additional content screens need to be designed. In

Importance	Attributes
4	The project is core to a business strategic goal The project is a component of a system or architecture that will be used by many other systems The project is in the largest 10% for the business
3	The project is a part of a system or architecture that satisfies a strategic goal, but there are few dependencies on it The project has budget falling in the middle or the organization's projects
2	The project is a useful tool but is not in a critical process path The project has a relatively small budget
1	The project is a temporary solution on the way to a more permanent solution The project is in the lowest 10% of project budgets

FIGURE 3.7

Business importance example.

Importance	Attributes
4	Major new UX platform or new-to-the-world UI
	Requires designing the full UI architecture
	The user experience is central to the business value of the project
	Many users, and the UI is used frequently
	Successful usage heavily impacts customer or partner satisfaction and loyalty
	The quality of the design impacts the brand
3	Complex UI or difficult UI design problems
	Requires redesigning major areas of an existing UI
	The user experience is one of the major goals of the project
	User errors may result in critical data loss or other system problems
	Successful usage impacts customers directly or indirectly, and is important to business operations
	The design impacts the experience of other products
2	Solving major user pain points
	The user experience is part of the business case of the project, but not a major one
	Many users but used infrequently; or few users but used frequently
1	Incremental UI improvements
	The UI is not central to the success of the project
	Few user or the UI is used infrequently
	The project is a useful but not vital tool for users

FIGURE 3.8

Interface importance example.

the middle of the dimension might be interface improvements that represent solutions to major user interface problems but without a wholesale redesign of an entire site.

Neither of these judgments is easily automated. The answers to the questions are judgment calls and the power of the tool is in the discussion it provokes. The goal is to have a conversation with the requester and negotiate the right assessment. The negotiation is educational and positions the way you want your work to be positioned in terms of its business value, and the user experience design and research activity required to deliver the value.

Given a position on the table illustrated in Figure 3.6, you can define a recommended level of engagement. For example, projects falling into the A cells might call for full support. Those in the B cells might only need partial support. Those in the C cells might only need consulting support, and those in the D cells might not require UX support at all. Teams owning projects in the D cells might be directed to

Description
Full support. The full range of deliverables and activities supporting creative, user-centered design are typically provided; and are integrated across the development process. The deliverables are essential to product definition and development, and begin by informing the very earliest phases of the project. Scope tends to be the entire solution.
Partial support. Not all skills may be provided by full-time user experience (UX) professional, and typically the full-time staff are supplemented at various points by vendors and will mange them. UX may not be fully engaged through the entire development process. The subset of deliverables will be clearly defined, and typically will be the core artifacts needed for the design. UX contributors are typically not dedicated 100% to the project. Scope tends to be the key user experience focus areas within the solution.
Consulting support. Full-time UX contributors are primarily in a consulting role, providing advice, direction, information, and pointing to reusable assets and best practices. They may provide sign-off and/or review services to user experience work produced by others. If specific targeted services are provided, they tend to be "discount" and are intended to address just the most highly leverageable experience issues, and selected fit and finish or production needs as needed. The needs of projects with higher levels of support may take precedence.

FIGURE 3.9

Levels of engagement.

examples they can copy and guidelines that have been created. The descriptions of these levels of support are listed in Figure 3.9. The original table I used was developed by Tjeerd Hoeck when he was a director of design for one of the Windows releases. I took his table and modified it to fit our IT environment and the approach we were taking to staffing projects. The version shown here is a further adaptation of that revised version.

Again, every project does not need an all-out UX effort. You want to concentrate the UX resources where the business return justifies them, and to the extent that users benefit. This approach can be at least as important as abstract ROI arguments in demonstrating the value of UX within a company.

The target level of funding of around 6–10% of a project's budget represents full support in this engagement model. The budget could conceivably be even greater for particularly difficult design projects. At the incomplete level of support the budget is at the 3–6% level; at the consulting level of support it is usually a portion of a single full-time UX person's time and is then supplemented by consulting. Interestingly, at one point I went through an exercise where I estimated the desirable level of funding based on the appropriate levels of engagement. I was only able to persuade a fraction of the teams to fund our team at the right levels. But when

I looked at how much the organization ended up spending over the course of the year on consultants and vendors along with full-time user experience staff, it was very close to the estimated need from the top-down analysis using this view of creating a portfolio of projects across the engagement levels.

One of the things I do argue for when I negotiate with teams, however, is the expectation that when planning work they should be planning for about 80% of an individual UX person's time, not for 100%. The 20% is needed for activities that keep a vibrant UX team going and for administrative tasks. It provides capacity for turning their work into reusable assets that benefit everyone. I have found that the managers I work with are comfortable with this as long as they feel *they* will get some of that benefit. If others also benefit, that is okay too. When they feel like they are paying for someone else to reap all the benefits in a direct funding model, managers get a little touchy. One example is a CSS framework, built by one of my designers with a development background, which made it easy to create design patterns, to assemble them, and to give them a brand identity. The sponsor was willing to share the work as long as his team was directly benefitting. This type of sharing model means that each team is also sharing in the assets created by the rest of my team, and it can be leveraged to make teams feel the support they are getting is beyond expectations.

3.1 POSITIONING WITHIN THE COMPANY

By Edmond W. Israelski, PhD, Director of Human Factors Abbott Labs, Abbott Park, IL, USA

Where should teams be positioned within the company? This question is common and the answer is not always simple. I personally have managed Human Factors groups in Systems Engineering, Software Development Engineering, Product Management (Marketing), and Quality/Regulatory. HFE groups might also find homes in Medical Affairs, Training, Documentation, System Test, Market Research, Manufacturing Operations, Safety, Occupational Health, and Industrial Hygiene among others. The guiding principle is that it should be where design decisions are made in order to have maximum influence on the usability of products and systems. Being in an organization that is considered a "consulting" organization is not optimal for having impact on design. You may not be taken seriously, or worse, be marginalized.

Another consideration is the mission of the HFE group. If the group is new and is trying to establish its presence with a beachhead, then being in a corporate organization is more influential in getting various divisions to incorporate HFE. But, ultimately, HFE needs to be near the product/system/process design action. If the starter group is in a corporate oversight organization that looks out across the entire corporation, then it would be better to dedicate group members to specific full- or part-time product or project teams depending on the intensity of the HFE efforts. This way the design teams feel that the HFE professional is a true valued and trusted stakeholder member of the team, rather than a remote or disinterested consultant. Being physically collocated with the design team is ideal to foster formal and informal (lunch, hallway) communications.

A related question is, "Should the HFE group be centralized or decentralized?" The answer depends on the many factors including:

- Company organizing philosophy
- Product line diversity
- Geographic diversity

1. Designing a product for global consumption
2. Modifying an existing product for local consumption
3. Designing a totally new product for local consumption
4. UX team as guidelines police force to oversee local (outsourced) developers
5. UX team embedded within IT organization doing internal systems design
6. UX as part of consulting practice (local or global)

In the first scenario, the local organization must be designed for daily coordination with other design locations as well as engineering and marketing in a highly distributed fashion. The communication skills and a shared design methodology are second only in importance to a high-quality project management approach to ensure that no deliverables are dropped. In the second and third scenarios, an organization with more local autonomy is preferred with a small and predictable amount of oversight from headquarters. This can work particularly well when other product stakeholders such as engineering and marketing are also local. It looks more like the first scenario when it really is not.

The fourth scenario is the most problematic from a management perspective. It is best to avoid this one because the work will be boring for a high-quality UX team. It provides little ownership and very little opportunity for creativity. This scenario is a recipe for high employee turnover and low morale.

Scenarios 5 and 6 provide additional challenges primarily depending on whether the internal or external customer is local or globally located with respect to the UX team. In a typical outsourcing situation the UX team is not collocated with the customer or problem owner. In the global case a significant travel budget is generally needed during the requirements and validation phase. The most common reason for project failure is the desire to save money combined with the assumption that conference calls are as good as face-to-face communication, particularly in the requirements gathering and validation phases where observational techniques are more relevant than interviews.

Another critical challenge is to define whether the local UX team is totally self-contained and has the full range of required interdisciplinary skills locally; for example, interaction designers, user researchers, information architects and visual designers. In the first scenario outlined above, there is typically a difference in global role distribution compared to building a stand-alone product or a module for a larger suite. In the case of software suite vendors, UI guidelines and visual design are usually centrally owned within a UX team at the headquarters location. The local UX team will need to learn to work within those UI pattern and branding constraints. This in turn impacts the type of designers that can be hired. For example, a Web designer used to concurrent ownership of visual design, information architecture, and interaction design generally will not adapt well to a globally distributed product UX organization where these skills are specialized and concentrated across different geographic locations.

As the dimensions previously identified indicate, globalization is a complex multifaceted topic. My best advice is to start with a clear understanding of the long-term goal and design each globally distributed team to match that goal. Otherwise you run the risk of building a UX team capable of delivering short-term cost savings that cannot scale to do independent design as both the team and the business mission mature.

Equipping the Team

4

THE ENVIRONMENT

Innovation needs teams. And teams need places to thrive and grow.

Tom Kelley

One of the characteristics of a job that distinguishes it from others is the physical environment in which people work. Do they have the tools they need? Is the environment pleasant? Does it inspire creativity? Does it support collaboration and bring people together in a way that enables each person to be the best that they can possibly be? Does it define who they are as a team? I have been in environments that range from an office with several people packed in it, to a light, airy office with windows that opened to the outdoors in a brand new building, to a design studio environment in the trendy downtown area of Denver. I have been in more formal work environments that had mail delivery robots moving by periodically and those where people zoomed by on scooters, played foosball at every opportunity, and those where a remarkable amount of partying was a regular part of the work environment. I have had a variety of awesome labs that I have been able to design, I have worked where the lab infrastructure was shared, and have worked where we just had to cobble together whatever we could to collect user data. Through it all, one of the things I have learned is that the physical environment you create can go a long way in shaping a team identity and climate, projecting that identity to the company you are supporting, and engaging those people in your work.

Lab Space

Fundamentally, user research requires little more than a pencil and paper and an astute observer. However, the space for usability testing is more than just a tool to run user studies. It is also a powerful tool for making those studies more effective.

Bringing managers, project managers, developers and others into the lab to observe users working with a prototype involves them in your work and educates them. At times it can be too successful. I remember one manager who was sitting, watching her favorite feature being used, and listening to the user saying things like, "This sucks. Who could ever think this would be useful?" She immediately picked up her cell phone, called the developer, and started redesigning the feature in real time. I had to caution her that it was worth at least seeing a few others using the feature before we wrote it off entirely. Today it is clearly also valuable to broaden the potential audience and leverage the public relations value both by streaming the studies as they are occurring over your intranet, and circulating video clips highlighting particularly interesting moments during the testing. But it is the live viewing of users that creates the greatest empathy. One additional advantage is that the team members can generate their own questions, and when the researcher is able to fit them into debriefing and other portions of the testing, it gets the team's fingerprints on the results and helps get their buy-in.

Back in 1994, Jakob Nielsen edited a special issue of *Behavior & Information Technology* devoted to usability labs around the country that still has much to say about current lab design. Technologies have improved, but many of the patterns observed then still apply. I wrote an article about the lab I had designed for Ameritech (Lund, 1994a) in which I described a series of requirements for the lab and their priority for the kinds of testing we were doing then. The requirements included:

- Space to simulate the eventual usage environment (ideally easily reconfigured as needs evolve)
- Cameras to record the face and the user's activity, a microphone to record the user's remarks, and recording equipment with the ability to synch to time
- A way for a remote experimenter to observe the user's activity (especially as being recorded) and to communicate with the user
- A staging area for users to help ease them into the test environment
- An observation area for observers (e.g., sponsors and team members)
- An environment for managing the lab and annotating the recordings that is easy to use for the researchers

Variations on that arrangement supported most of our needs (including both summative studies with researchers sitting in the observation room, and more formative studies where the researchers sit with the users and probe in the course of the interactions). When we built the lab, we used the traditional one-way mirrors between the observation and testing areas, but the available video technologies have advanced considerably since then and we have seen value in enabling remote observers to have active discussions during the study. These kinds of discussions typically need to be remote from the testing environment so the users are not disturbed. At Compaq I recall there was an area specifically designed for people to observe the observers.

Since most of our work involved workstations, for many studies we recorded directly from the monitor with a splitter, and used the cameras to focus on the face and the hands. Back in those days we also laid a track of SMPTE time code so we could synchronize the streams when we edited summary videos, and ran them through software that let us annotate the videos for later analysis. Today the video is immediately digitized, and observers can annotate (often collaboratively) as the video is being created. The coding allows the video to be more archival and to provide value beyond the individual study for which it is being recorded.

In that same double issue, Nielsen summarized the 13 labs that were described. The median floor space for a typical subject room was about 13 square meters (with a mean of about 19). Most labs had around 2 or 3 rooms. In general, there were 2 cameras per room (a few had 3), and in general half of the time they used a scan converter as well to record directly from a screen. Most (but not all) used a one-way mirror, and all had some staff whose responsibility it was to support the lab. The median ratio was 1 support person for 12 people using the lab. Another good source for usability lab examples is the Appendix in *A Practical Guide to Usability Testing* (Dumas & Redish, 1999).

Since then, usability environments have expanded in several directions. The concept of simulating the usage environment has caused more and more groups to build labs that duplicate a wider variety of environments. At Ameritech we built a teleconferencing room specifically for research, and eventually constructed a small home in the lab to study smart home control use. At US West Advanced Technologies we built a living room lab. I made a slight mistake there in that I had a new graduate select the furniture and decorations for the room, and it ended up looking suspiciously like someone's fantasy bachelor pad. Since then I have seen IT environments where people are studying how administrators rack and manage equipment, and I have visited the headquarters of a drugstore chain where they had a simulation of an entire pharmacy.

As user researchers adapt more methods from market research, as participatory design methods are used, as information architects continue to use techniques such as affinity diagramming, and even as teams collaboratively sketch solutions to design problems, larger spaces make sense and a method of recording what is taking place can be useful. When a UX effort grows beyond a group, a larger space optimized for studying group activities can sometimes be justified. A large space, whether in a lab or in a hallway, is often a powerful tool for data analysis. Qualitative data can be placed in it, organized into meaningful units, and turned into a variety of models of users, their experiences, and their behaviors.

One of the finer examples of a lab I have seen recently is the lab seen in Figure 4.1 (designed for the Microsoft Servers team). The lab is completely digital and leverages the latest in data logging infrastructure created by the UX Central team in collaboration with the Visual Studio team. It has ample space for exploring information worker, administrative, and group activities (since a large amount of real-world IT work is social in nature). It is easily reconfigurable. The design elements of the lab have been chosen to make the users comfortable and create quality video.

FIGURE 4.1

Usability lab.

Published with permission from Microsoft, photograph courtesy of Paul Elrif and Tyron Chookolingo.

Design Studio

When I joined Sapient, they had already started the process of creating identity among the user experience community and then quickly incorporating new employees into it. Some referred to it as "drinking the Kool-Aid," but it was rare to find someone who regretted it. Many of the colleagues I have continued to stay in the most contact with over the years came through Sapient. Part of that identity-building process was to go through a multi-day introductory workshop.

At one point during that introductory workshop there was a tour and field work at one of the Sapient design studios in Chicago. The studio had been one of the E-Lab locations before it was acquired by Sapient. I remember that we were all excited about the new job. Sapient had an incredible reputation for user experience during those pre-Internet bubble bursting days, and it was truly exciting to be a part of the latest "class" of new recruits. We walked for blocks and blocks through the Chicago late Fall chill. I remember talking with someone about their interest in marathoning, and briefly wondering whether that might be something to tackle someday. We arrived at a classic Chicago brownstone. This was the kind of building in Chicago with old wood with dark varnish and brass fixtures, with lathe and plaster in the old parts; the kind that smells a hundred years old, but in a good way. It was downtown and there was plenty of urban energy. We went upstairs and then came into this amazing space. It seemed mostly open, except there were exposed brick walls. On the walls were collages of pictures and notes from research that was underway with stylized stickies to help organize the information. There were design posters on the walls. There were strange toys, bicycles, inflatables, and other things hanging from ceilings. The whole place was filled with the creative clutter that decorates the minds of many user experience people, and which supports the kind of serendipitous connections that generate new ideas and insights. There was a definite excitement in the place as people moved throughout, and there was talking and laughter everywhere.

When we built out the Sapient Denver office it was a blank slate. As with the former E-Lab location in Chicago, the Denver office had an urban feel as it was located in the LoDo (Lower Downtown) district. The area was very trendy with lots of little boutiques, great restaurants and clubs, and warehouses converted into condos. In our building a floor had been knocked out in the building we were in, and large open spaces were created. The exterior walls were large windows looking out on the city and the Rockies. The remaining walls were virtually floor-to-ceiling whiteboards generally covered with designs, code, research, project status plans, and other artifacts of the process. Off the rooms were smaller breakout rooms where the walls were all whiteboards in which working groups could go to collaborate on designs. In the open spaces we sat at moveable tables that could be reconfigured as needed, and everyone working on a project was physically located together. The breakout rooms held couches, foosball tables, video games, and so on, to break up the long nights. Off one end of the building was a huge outdoor patio area wired with Ethernet so people could get quiet time and work in the fresh air, and where there were frequent BBQs for people to bond. There was an impressive lobby where the Sapient brand and successes were clearly displayed, but once the clients moved past the lobby they were immersed in our process and activity.

Tom Kelley (2001) argued that innovation flourishes in greenhouses. He argued that a greenhouse is a workplace designed to foster the growth of good ideas, a place designed to support collaboration. IDEO considered their spaces a primary asset, as did Sapient. Visiting the offices of leading design vendors in the Seattle area and some of the most innovative teams with whom I work, I see a similar design studio vision repeated again and again. Kelly argued that, in general, when putting the space together the fewer the rules the better. He does flesh out several principles in the course of his book, noting that you

---

Start by building neighborhoods and thinking in terms of projects. Make building blocks to create playful, flexible foundations for your workers. Throughout the process, remember the spirit of prototyping. Space should evolve with teams and projects in much the same way as do your plans for an innovative new product. Encourage hot teams to find or create a team icon. Finally, don't forget that your spaces should tell stories about your work and your company.

Furthermore, your spaces help project the identity for the team.

Within my current role I have been moving in this direction myself. Space is limited in our area so when we were a smaller team we arranged with the administrative assistant owning the space to let us have a large lounge area on one floor and we turned that into a design studio. When all the teams in the organization were being moved around, we started looking for unused spaces. We found a lab that had originally been used by the games group and arranged to get access to it as a design studio in exchange for the cost of painting and cleanup. The full space included a small usability lab, some rooms that had previously been usability labs that we are going to turn into breakout and project rooms, a very large conference room that we treated as the center of the team space, and a room with cubicles that had been used for mass games testing that we converted to house contractors and vendors. The next step was to arrange for my team to have our offices consolidated around the space. We pushed the artifacts of our design process and examples of our best work out into the halls around the space.

Ambient Spaces

Space shapes our attitudes, how we interact, and in many ways how we think. Every place where I have seen a vital, influential user experience team I have seen a space that reflects their creativity. At Sapient part of the signal of what we wanted to be about was floor-to-ceiling whiteboards and whiteboards that were covered with sketches, diagrams, and plans. The walls were covered with posters, clippings, and printouts of data and screen shots. People were standing next to them gesturing and drawing in groups. The whiteboards were a living environment and yet they also persisted over time to support asynchronous collaboration and the reinstating of previous trains of thoughts.

Around many companies you know you are walking into a user experience space because you start to see designs on the walls. You see data and figures laid out and experience models taking shape before your eyes. At times there are more organized signals of the kind of space you are in. There may be more ordered comparisons of design screen shots, or personas laid out next to each other, or photographs capturing images that stimulate the emotions that are being targeted, or posters of style guides. There may be framed versions of past design milestones and successes. There may be spontaneous art projects. There may be representations of the design language being used by the team.

Turn the walls of the halls into design spaces (Figure 4.2). It encourages each member of the design team to look at what others are doing and engage with it. It brings the perfectionists out of their shells a little, and forces them to share incomplete design and open themselves to others feeding into their design process. It enables those engineers who may work sitting behind their screens to really see what is behind the evolving design, and that while it is messier than they may be used to, it also is informed by principled ways of thinking and talking. Furthermore, pushing the design out into the public spaces invites that public into the design process, because when walking through the halls they cannot help but engage at some level (and may actually have to push their way *through* the design process in action).

FIGURE 4.2

Collaborative MS IT hall art.

TOOLS

Engineers have impressive tools. Most of the organizations I have been in have hardware labs on raised floors with racks and racks of equipment and blinking lights, and much of the budget discussion each year is around the servers in these rooms, the automated test tools, and other things that you can see. The only things missing are those tape drives from the old science fiction movies and there are not nearly enough blinking lights. I have always enjoyed building and managing UX labs. They are a visible example of what we do. But I admit I've also been a little envious of the toys the engineers always seem to have.

UX also needs tools. Designers need really zippy machines with the horsepower to drive the various programs they are using. They need big (or multiple) screens to work on. They need laptops that are similarly powerful and often with larger than normal screens so they can take the work on the road when they go sit with developers and work. Conference rooms today typically have projection systems for sharing designs, but if there is extra budget you might want to arrange to have access to an easily portable projector for their laptops in case it is needed. Admittedly, given the ubiquity of projectors this is a pretty low priority. Make sure the computers have the usual design tools (Photoshop, Illustrator, etc.), and remember they can be quite pricey. Even upgrades are often expensive and you will want to plan to keep the software up to date.

There should be some kind of collaboration environment for storing and sharing designs. At Microsoft that is called a SharePoint site. We usually float between sites we share with the teams that we are collaborating with and a team site that makes it easy for everyone to see what everyone else is doing.

At one point our CIO worked in the auto industry. The vision he outlined for how design worked there is compelling and is something we are working toward. It begins with sketching, paper vision prototyping, and other activities to get ideas out on the table. These prototyping tools may include PowerPoint or Visio, paper, or even whiteboards (or whiteboards that can be easily digitized). Alternative designs are captured and saved on the walls of team rooms, hallways, and in other areas where they can stimulate creative solutions to the needs represented in the user scenarios.

PowerPoint, Visio, and even Excel can be used for simple wire framing. We have created libraries of templates and common controls to simplify this early envisioning. The goal is to move these sketches into a digital form and start to piece together low-fidelity prototypes for how the interaction is going to work and that embody the information architecture. There are a variety of tools on the market for facilitating this rapid prototyping stage. Balsamiq is an example of one of these. It is light, easy to use, and inexpensive. It gives a feel of the basic interaction. SketchFlow in Microsoft's Expression suite is a richer tool, but with that richness comes a little more complexity. Sketches can be imported in a variety of forms and you can rapidly build an interactive prototype. The prototype can be "published" for users to comment on as they interact with it. The design can be fleshed out and feeds common development tools, and documentation can be automatically generated about the design.

This early prototyping serves to bring everyone together around a common language for the design. These prototypes ideally are suitable for user research. What you want is to build out the fidelity of the screens as they become complete and to attach simulated data to make sure the interactions work right. In the next stage these designs need to feed the development tools, so they need to either output code in the appropriate format that can be input into the tools, or the tools need to be part of an integrated environment. While development is going on, the ability to have both a designer's view and a developer's view is useful. Each works in their own environment and you want them to see what the other is seeing. You want to be able to output through this process to a form that can be used for testing. Ideally you can track generations of the design and comments that lead to changes in the design (e.g., from research).

Researchers need a user testing environment (described earlier), and they need software to analyze the data. Labs now are usually entirely digital and the various sources of information all feed a single database. As the data are collected they are annotated so they can become intellectual capital and inform decisions far beyond the specific studies for which they were originally collected. Excellent tools are on the market to support usability labs, or you may choose to develop your own in order to achieve a full integration of the wide variety of sources of information you are collecting locally and remotely. Whether buying or building the software, it will need to be planned for in your budget. Video editing software makes it easier to turn the data into clips that can be attached to reports and circulated among stakeholders. Researchers may need a questionnaire tool that has to be budgeted for, and tools for affinity diagramming and analyzing field data. Some labs (especially those focused on Web design) have an eye tracking system. We document studies in research reports, and have a database where those reports can be stored (so they can be used to answer future questions, much like the data). Laptops make sense for researchers, even if they also have a workstation. Laptops are used in the field and for presenting work to teams. A variety of mobile labs are typical for many teams (Lund, 1994a) and are easy to assemble, especially given affordable video cameras and Internet streaming for sharing the studies as they are underway.

In addition to the usual research tools your team with also need access to users for testing. For some projects you may need to work with field people to get access to customers and other users. You may need to create your own database, continually populate it with the names of users, and track which studies those users have been through. The creation and administration of the database and the costs of recruiting (e.g., through recruiters and advertising) need to be in the budget. At some companies a centralized user experience organization does the recruiting through advertisements, through the corporate Web site, and through other channels. In addition to the costs of acquiring people to test, you will need to provide for some form of gratuity to compensate people for participation. At Ameritech we paid approximately $50/hour, and at software companies you might pay with software. When we use employees we often repay them either with small gifts or with gift cards. Note that when payment exceeds certain levels you may need to report it as income for tax purposes, especially when paying for research outside the United States. Another issue that has arisen is around policies governing "gifts" of products and whether a gratuity is payment or a gift. You may need to work with your legal department to shape a policy that makes sense. For international research considerations a good reference is Schumacher (2009).

An additional consideration at most companies will be to work with legal to ensure forms are created to cover non-disclosure of corporate secrets (e.g., the designs of the product prototypes you may be testing). You will need to create a document that the legal department reviews to protect the privacy of the people you test, yet that allows you to use video and other data you collect with the teams to inform design. You should define a policy around archiving the data and how long it will be held, and when and how it will be destroyed. Most companies have limitations on how long they keep various kinds of documents in their files.

While I can honestly say I have not seen it being done as much as I would like, I believe that it would be good for your user experience team or community to define a set of ethical policies that inform how you treat the people who participate in your research. That belief probably goes back to when I ran the human subject pool at Northwestern as a graduate student, but it does seem the right thing to do. First, determine the limits of deception. In general there does not seem to be the same legal requirement for these kinds of policies as the non-disclosure and the release documents, so it probably could be defined simply as another step in building the identity of your team (since it will be tied to your team's values). However, if you are testing kids (e.g., a gaming application), that requires a careful collaboration with the legal department to create the right set of documentation and policies. There are a variety of issues about compensation, the nature of the content the kids will see, who will be alone with the kids and when, how distress is handled, and so on that will need to be anticipated.

BUDGETING

The blood that keeps your team alive is your budget. If your team is positioned lower in the organizational structure, your budget will probably be handled by a higher level manager and it may be hard to actually see it broken out by category. Not having your own budget reduces some of your flexibility, especially if you might be able to move money between line items as long as your overall budget is on track. The higher up you are in the organization and the larger your team, the more likely you will be able to manage your own budget. Whether you control your budget directly or not, you would like to be in the position to request and receive a budget that will help you make the bigger leaps toward your vision — the budget that you can invest in key strategic activities. When I have been in a team devoted to a single product, my requests were treated (and evaluated) the same way as business cases for features within the product. The budget also needs to provide for costs that are unique to user experience teams such as recruiting users and funding research.

Figure 4.3 shows a portion of one of my budgets. It is a snapshot of one quarter, and the full budget report would typically show the budget for the year, the year-to-date spend and budget, and the most recent month. In some teams I received a monthly update and in others the budget was worked through quarter by quarter. Another task in some companies has been to not only project a month-by-month expected spend, but I have also been asked to periodically update the projection. This can be quite a challenge since for most of my teams I have really only had visibility into the activities over the next quarter. Projects change so quickly that the design and research activities need to change with them and those changes clearly impact the budget. Since finance people generally do not care about details like actual confidence in the budget, the projections often have to be based on past trends and then adjusting based on what I expect demand and activity will be like, rather than basing them on hard project plans. More recently these budget adjustments have become critical, because at the top of companies they have started the practice of looking at underspent budgets (based on projections) and then pulling

	Q3 Actual	Q3 Budget	% Spent
People (salary and benefits)	$479,969	$851,095	56.4%
Infrastructure (offices)	$59,501	$99,388	59.9%
Travel and Entertainment • Transportation and Lodging • Meals and Entertainment	$9,439	$7,336	123.7%
Morale	$499	$1,888	26.4%
Employee Development Training and Conferences	$3,410	$3,203	106.4%
Computer Expenses	$29,043	$18,250	159.1%
Dues and Subscriptions	$597	$41	1459.5%
Freight/Supply	$2,101	$1,713	122.7%
Contingent Staff/Interns	$106,529	$283,294	37.6%
Outsourced Resources	$15,057	-	NA
Product Development (special projects, research cross-charging)	$72,725	$496,500	14.6%
Lab Equipment	-	-	NA
Other Expenses	-	-	NA
Grand Total	$733,781	$1,730,277	42.4%

FIGURE 4.3

Example budget.

the unspent dollars back to reinvest in the corporate priorities. This is an attempt to avoid the practice of teams spending anything in the budget that has not been spent before the quarter or the end of the year is over. The downside is that efforts to save money today to buy something bigger tomorrow can be hard. Thinking through the budget, even without the data you would like to have to do it, is therefore often critical for the operation of your team and the growth of your user experience effort.

In the budget in Figure 4.3 the biggest line item is clearly the salary, bonuses, and other compensation for the full-time staff. The next biggest is the budget for the special, strategic projects that were added to the budget. This item also includes the cost of doing our research. Some of those projects involved hiring vendors and others involved major research investments. The third largest portion is the contractors (who are distinguished from vendors) and interns who give me flexibility in my staffing. Other budget items included the infrastructure (e.g., cost of office space) that comes with having full-time staff. Travel and entertainment, employee development and conferences, and computer expenses are about the tools used to get UX jobs done and to grow people. The morale budget was specifically for team-building activities. Other items can easily vary from organization to organization and company to company, but these major ones are typical across companies.

OTHER OPPORTUNITIES

You do not always have the budget for what you want to do and the rules for getting it may not always be obvious. One of the virtues of a startup is that while things are lean everyone does whatever is needed to move the business forward, and while you are all in it together you are ready to improvise. When I was going through the welcome-to-Sapient training one of the things that was impressed upon each of us was people are not always going to tell you how to get what you need. You need to go find it. If you are on a consulting gig go find the supply room, talk to the administrative assistant, work out of Starbucks, do whatever you need to do. One of the things that makes or breaks people in large corporations is whether they feel constrained and limited by all the rules and structures, or whether they see the size and then see the cracks between the processes and rules as opportunities that they can leverage when trying to get things done.

There are times when you need to push the limits and take reasonable risks. We have talked about putting things on walls to create an ambient design space. If you actually track down the building manager to ask permission the answer is very likely going to be no. If you just put something up, what is the worst that can happen? Someone will take it down and ask you not to do it again. If they do, then that lets you start a conversation about how that kind of space is important and you brainstorm together about how to accomplish your goal. Can you put up corkboard? Can you get a team room? Are there spaces where it might be okay? In many of these situations the phrase "don't ask permission, ask forgiveness" makes a lot of sense.

One of the things I start looking for in a new organization is who manages the space and whether there is a separate budget for decorating that space. Often the space budget sits somewhere outside of daily operations and is only used for major moves, repairs, and so forth. In one team, we tracked down the administrative assistant who owned it and uncovered a couple of small conference rooms that people were not using for offices. We found budget for the space, and convinced the administrative assistant to let us turn the two small rooms into a design studio. If we ever moved, they would still have a big conference room. We then used the budget to buy a large screen, a projection system, and several computers along with couches, chairs, and tables. Several members of my team went to the hardware store and bought those really big whiteboard sheets and mounted them to the walls (and having extra, went around and redecorated some of our offices). The whiteboards let us sketch and explore design ideas. The studio became the center where we held our design critiques, and where we could post designs and leave them in place for extended periods.

One of my team members discovered in the process of reorganization that there was an office that had not been assigned to anyone. It was an inside office, so it was not under heavy contention. He talked nicely to the administrative assistant and argued he could really use a team room dedicated to his project for a few months and she said okay. He then went to the hardware store, bought bright green paint, and painted the office with it. (Immediately that reduced the likelihood that someone would want to take it over.) He found a furniture budget that had not been used in years and bought a bunch of Aeron chairs for the room and a great table. He had a special sign made with etched clear plastic that said "The Green Room." That became a part of what we were as a team and a focal point for the sub-team that he was leading.

Another example came at the end of the first year in my current organization. We were looking for a space that could be used for a team room for design critiques and participatory exercises and as a lab space. I found the administrative assistant who handled the space and we had a great talk. There was a storage room that she said we could have that was not being used for anything. Another space that I believe Pam came up with was a lobby area on the third floor of our building. A few chairs were sitting there if I recall, but it was not being used for anything else and it was just outside my office at the time.

For the storage space the first thing Pam did was to put a lock on the door to protect the space, and later we set up a reservation system to manage it. Initially we were thinking about turning it into a discount usability lab, since my researchers had to travel a half an hour or so to the main campus in order to do research. I wanted something that would enable more of our team to observe the tests. The team who manages the labs for the user experience community arranged for the building people to come and join them in evaluating the space. It turns out that when you are building labs like this you have to worry about where the air is flowing, fire danger, where the wires are piped, and so on. We learned it could cost a lot to turn it into a standard usability lab. So that ruled out our initial approach.

But then one of those opportunities emerged that you need to seize when you can. We were getting toward the end of the year and my boss had a lot of surplus money in his budget. The one constraint was that it had to be spent, and whatever it was spent on, had to happen within a month. Pam took this project on and with frequent trips to Ikea, to the hardware store, and many calls to a few vendors, the two spaces were turned into effective collaboration spaces. Both had projection interactive whiteboards where you could sketch and record the digitized images on your computer. We could store some of the field research equipment in the storage room, but both provided spaces where we could mount designs and research, and let them stay up over extended periods of time.

We have also been successful in working with some of the teams we support and in keeping our eyes and ears open to see when they have a little extra budget. We have been able to get them to fund anything from software upgrades to travel outside the standard travel budget, to vendors for special projects, and most recently, replacement laptops for the team. As a manager, one of things you should make sure you have is a list of things you would like to have if money becomes available. You can use such a list if you do come up against budget deadlines and when someone asks "Is there anything we need that we should spend this money on?"

The other phenomenon I have noticed is that sometimes being more outrageous in the dream is better than being more modest. You might not be able to get a few thousand dollars to upgrade your team's equipment, but if you ask for a million to rethink the entire vision of your space and turn it into a design studio you might be able to find it. Again, the money may come from a different budget and something as bold as an entire design studio may serve the needs of an executive who is looking for a way to make her own statement to senior executives about the leadership she is providing.

HINTS FROM EXPERIENCED MANAGERS

Boldly delegate responsibility to your team. It helps them grow and allows you to scale. It also gives them ownership and ensures that you are not the single point of failure.

Andy Cargile, Director of User Experience, Microsoft Hardware, Seattle, WA

Do the work too. Don't just tell people to do it. Your staff has to know you can and will pitch in when needed AND that you can lead by example.

Robert M. Schumacher, PhD, Managing Director, User Centric, Inc., Oakbrook Terrace, IL

4.1 BUDGETING

By Robert M. Schumacher, PhD, Managing Director User Centric, Inc., Oakbrook Terrace, IL

The good news about budgeting for user experience researchers is that, for the most part, this is not a capital-intensive business. Nevertheless, it is important to make a priority to ensure our staff have the tools necessary to do their jobs with excellence. In our experience, the capital expenses fall into one of three general categories: lab space, lab equipment, and technology for the researchers/consultants.

Rent takes the biggest chunk of the budget, and cost will, of course, vary depending on where you are. One of User Centric's offices is on Michigan Avenue in Chicago, which is an expensive location. But it's where our clients expect us to be, and it's where participants can find us, so we accept the expense as necessary for running our business. No company wants to overspend on space, but it's crucial that your offices and labs have a high-quality feel and project an appealing, professional image.

The next highest equipment cost comes with setting up labs. There are two areas to consider: technology to do or deliver the research, and technology that is being researched. To do the research, you need to be forward thinking about the kinds of services you plan to provide, and invest in a quality environment where researchers can work to their highest capability. In this day, it means having large-screen monitors, HD cameras, and lots of gizmos and gadgets that can do important technology tricks. We research a lot of cool tech products, so that we can make sure our labs have high-quality audio, video, software, and other technical capabilities. Capabilities like recording software or streaming require budgeting for the infrastructure and software, and maybe the technical resources to run it if the researchers are not able. As for technology that is being researched, if you work with particular devices (e.g., TV services or kiosks or mobile devices) you must budget for continually upgrading equipment used in tests, as well as for the service necessary to run these. For example, if you work with digital TV, budget for cable systems and possibly HDTV service in addition to the televisions themselves.

The capital expenses required for setting up a lab are significant at the outset. However, we've found that with each lab space we've built, the capital requirements to do what we've done in the past go down. It's very important to keep labs state-of-the-art. To this end, you must dedicate part of your annual capital budget to improving (not just maintaining) technology resources to keep up with new lab technology used to test and new technology used in testing.

Equipping individual consultants is relatively modest, but varies depending on the individual. In general, the majority of researchers fare well with a reasonably powered laptop, a cell phone, and typical office productivity software. For designers, the hardware and software demands increase considerably. Prototyping and visual design tools tend to be quite pricey. Then there's software that is required to run the business that is expensed month to month (e.g., time and expense reporting systems, screen sharing tools, VOIP systems); these tools can easily add an amount on a monthly basis that will impact the budget over the year.

Other expenses may come into play if consultants will be doing international testing, or work involving specialized equipment like eye trackers or driving simulators, but these are more exceptions than the rule. The useful life of most consultants' hardware is 12–24 months, so there should be allowance in the budget for updating researchers' capital resources.

While expenses for a user research team may be less than some other businesses, it's still important to be aware of where you can and cannot cut corners. Since what we as user researchers sell is knowledge and expertise, it's important to budget for regularly maintaining up-to-date facilities and equipment that will maximize your capabilities, as well as convey a sense of competence to your clients.

There is one other thing, our clients are watching. I had a client say to me the other day "I like to see what you usability guys are using." No pressure.

Focusing the Team

5

FINDING YOUR SOUL

Great teams have a kind of soul — something that defines who they are. It infuses their identity and it is woven through how they appear to others, their vision and mission, and their messaging. Some teams are all about brand. Others are all about the essence of design as a practice. And still others are all about designing from user understanding or even about improving usability. When a team has identified their soul, it is quickly obvious what it is and what they are passionate about.

The other thing that I have noticed is that the soul — the energizing principles and language — most often comes from the leader of the team. In other words, the manager is the flame that gives life to the core of that soul. Making the ideas explicit, therefore, begins with you making them explicit for yourself. Often this is done in interaction with the team so they feel their fingerprints are on it. For my current team, my previous boss at one point, in a one-on-one feedback discussion, said that I had clearly defined where I wanted the team to head and why I wanted us to head there, but that this vision was too far beyond what the team understood about themselves. I needed to step back, he argued, and bring the team along. They needed to incorporate their own ideas into how they were thinking about their work.

On the other hand, one of my colleagues (Monty Hammontree) has done a wonderful job in evolving his vision of design thinking, human and design patterns, making by doing, and driving creativity and innovation into his team's work. He has been able to communicate his ideas through compelling visual representations and move his team to better implement these ideas. The heart of Monty's team is a set of ideas that spans research and design activity, and the set is communicated through both the design and the process used to create it.

Steve Kaneko, who currently heads the UX Leadership Team, has always impressed me with the culture he creates within his teams. He is an excellent visual designer and gathers similarly gifted product designers around him. Everything I see from his team is expressed with a strong design language, even through the user research that happens on his team. While Monty's messages often connect most with the head, Steve's messages most often connect with the eye and the heart. Both have strong ideas. Both think strategically. But the ways they express what they do, where they are heading and why are communicated in very different ways — ways that lend themselves to different team cultures. Monty's world is clearly about engineering, whereas Steve's world is currently about entertainment and making technology personal.

Ideas Shaping My Approach

The story of how my approach to designing experiences evolved illustrates how your perspective can influence how you position your team within the processes and culture of your organization. When I started at Bell Labs as a researcher, one direction the work was taking in my department focused on the paperless office. By the time I left, while research continued to look for new experiences and the value they could bring, much of the industrial user experience work was focused on usability. Usability as a discipline was taking off and its focus was clearly on removing design problems. Many of us have offered critiques of usability methods even as we employ them. They have been useful and fit within the way user experience is implemented within corporations, but many clearly come with inherent limitations and have created a practice that at times is less rigorous than it should be (Gray & Salzman, 1998; Lund, 2006; Lund, 1998). When I was at Ameritech I began to realize that we could remove all the design problems and still have a disastrous product in the marketplace.

At Ameritech, because some of our budget was in the form of common funding that did not depend on individual projects, we were able to study how to create not just error-free products but more important, successful products. This research brought the kinds of insights to the business that resulted in a new brand promise for Ameritech and a new ad campaign. Ameritech was already pivoting around our elevator pitch at that point, and the consumer business unit proposed to put a human factors seal of approval on their products. Unfortunately, no thought had been given about the metrics that would qualify a product for the seal. As a result, we began a project in collaboration with the researchers within the business unit's market research group and the University of Michigan Business School to understand what made successful products (Schwartz, Thomson, Seifert, & Shafto, 1996). This was the kind of project that provided high executive visibility and made it clear UX could shift an entire business plan.

The study took a wide variety of experiences in people's lives and evaluated them on a set of experience dimensions. We then looked for clusters in the data that predicted various aspects of the experience. After the study we were able to say things like "Using Caller ID is easier than using a light switch." That was such a powerful idea that the marketing people represented it in one of Ameritech's ads (Lund, 1996b and shown in Figure 5.1).

"The Human Factor: Train" :30TV

Ameritech
Your Link to Better Communication

(SFX: TRAIN SOUNDS)
(AVO): Meet Ardi Kramer...

of Ameritech's Human Factors
Department.

ARDI: (CLEARS THROAT) This
picture seem clear to you?

MAN #1: No.

(AVO): He studies how people use
new technology...

ARDI: This picture...seem clear to
you?

MAN #2: Yeah.

(AVO): To make sure, it's easy to
use.
ARDI: Are the buttons big enough?

(AVO): Because we believe...

that if technology doesn't work for
people...

ARDI: (CLEARS THROAT)

Is this picture clear enough?

(AVO): ...it doesn't work.
WOMAN: A little small, isn't it?

(SFX: TRAIN SOUNDS)

Ameritech
YOUR LINK TO BETTER COMMUNICATION

(AVO): Ameritech. Your Link to
Better Communication.

© 1995 Ameritech Corporation

Fallon McElligott

FIGURE 5.1

Light switch ad.

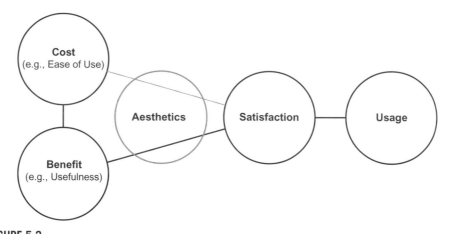

FIGURE 5.2

Adoption model.

Using data that let us study how the factors predicted usage, we built the model shown in Figure 5.2. The parts of the model that we feel the most confident in shaped the way we describe our vision and mission as well as metrics we have defined to track progress towards business impact. The argument we make is that satisfaction is the biggest driver of usage, so the expectation of satisfaction is the best predictor of adoption or intention to adopt. The biggest predictor of satisfaction is the expectation of usefulness (or past experiences of usefulness). Ease of use also predicts satisfaction, but it appears to operate through usefulness by "revealing" the usefulness. In other words, poor ease of use gets in the way of usefulness.

The nice thing about this model is that it makes it very clear how and why the work we do impacts the business benefits of products and other solutions on which we are working. This set of factors interestingly maps nicely to the ISO 9241 (1998) definition of usability as including efficiency (similar to ease of use), effectiveness (similar to usefulness), and satisfaction. That means as we talk about our mission, we can also ground it in international standards and when needed we can draw on tools built around those standards such as the CIF (the standard research reporting format for summative data) and the CIF-R (the emerging standard for user requirements) to support arguments we are making (ISO/IEC 25062, 2006).

As I was doing this work, I found that it converged with research in the MIS area on a Technology Adoption Model (TAM) based on expectation theory (Davis, 1989; Davis, Bagozzi, & Warshaw, 1989; Venkatesh, Morris, David, & David, 2003). Furthermore, people were beginning to extend the TAM model and related questionnaire instruments to product areas like those in which we were working. This research as well as exploration of models continues to improve the prediction of technology adoption. It has been gratifying to talk to companies who have applied this view of what drives product adoption and success to the organization of their user experience teams, and to see the broad use of the USE questionnaire as a means of assessing user experiences along the dimensions. Whether you have a model like this one or another you like to use, having a clear point of view about how you deliver business value is a powerful tool in defining your team's role within your organization. It also provides a framework around which you can build standard tools and processes and rationalize their use.

One of my first conversations with Monty Hammontree was about this model. I remember sitting in a conference room with him in the building where I had my office. We were sketching alternative models on the whiteboard that showed what makes great experiences and our thoughts about what we should do to raise the bar on product quality. It has been fascinating to see Monty take the ideas we brainstormed and combine them with the ideas he had been developing and other insights he has gained since then (he is one of the best read user experience people I have ever met in the area of the theory of design and innovation) to develop the vision that he used to energize his team and to transform the broader user experience community.

While educating the organization about why UX work is important for the business, I have been extending the model in a couple of directions. These extensions are based on my interpretation of some of the more recent data on the TAM model, as well as our experience in practice with more personal technologies such as Tablet computers. First, we overlaid the aesthetic factor on the model. There is a suggestion that the visual characteristics (the aesthetics) of the design say something to users about what the functional and ease of use characteristics will be (e.g., see Cheskin & Sapient, 1999, for a discussion of aesthetics and trustworthiness). This appears for some products and applications, but not others. I am still working out how best to present the model, but the version in Figure 5.2 works for most situations within the business. In general, this factor is intended to capture both the aesthetics and therefore much of the visual (or sensory) attributes that are associated with brand. It seems to operate at the point of first exposure by attracting the user to the solution in comparison to other alternatives. A well-designed object has a tendency to lead users to expect ease of use and usefulness even before they touch it.

The visual or sensory aspects of applications can be the goal that a solution is designed to satisfy (like an entertainment product). So we have also expanded the concepts of ease of use and usefulness to the broader concepts of cost and benefit, with the argument that users implicitly or explicitly build expectations of the trade-off between the two as they decide whether they will be satisfied and decide to use something. The costs may include the time it takes to learn, to change from something familiar, the social pressure they will receive, or risk to their data or other factors in addition to issues with ease of use. The benefits may be delight, personal expression, or social praise, as well as functional value.

This model gives us a language to talk about how we deliver value to the business. People tend to get it. We can also talk about the role of visual design as it delivers on the aesthetic, brand, usability, and emotional connection; interaction design as it builds usefulness into the user interface and contextualizes the experience to ensure ease of use; and research as it helps uncover and validate usefulness and as it identifies problems that reveal the usefulness. We can talk about how we need to be

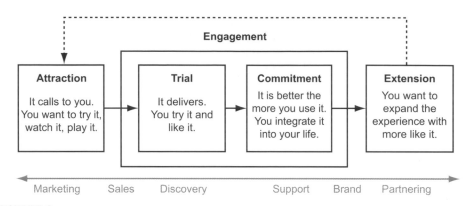

FIGURE 5.3

Model of technology diffusion.

involved very early in the process where we can help uncover new opportunities for value. We want to be involved early in the process because that is where we build in the usefulness (saving downstream costs that come from trying to fix things that are very expensive to correct by that time). We also want to be involved later where we polish off the rough usability edges and after release where we can measure how well we have delivered on the initial goals. The model even gives us the language of quality in use, and the metrics that the organization should be focused on throughout the process (using questionnaires like USE for the subjective measurements to complement efficiency and effectiveness performance measurements).

An additional implication of the model speaks a bit more to the end-to-end life cycle story around user experience. One way to look at technology diffusion is seen in Figure 5.3. In this model, people have to become aware that the solution will be useful (they can expect satisfaction), and that the value outweighs the value they receive from current solutions (the value proposition). This happens in the attraction stage. They hear about the value from their friends, press, or advertising. When they see it on the shelf, its design calls to them. The brand leads them to have expectations about the value. UX contributes content to these stories, and this provides a rationale for trying to build a close partnership with the marketing and market research teams within your organization.

If users believe there is a possibility of value, they are more likely to try the solution. The trial stage includes activities like playing with the model at a neighbor's house; testing it in the store; and taking it out of the package, turning it on, and taking those first few steps to use it. As we design and evangelize our designs we lift the use cases for the core value high in the interface so they pop in the experience and are intuitive to use. These have to be very easy. The ambiance of the design is a part of the initial experience, and the experience must not violate the brand promise and the promise of the aesthetic. If in that initial trial stage the person discovers yes, there is value that justifies the cost of adoption, they begin to move into commitment. Traditional usability, embedded assistance, and high-end design are all critical in shaping an experience that leads to commitment.

This jump into commitment typically takes time and effort. As users step through the commitment process, they need to feel they are getting more value and the experience is becoming easier. To design to reduce the friction of committing to a product requires a deep understanding of the users and how they achieve their goals in context, and the designers need to collaborate with the architects to ensure the solution is architected in a way that supports the expected scenarios of use. This type of research tends to be more ethnographic in nature. This work also uncovers the kinds of stories and scenarios that marketing and sales will want to use. This is another great place for collaboration with marketing, and when you engage project management and development (and ideally even test) up front, they become advocates for the design and the user throughout the design process and are more effective participants in increasing the innovation of the design.

One of the insights gained when I was in the Tablet group was that the life cycle does not stop with commitment. We heard an interesting talk by a consultant from Doblin where the notion of extending the experience was presented. If Disney can get you into the movie, they can get you to buy the toy. With the toy, they get you to Disneyland. From Disneyland you are soon buying the clothing, and going back to the next movie. For many of our products, what we really care about is not just the isolated product but having you buy into the entire ecosystem so that you are buying products not just from us, but taking advantage of the innovations created by our partners. Because you have the products from the partners you continue to be excited about ongoing innovations in our platforms.

I am describing the approach I have taken because it provides the rationale for the strategic plan I developed for my current organization. Other models and areas of focus are certainly possible and could make sense for your context, but what you learn here is that your point of view about how to deliver value provides the rationale for your strategy. It gives you a framework for thinking about what you are doing, how you deliver value, and how you talk about it.

A STRATEGIC FRAMEWORK

> Our plans miscarry because they have no aim. When a man does not know what harbor he is making for, no wind is the right wind.
>
> **Seneca**

Startups benefit from a strategic framework to ensure they do not lose sight of their ultimate goals in the midst of day-to-day activity. A strategic framework is a set of artifacts that ensures the plan for the company delivers on the strategy designed to achieve its vision. The goal of the framework is to inform decision making and to provide a basis for more detailed planning. It helps to explain what you do to

---

HINTS FROM EXPERIENCED MANAGERS

Establish a Vision, Strategy, and Priorities

Be sure to establish an experience vision and strategy for achieving that vision with your team. And, set priorities for the team. I recommend doing this collaboratively with the team overall. Focus on things that will deliver value both to the customer and to the business. (I have found that some experienced researchers/designers forget the importance of a business justification for what we do.) I like to call this customer-centric and business savvy experience strategy. This strategy and these priorities should evolve over time in response to the changing customer and business needs, along with the growing knowledge and experience of the team. The strategy and priorities can help when gauging the effectiveness of the team or when making decisions about what activities to invest in.

Marilyn Salzman, User Experience Strategist, Salzman Consulting, LLC, Louisville, CO

Don't underestimate the power of a strong vision. If you just focus on managing, no matter how good you are, you won't capture people's imagination. And it will be the person who can who will be able to steal them away.

Andy Cargile, Director of User Experience, Microsoft Hardware, Seattle, WA

---

others in order to inform, motivate, and involve, and the framework underlies your communications plan. It further assists in benchmarking and performance monitoring, and it stimulates growth and takes your impact to the next level as the team matures. The strategy that emerges from the framework should be visionary and directional, flavoring the way you approach your day-to-day work. It should be realistic and attainable, but should relate to the 3- to 5-year time frame.

For a UX team, a strategic framework begins with a vision for the future you want to create and a mission statement that describes who you are and what you do. Both of these are grounded in the soul of your team, the big idea, and your passion as a manager that energizes your team. This framework is based on how you deliver value. An elevator pitch is a summary of that soul and mission, and serves to organize messaging about your team and communication about your mission. The vision and mission also build upon the shared values of your team. A strategy (with your goals) is then developed that describes how your mission will be exercised to achieve your vision, objectives are set, and tactical plans are defined. The tactics are shaped according to the organizational context in which you find yourself. Metrics should be defined to ensure that you are on track to achieving your strategic objectives and to provide control over the process.

That context can be characterized by a SWOT analysis. If you are not familiar with this tool — and I was not until coming to my most recent job — it uses a framework that sorts the contextual forces into those that are helpful to your goal and those that might be harmful, and into those that come from outside your organization and those that come from within. The resulting table shows groups that represent strengths and weaknesses and opportunities and threats. In Figure 5.4, some of the forces that two colleagues (Peter and Louise) and I identified within our organization are listed. Within the strategy and the tactics to implement the analysis you can ensure that you are building on the strengths and compensating for your weaknesses. You can also ensure that you are addressing your opportunities and mitigating the threats to reduce the risks.

	Helpful	Harmful
Internal	**Strengths** • Deep competency • Strengthening community • Enthusiasm to innovate	**Weaknesses** • New to the organization • Fragmented UX teams • Missing skills • Immature success metrics
External	**Opportunities** • Growing awareness of impact • Cross-discipline accountability • Demonstrated wins	**Threats** • UX not visible in standard development process • UX missing from planning staffing ratios • Lack of scalable funding model

FIGURE 5.4

SWOT analysis example.

DEFINING YOUR VISION AND MISSION

I have been asked to generate new vision and mission statements for every company I have been in and nearly every time there has been a major organizational change. Often the exercise is driven by senior management mandate, but when it is done with your team's engagement the real benefit is that it becomes a tool for building team identity. At times the direction has been to align with the vision and mission statements of the organization; even without that direction the most effective mission statements take into account the direction in which the organization is heading. As you will see later, this is at the heart of positioning your team to deliver the strategic value that matters most to the organization and the company as well.

Vision Statement

Aim high! Trivial corrections usually are as hard to make and as staunchly resisted as fundamental changes.

Peter Drucker

The vision statement answers the question Where are we heading? by painting the picture of the goal with words. Like a vision for a design that aligns the roadmap of planning, the vision for your team should provide a focus and inspiration for your strategy and your tactical plans. It is the destination of the journey. It should not sound like everyone else's vision statement. It should capture something unique about what you and your team want to do. It should be aspirational but plausibly achievable.

The vision statement typically is internally facing and is a tool for the team. Given its function, it is the kind of statement that should be created by the team.

With every team member's fingerprints on it, it is more likely to engage them all, align them, and energize them to attain the vision together. There is no size limit typically, but it is usually one or two paragraphs. You do not want it to be so long the statement gets fuzzy, but you want enough description for the vision to be clear. Beware of a statement that is so ideal and visionary it could never be achieved and so ambiguous that it could apply to any team.

Here are some ideas that will help to create a vision statement:

- Review the corporate and organizational vision statements you already align with.
- Begin with your mission statement (if one has been defined) and your value proposition.
- Dare to dream big and focus on success. Imagine five years out and what you want your products and world to be like from a UX perspective. What will your team have accomplished? Paint a graphic word picture of what you want.
- Infuse your statement with passion.
- Fit it into a framework like "Five years from now, I envision…." You may drop these initial words, but they will get you started in the right direction. Then explain how you will think and act to get there (several distinct characteristics or values that make your team unique).
- Find other compelling vision statements to emulate.
- Think about how you will take action on your vision statement and build it into your strategy and tactics.
- Plan on using it with your team, revisiting it periodically, and testing your activities against it. You might usability test it with this scenario.

One approach is to have your team gather, and after reviewing other relevant vision statements and your own mission statement, set the stage for the dreaming and brainstorm elements of the vision. Put the ideas up on the board. Ask probing questions to stimulate additional brainstorming as the ideas slow down to ensure that you have thought about the future from the various perspectives that might be relevant. These might include the categories in the SWOT analysis; the perspectives of your users, your company, and your organization; and your own passions. Then use affinity diagramming to organize these ideas into clusters of elements that the team wants included in the statement. Finally, grab representative phrases that capture the clusters and put them into some type of logical order. Avoid spending too much time fighting over the wording as a group, because it is easy to get caught up in fighting over individual words and stall the progress. Just ensure you have the main ideas that everyone thinks should be represented in some fashion, and then go away and try to do an editing pass to tighten it up. Take the proposed wording back to the team and do an additional pass or two for refinement. Keep the accountability for the final statement rather than delegating it to the consensus of the team or a

A, broadcast it to the company, people would start working on it, and the growth in the business would remain exactly the same — a steady single digit growth rate year after year. The problem was that this was at the beginning of the emergence of the great current technology companies who were turning out not just double-digit growth rates, but *big* double-digit growth rates. Investors were not sticking around for the dividends any longer. He would then introduce initiative B with the same result.

A book came out about that time called *The Fifth Discipline: The Art & Practice of the Learning Organization*, by Peter Senge. One of the ideas that struck me in that book was that when you try to change an organization, especially an organization that has grown a set of processes and a culture around them that have worked reasonably well, the organization functions a little like an organism and the change is treated like an infection. Organizational antibodies begin to form around it to prevent it from succeeding. The people in various power positions know how to succeed in their jobs and get raises under the existing set of rules. The last thing they are motivated to do is to change things. What I have observed as the industry has gone through bubble and burst phases, and with assorted corporate takeovers, is that these earth-shattering events loosen up the bureaucracy, the habits, and the culture enough to open tremendous opportunities to drive change. Bill Weiss decided to force that level of change on his company.

He began by replacing his senior lieutenants with lower level executives drawn from around the company who were known as change agents in their organizations. Then he set the executives against each other to see who could drive the most impactful change; the prize was his job when he left the company (Tichy, 1997). I was in the organization of one of them, Dick Notebaert. The rumor mill already was circulating great stories about this head head of Ohio Bell, and how on his off time he would wear a magnetic earring, get on his Harley, and ride.

I remember the first management meeting Notebaert held when he started. I was sitting in the large meeting room on my stackable, industrial chair, waiting for him to be introduced and start to lay out his plans. The room held probably 100 to 200 people as I recall, and had that large multi-purpose room, fluorescent feel. It was filled with the energy of anticipation, both positive and negative. At the moment the podium at the front was empty and there was nothing on the screen. There were a few managers that I knew and those I did not were milling about at the front of the room. Suddenly someone sat down next to me and said "Hi! I'm Dick Notebaert." I introduced myself, and then he said "What do you do?"

This was the turning point for my team. I did not know it at the time but that is exactly how it turned out. I spoke from the heart and out came the elevator pitch. "My team designs products to meet our customer's needs." Dick had come up through the ranks at Ameritech mostly on the sales side when he was younger. He was a salesman at heart, so he got it. He really got it. At one point in my career I was a management trainee for a jewelry store, and when I sold jewelry I knew that the goal was to try to get to know what customers needed and wanted, and then to convince them that what you had would satisfy those needs. For someone like

Dick Notebaert who had made a living understanding customer needs and trying to sell things to satisfy those needs, finding a group in his team that actually used the same information to design the products he could sell was incredibly powerful. This connection resulted in the entire company pivoting on our mission, a three-year ad campaign based on our team's work, the product strategies for many parts of the business shifting to leverage our work, and more.

All this is to say you never know how important your elevator pitch may become, but it is one of the key tools in your UX management arsenal. Being able to articulate the heart of your vision and mission in a few words that flow easily from the tongues of you and your team will help align you as a high-performing team. It will begin to define your brand as people remember it, and it will guide and motivate funders to help you grow.

The elevator pitch does not have to remain the same and there is no one pitch that is ideal for every team. Pick your elevator pitch based on the strategic goals of the business, the culture of your organization, and your audience. I happened to say the right thing at the right time in that context. Over time, as the advertising people began to work with us, we crafted a pitch that aligned with the new brand promise of the company. The phrase that was developed by the advertising people was "If technology doesn't work for people, it doesn't work," and I have continued to find myself using variations on it as I talk to developers across the companies where I have worked.[1]

The elevator pitch concisely and confidently answers the question: What is UX all about? As we all know, for better or worse what politicians and others who have to deal with the press have learned is that they need to stay on message. Often the message is their elevator pitch — the short, pithy statement that they can use to ensure consistent messaging. The idea is to have a consistent message that you can express confidently, passionately, and consistently whenever the appropriate opportunities arise, and that you can build on if you have more time. The goal is to communicate what your team and program is about and to get the listener to want to know even more.

It is not a vision or mission statement. It is about your value. It is not all the detail; it is just the right detail. It is a teaching tool that provides an introduction to your sales pitch for UX. It is about getting to the point in a way that ensures the listener will retain it, but creating a demand so if there are future opportunities they will want to know more. It is about giving the listener a sense of what is in it for them and the issues they care about.

Some argue there should be both a short and a longer elevator pitch. The longer elevator pitch is for that 45-second elevator ride and is a slightly richer statement of the value proposition for your team and program. The short pitch is the one- or two-sentence statement describing what your team or your UX program is about. Ideally

---

[1] The slogan continues to live as the "If technology doesn't work for people . . . it doesn't work!"® slogan for User Centric, Inc., and my good friend and colleague Susan Dray has used a slogan that captures the same idea ("If the user can't use it, it doesn't work.") since well before Ameritech came up with ours.

it should have some stickiness to it, something that enables your team to use it consistently and the listener to remember it when you reference it again.

There are several characteristics you might consider for your elevator pitch:

- Who are you focused on?
- What problem are you solving?
- When you try it, does it come across as short, clear, and memorable (perhaps with humor)?
- Does it convey your energy and commitment? Are you credible when you share it?

CREATING A STRATEGY

However beautiful the strategy, you should occasionally look at the results.

Winston Churchill

One of the things UX has going for it is that when teams get a little taste of user experience work, they typically want more. What we do is attractive because it brings value both to the user and to those who engage us, it is emotionally compelling and aesthetically delightful when done well, and it is about human stories with which people can empathize. But relying entirely on the addiction of client teams to user experience can also lead to a service model that only provides incremental benefits. To advance user experience in your organization you should find the areas of maximum impact and implement a strategy to get there.

Strategies can take different forms. Eric Schaffer (2004) does a nice job of laying out one approach that is very direct. There are long-term strategic plans and near-term strategic plans. An example Schaffer provided includes areas such as training, methodology, facilities, tools and templates, standards, showcase projects, and organization and staffing. He pointed out that you want to select and sequence activities to drive your goals, optimizing practicality and efficiency. He rightly suggested that you bootstrap the success of small early activities to justify the investment for larger tasks and goals.

A Case Study: Creating a User-Centered Culture

The approach I having been using in the IT organization was recently summarized in Lund (2010). The situation is similar to the one you might face when starting UX from scratch in a company or large organization. The IT organization is made up of several thousand employees and while the majority of the employees are based in and around the Seattle area, significant numbers are based in India, China, and elsewhere around the world. Even in the Seattle area the IT staff is distributed widely across various buildings. IT produces hundreds of applications each year to enable the company to create its products, to support employee development and productivity, and to support operations. It also produces applications used around the world by our many partners, and applications that support our customers as they buy, use, and receive support for our products. The role of IT in helping create a relationship between the company and its customers and partners has been growing even more critical in recent years. When I joined IT it was because there were champions in senior management who believed that user experience is critical to help the company to achieve its goals.

While the user experience population across the company is sizable, within IT the population consists of a relatively small number of professionals primarily distributed across my group and a group supporting internal applications (e.g., Human Resources). If the proportion of UX within IT was based on the demand of a company with a similar size (Lund, 1994b) or based on a proportion similar to the product groups, it would be many times larger. Many in IT, as with most large corporations, fell into the trap of assuming that employees are captive users and will have to use applications whether they like them or not. They neglected to realize that poorly conceived and designed applications hurt the productivity and effectiveness of employees, and therefore of the business, even if they do use them properly. Research and experience at many companies demonstrates that employees may be "captive" in the sense that if told to complete a form they will, but that does not mean the form will be completed accurately and used in the way senior management imagines. We continually run across situations where people work around the system to check off the list of requirements without actually having to experience the pain of the application. They get their jobs done in spite of the applications, not because of them. As a result, decisions further upstream are based on inaccurate information and therefore ultimately hurt the business.

The approach that is wired into many of us in this situation is to grow by making the return on investment (ROI) case, and demonstrate either the bottom-line value that UX brings or at the very least how UX satisfies the strategic goals of the business and of management (Karat & Lund, 2005; Lund, 2007; Lund, 1997a). Even management occasionally asks for the ROI justification, although when provided it does not seem to be as persuasive as people would hope. Dan Rosenberg (2004) eloquently pointed out that these arguments alone in the best of times do not seem to be particularly effective in actually driving UX growth. Often it is far more important to either have a strong advocate in senior management or to leverage the direct value that a team experiences as they receive the benefits of UX work when driving growth. We have been fortunate in having advocates within senior management ranks who seeded user experience and nourished its start. Growth in these circumstances, however, is often slow. On the ground, an organization has to decide whether a vacancy is going to be used to bring in another developer, tester, or project manager or to use the vacancy for a user experience person whose role they are only beginning to understand. Even if growth was not an issue, it would take years to grow to satisfy the need within IT; in the recent economic climate that rate of growth would be unrealistic. These challenges are faced by nearly any large organization or company where UX is just getting a foothold.

The approach that I have been taking is to step back and instead of relying on the incremental approach, to think about what it means to transform an entire organization of thousands of people and to grow a user-centered, design-thinking culture across it, and to do it with a handful of designers and researchers.

The Approach

I should be clear on the scope we are attempting to address. Within an organization as large as IT or an entire company there are various groups within the organization that will have their own cultures. Across the entire company there is often a corporate culture that is the collected set of values, traditions, and other elements that characterize the company, which senior management often tries to steer. I am interested in influencing the IT organizational culture — "the specific collection of values and norms that are shared by people and groups in an organization and that control the way they interact with each other and with stakeholders outside the organization" (Hill & Jones, 2001). In essence what I want to propagate throughout the organization is a system with a common vision that is shared across the organization, a language that all can use to talk about it, a reinforcement structure that motivates people to take the appropriate actions to improve the experiences created and that shapes how individuals interact, and enhance the way they think about and interact with the artifacts they create. Furthermore, the goal is to design this system around a kind of virtuous cycle of self-reinforcing activity whose impact grows as it operates across the organization.

In raising the design-thinking IQ of an entire organization the quality of the hundreds of experiences created improves faster than if you have to rely on the small UX population and the projects directly supported. It scales the efforts of UX up, and indeed allows them to scale indefinitely as the greater organization grows. It transcends both geographic and discipline boundaries. It should build into the organization shared belief in the value around UX and drive the kind of demand for expertise and value that may lead to bringing in more designers and researchers (e.g., full-time staff, contractors, or vendors).

I also want to be clear that an implication of this approach is that non-UX people are being given more UX skills. I recognize up front that this is a frightening or at least disturbing prospect for many, and growing a UX empire would certainly be better for my personal career. If non-UX people grow their skills will they conclude that UX is no longer needed? Will they do a terrible job and ruin the "brand" of UX? Both have occurred in the past and will occur again. On the other hand, it is not clear whether it has been because of the training or in spite of it. Developers, project managers, and others will drive user interfaces without UX. Whether or not UX people are working on a project, an effective user interface and a great experience is a collaborative effort. If approached by everyone based on a foundation of sound design thinking the design will be better.

My experience is that the more people know about user experience, their own impact on the experiences improves and they come to respect the expertise of professionals even more; that respect often leads them to be evangelists for hiring more

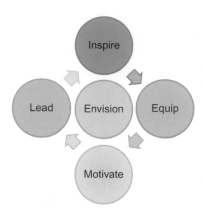

FIGURE 5.6

Virtuous cycle of culture change.

user experience people and getting them involved. These evangelists in turn do a better job of collaboration with the user experience people with whom they work (often challenging them, but in the process driving a better result). Furthermore, they often continue to grow their own skills and in some cases become professional UX people, bringing their own diverse experiences to enrich the field and projects. In short, I have found bringing more people into the UX tent has the benefit of being the engine that leads to growth. The alternative, where UX is owned and driven only by the UX team, would take longer and potentially be less impactful than when large numbers of people with higher levels of design thinking are engaged in the process.

Project managers should be better project managers and when they work with user experience people, they should be able to facilitate the creation of even better experiences as experience producers. Developers should be better developers as they build the support of great experiences into their code. Testers should complement user feedback by not just testing the code for traditional bugs but by empathizing with users as they ensure users can achieve their goals through the targeted, contextualized scenarios.

Engine of Culture Change

The approach I have taken is to define a model of culture change, a virtuous cycle that as it operates and the cycle iterates the culture evolves. It is illustrated in Figure 5.6.

At the heart is the vision for the experiences we want to create. This vision provides the language for the common direction and the business rationale for that direction. In the approach we are discussing here, it includes the core ideas that drive business value and adoption. It includes the experience attributes we want to deliver, the design experiences we want to create, and the themes we are trying to push through our designs. For the IT organization, at the core is delivering compelling, useful, and easy-to-use experiences that satisfy the brand promise.

Organizations are not necessarily motivated by models and supporting research. They are motivated by sticky ideas — by stories and images that grab their attention. As a result we are developing ways to grab their attention around the vision. We have been exploring how to further refine this vision in the form of concepts that capture the relevant elements. For the division we are in, the core concept has been growing the relationships between the user (whether customer or partner) and the business.

Deliver and Inspire

There was pressure in the first year my IT team existed to avoid supporting specific projects and to concentrate on creating standards for user interfaces. My experience has shown, however, that the best standards and guidelines are grounded in success-ful design rather than pulled out of the air. We have persisted, therefore, in pushing to ensure that the user experience teams are focused on the most important projects within the organization — and to identify those projects that are strategically impor-tant and where the user experience is in the critical path to success — and to get involved in those projects. In addition, we continually search for the difficult busi-ness problems facing the organization, and identify problems within that set that are centered on the experience. We work on breakthroughs for those problems based on design exploration and user research.

Our goal to move into new areas is to invest in setting the direction, the vision of where the design should be several years out (even before there is technology to support it), and to ground that vision on the user's needs and desires (the usefulness that drives the satisfaction). That vision is where we attempt to drive innovation in what the experience could be for users. Against that vision we work with teams to create road maps of how we will get there, and then the bulk of the team's work is the beginning-to-end involvement that delivers on the road map.

When great design is delivered it raises the visibility of design thinking across the organization. Senior executives get excited about the vision and even about the solu-tions to their problems. They get excited about the fact that their users are engaged in the process. The executives become evangelists for great user experiences, and become the sponsors for implementing the new ways of talking and thinking about the experience artifacts and how experience is woven into the design process and the teams that engage in it. The great design also becomes a source of the reusable assets and best practices, and by their strategic weight the design lends credibility to those assets. Finally, there is great design that teams without user experience can copy when appropriate.

Equip

An underutilized area where the user experience impact can be extended is through the architecture and the reuse it enables. The architecture we build our solutions on assumes Microsoft and partner platforms. On the platforms, there are a variety of data sources required for the business. In the middleware layer, systems corre-spond to business capabilities. Above the middleware layer, capabilities are com-bined to support user applications. The applications are then rendered to support an expanding ecosystem of devices as users move from device to device, and to support groups of users collaborating as part of various activities. This is where the usefulness is delivered, and contextualizing the experience through end-to-end user scenarios that are supported in the design is how we intend to deliver satisfaction. Integrating user experience into the architectures used by the teams is one way to insert the experience into the DNA of the organization.

When I started with my current team an architecture review meeting was held. I noticed that the presentation of the architecture only had a small annotation that there were user interface issues. We volunteered to create the poster that would show off the diagram, and I volunteered to co-author the architecture document. By the time we finished, more than half the diagram consisted of layers that connected the underlying systems with the users in context. There is a lot of power in being the author of the meeting notes, and there is a lot of power in being responsible for communicating the architectural ideas visually. Just through the involvement in the communication process we were able to change the language and the mental models of the teams.

The goal of the architecture we created is to create user interface building blocks that can be combined in various ways as new solutions are created. By using the same building blocks across applications the users will associate the family of solutions with the same brand and use the branding as a cue that triggers scripts that will help them know how to use new solutions. It should set up expectations about ease of use and usefulness. In addition, the goal is to assemble blocks into groups and groups into higher order groups based on common needs. The primitives should reflect sound usability principles, and the higher level design patterns should be both useful and easy to use; skinning with various brand identities should change the voice and suggest the support for families of scenarios, but should not be the basic ways people use various controls to get things done. This model placed our work on common guidelines and reusable design patterns at the heart of the strategy that was being used to turn the organization into a more efficient development team.

As part of this strategy we have taken several steps. I became a senior UX sponsor for a cross-MS icon database and a cross-UX community design pattern wiki project. We have led or participated in IT standards efforts around measuring user satisfaction, implementing accessibility and internationalization, and we are planning standards for usability measurements and branding. A major project of the team has been to build a UX Pattern Framework for implementing UIs so they can be easily rebranded and support the pattern architecture. We have housed this evolving set of patterns in a developer library and implemented it for several projects. We are working with another design team to create a library of reusable design assets and page templates.

The core idea is that IT should build from the conventions developed across the company and the partner ecosystem. In doing so, we leverage existing knowledge to enhance ease of use, add value to that ecosystem, and also serve as a customer that can provide user feedback into the ecosystem to drive innovation and improvement. We can also generate knowledge that can be transferred to our customers and partners about new ways they may also get value from the ecosystem. While executing this strategy I have been pulled in to talk to customers about how we leverage the ecosystem. The message is that user experience is integral to the success of that application development process.

The building blocks can be put together in ways that still result in bad user interfaces. To help with that, we have defined a set of common user requirements that should apply to all solutions throughout IT. These include accessibility requirements, for example, as well as requirements for supporting global localization and to support responsiveness in the user interface. If we succeed in creating truly common requirements then project managers, developers, and testers will become familiar with them, making them part of the standard practice, and they will only rarely need to be referenced. Education will then only be required around updates. Furthermore, to help obtain broad buy-in across the organization, the change management process is intended to incorporate requests from the organization to ensure that the practical day-to-day needs of UI guidance are reflected in the document; anyone can file bugs against the document to drive improvements within it. This process has the side benefit that the entire engineering organization is able to develop ownership of the evolving pattern of reusable assets available for designs created by the organization. An internal survey showed that the common requirements and the human interface guidelines are viewed as two of the most anticipated useful documents created by the UX team.

Having the right architecture is only part of the challenge. The blocks need to be assembled in a way that results in satisfying and compelling experiences. We began by defining the waterfall process illustrated in Figure 5.7. The starting point was the development process that had already been defined for our IT organization, a process that is typical of one with a planning phase, a requirements phase, a design phase, a development phase (including testing), and then deployment and maintenance. The process is somewhat complicated by the organizational stakeholders. For most of the projects within IT, certainly the most strategic ones, there is a business organization that sponsors the initiative and drives the business plan. Within IT, there is an organization whose responsibility it is to translate the business goals into business requirements. When I started my career back at AT&T Bell Laboratories, this was the equivalent of the systems engineering organization. The business requirements are then taken by engineering and turned into specifications and coded. At AT&T Bell Laboratories, this was the development organization.

We overlaid onto the existing process the set of user experience activities that should take place within each of the phases if teams have full user experience support. The core concept is user-centered design. Understand the users, translate that into design, test, improve, and iterate, and do it from beginning to end. This is enhanced with the idea of engineered creative design thinking, baking in a process of broad exploration and then prioritization, focus, and renewed exploration for the next phase.

For teams that are encountering user experience for the first time one of the questions we are asked is What do you do? Another question is What do I do with it? which can be read as Why should I care? In describing how user experience

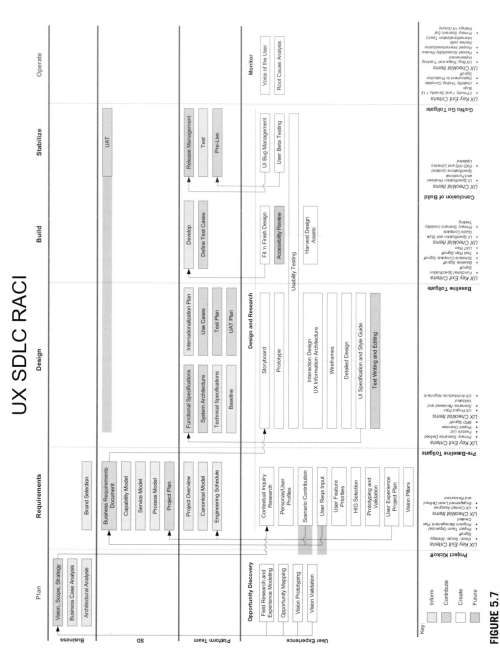

FIGURE 5.7

User-centered waterfall process.

fits within the existing development process, we showed how our deliverables are influenced by the deliverables on other teams, and how our deliverables influence subsequent deliverables and make them better. The goal is to describe more clearly how the quality of the user interface development and the success of the project is enhanced by engaging user experience throughout the project, and how design thinking and user understanding can influence every phase of the project from uncovering new business opportunities, to development, and to validating that the project was successful (e g , through the satisfaction and other metrics described previously showing the impact of the work). In particular, we have been able to show where user experience activities improve the usefulness of the result and where they address ease of use. We use this framework to lay out a very clear description for who is responsible for what and to inform project planning.

The goal is not just to focus on what the UX team does for projects, but rather to provide a user-centered perspective that any team can use. When UX is involved, the process should work better and achieve an even more spectacular result, but every project should benefit from design thinking. There certainly will be some teams with full UX support, some with support that will come from engaging contractors or applying a smaller UX team for specific tasks, and some teams without any UX support.

One particularly effective approach to defining a set of tools that raises design thinking across the organization has been to drive a scenario focus into the development process. It began with a quality initiative within the organization. We defined quality in terms of process changes we wanted to make to raise quality. These included building it right (with a focus on things like release management and test automation), but also an effort around building the right thing. Building the right thing focused on clearly identifying the users, defining the scenarios that drive business and user value, and then ensuring the scenarios are delivered. We used this as an opportunity to take many of the concepts and tools built around user-centered design and integrate them into the scenario-based development process.

One issue that arose early was the diverse ways in which people define scenarios. I remember quite clearly sitting in the evening in front of the TV surrounded by books, articles, and materials from one of my sibling UX teams (where they had evolved an approach that pragmatically worked for their team) and coming to the conclusion that instead of trying to debate various types of scenarios, I would just define the terms in the way we would use them across IT. The goal was to define terms like *scenario* and *use cases* in a way that would allow the creation of a development system that would support creating usable design. From the definitions I created templates that would be used to transform our requirements and specifications documents. From those definitions it was then possible to create various tools such as scenario-based bug classification. This bug classification allowed us to build usability into what was otherwise a purely engineering-focused process.

We then began driving scenarios into the larger organization with the support of the general manager. Teams were required to create quality plans that explicitly laid out how they would implement scenarios. Over time the goal was to raise their levels in a maturity model that showed how they were using scenarios for user-centered design. I integrated scenarios into the release management process, and that allowed us to track progress publically in the organization. We built scenarios into the code management tool the developers used, and that allowed bugs to be filed against the scenarios to improve them. We put together training around the process and launched training and mentoring with the teams as well as drove it within the projects we supported directly. The person on my team who had been driving this effort (Peter) moved to report to my boss directly so he could drive the overall quality process. That continued to raise the emphasis on the scenarios work across the organization.

Serendipitously, the training organization was developing a scenarios-based emphasis. We fed what we had been learning and developing to them, and they integrated scenarios training with a user-centered design course for non-UX people. They began rolling that training out more broadly. Peter, in turn, moved to the IT version of a training and engineering best practices organization, and he took the course and contextualized it for IT using our scenarios approach. He then took on the charge of driving the training through all of IT. As a result, thousands of people are being trained in user-centered design, and the demand for design and user research has been blossoming.

Personas and Scenarios

We have built and are continuing to expand a library of personas that teams can use. While there are differing views about personas, for a situation like ours where they stimulate empathy through their stories, they serve as an effective anchor to help teams begin to think like the intended users. They also help teams focus on specific users rather than on "all users."

We have defined a specific form of scenario, templates for how to structure the scenario, and guidance on things to do and things to avoid, and we have assembled best practice examples. The scenarios are prioritized, and the goal is to adopt something like the Kano model and Pruitt and Adlin's (2006) persona-based prioritization scheme to help teams think through the process of prioritization based on the needs and desires of the personas.

A new step we are introducing is to standardize the expectation that early sketching and rapid prototyping will occur as the requirements and scenarios are defined. The key for integrating UX and user-centered design into the development process is that this early prototype provides a kind of common model and language that all the stakeholders in the process can agree on, and serves as a representation of how the scenarios might be implemented. It is understood that it is not a final design, and indeed is expected to change as the design is more fully explored and tested with users. It is a starting point for testing with users, it demonstrates the feasibility of implementation, and it puts a reasonable size around the design effort (number of screens, number of controls and design assets that will be required, etc.). It also helps to identify where further and more detailed explorations will be required.

The scenarios are then turned into use cases by the project managers and documented in the specifications. The use cases serve as the implementation requirements for the specific application being built. Test cases are then built from the use cases, but testers also use the personas and the scenarios to ensure they are staying focused on the goals the users have and not just on the software itself. We are implementing a bug severity and prioritization scheme that introduces the user experience, the scenarios, as an equal player against the more technical bugs that can occur; and to build it into the way test, development, and project management think it is being built into the tool that is used to report, triage, and track all the bugs. Reports from the bug reporting tool are sent up the management chain who will then review experience bugs based on the targeted scenarios and require accountability around delivering the experience. Finally, traceability is defined and tracked from the test cases back through the use case and to the scenarios; this provides some assurance that what is being built is what users are saying they want and need.

The scenarios are the backbone of the user-centered process, and are an attempt to anchor the process at the beginning. When UX or market research is involved the research is better controlled — and will certainly have higher reliability, generalizability, and validity — but we believe that even without experienced researchers teams will be better off if they listen to users and adapt designs based on what they hear. Then our goal can be to improve those skills.

The scenarios, however, need to be turned into design. Teams without UX will produce designs in the course of project management and development. We can further extend the user-centered model, however, if we introduce some form of interim prototyping and validation between the requirements and the specifications. To do this, the plan is to leverage Microsoft's SketchFlow tool in the Expression Suite, and build the reusable controls and design pattern components (the building blocks) into it. Teams will be able to put the building blocks together to try different implementations to support the scenarios. Based on the experience either they will generate better use cases or be able to expose them to users to get feedback on whether they effectively support the implementation of the scenarios and then use that feedback to generate the use cases. Another tool that we have begun to leverage is one that allows prototypes to be exposed to user communities who then provide feedback based on the previews. The feedback should inform changes to the prototype. Furthermore, these teams should be able to draw from the libraries of design patterns and in some cases copy the best practices from the visible, highly strategic projects that the user experience team has been supporting directly.

The result is validation of the intent of the design with users up front and user-centered focus in requirements, design exploration and confirmation with users that what is being built seems to deliver the usefulness being targeted with the scenarios (and the context the scenarios reflect), user "surrogate" testing carried out by testers who are educated with heuristics and grounded in the validated personas and scenarios, and a feedback loop from the users once the application is deployed.

The feedback loop ensures that the problems will be pulled into the planning for the next release and teams can iteratively (albeit incrementally) improve the experiences they create.

Training

The most critical step in creating tools that transform the way people work is to create tools that are usable, useful, and easier to use than existing alternatives. But just making them is not enough. We need to support their use and grow design thinking (Brown, 2008) across the organization. That means we need to train and mentor. To do that, we have put together a curriculum for our IT organization that raises the design-thinking IQ of the entire organization. In addition we are engaging senior management support to grow the UX expertise of a subset of their project managers, developers, and testers. This combines courses my team created, those developed by the other IT UX team, and courses offered corporately. The curriculum is illustrated in Figure 5.8.

We have structured the curriculum into levels with basic courses, intermediate courses, and extended courses. Initially we thought we might emulate the Six Sigma Black Belt concept, but then felt that we did not want to imply that if you had a black belt you had everything you needed to be a fully skilled user experience professional. Instead, we decided to present the curriculum as teaching the ability to do very specific tasks. The tasks would enable teams without UX to do a better job in what they design, and would enable those taking the classes to partner with UX more effectively and for UX to scale their impact ad design direction beyond the simple number of UX people on a project. Since the designers and researchers need to deliver inspiring design as the core of their day job, part of the goal is to drive toward as many self-service courses as possible. We also want to leverage the existing training that the engineering training organization is offering, and complement it with the training that we create, which is specific to our local organization.

There is an introductory class that teaches design thinking, the vision, general principles of great design (Lund, 1997b), and the process and how to apply it. It also provides an introduction to the available reusable assets. There is a class in prototyping with wireframes, and a class in simple validation with users that includes several sessions and hands-on labs. There is a class on scenarios, and one on implementing the reusable assets and customizing CSS. There are also hands-on workshops that we are developing with the quality organization around resolving user experience problems. We are also working with the corporate training organization to see if we can leverage their registration process to track who is participating, and to bake the training into the objectives of individual project managers, developers, and testers who share responsibility for the quality of user interfaces.

What we are enabling are UI specialists within each of the disciplines. The UI project manager is someone who is responsible for the end-to-end scenarios that deliver usefulness and user satisfaction — not as the person who owns

Level	Course Level	UX Area	Course	Delivery Method	Provider	Supported Team	Self-service Team	Disciplines	Notes
Extended	360	D, R	Advanced Mentored Project	In Person	UX		O	All	Proposed
	341	D, R	MS UX Accelerate Workshop	In Person	CQ		O	All	Exists
	331	R	Affinity Diagramming Workshop and User Modeling	In Person	UX		O	PM	Proposed
	323	R	Branding	Video, SDK	UX		O	PM, Dev	Proposed, Deck Ready
	322	D	Creating Trustworthy User Experiences	In Person	ET		O	All	Exists
	321	D	Creating Customer-Centric Web Sites	In Person	ET		O	All	Exists
	312	R	Assumption Persona Creation Workshop	In Person	UX		O	PM	Piloted
	311	R	Conducting Site Visits	In Person	ET		O	PM	Exists
Intermediate	261	D, R	Metrics for Success	In Person	UX	O	O	PM	Proposed
	260	D, R	UX Champion Seminar	In Person	UX	O	O	All	Piloted
	252	D, R	UX Design Tips and Tricks	In Person	UX	O	O	All	Proposed
	251	D, R	Geopolitical Awareness and Content Quality	In Person	ET	O	O	All	Exists
	226	D, R	Accessible PMing, Development, and Testing	Online	CA	R	R	All	Exists
	225	D	Effective Technical Writing	In Person	ET	O	R	PM, Dev	Exists
	224	D, R	Information Architecture	In Person	ET	O	R	PM	Being Developed
	223	D	Guidelines-Based User Experience Design	Online	ET	O	R	PM, Dev	Exists
	222	D	Overview of Reusable Assets	Video	UX	R	R	All	In Preparation
	221	R	Creating Accessible User Experiences	In Person	ET	R	R	All	Exists
	211	R	Conducting Informal Usability Observations	In Person	ET	O	R	PM	Exists
	210	R	Connecting with Customers	In Person	ET	O	R	PM	Exists
	203	D, R	Scenario-Focused Engineering and User-Centered Design	In Person	ET	R	R	All	Exists
	202	D, R	EE Scenarios (incl. UX for Other Disciplines)	In Person	ET	R	R	All	Exists (based on capacity)
Basic	160	D, R	Mentored Project	In Person	UX	R	R	Dev	Exists
	131	D	CSS Framework and RXD Catalog	SDK	UX	R	R	Dev	Current Visual Studio Recommendation
	130	D	Expression Blend	In Person	Varies	R	R	PM, Test	Exists
	111	R	Usability Studies, What Are They, How to Use Them	In Person	UX	R	R	PM	Piloting
	110	R	Usability Principles	In Person	UX	R	R	PM	Exists
	106	D, R	Overview of the UCD Process	In Person	UX	R	R	PM	Exists
	105	R	Personas, What Are They, How to Use Them	In Person	UX	O	O	PM, Test	Exists
	104	D	Design Tools and Templates	In Person	UX	R	R	PM	In Development
	103	D	Seminar on Wire Framing, Storyboards, and Prototyping	In Person	UX	R	R	PM	Exists
	102	D, R	RXD Scenarios Framework	Video	UX	R	R	All	Exists
	101	D, R	Introduction to Accessibility	Online	CA	R	R	All	Exists
	100	D, R	Introduction to Quality in Use	Video	UX	R	R	All	Proposed

EE = Engineering Training
CQ = Corporate Quality
CA = Corporate Accessibility
R = Required
O = Optional

FIGURE 5.8

Example course curriculum.

developing the experience, but as a producer who engages others to design and develop the experience and facilitates its creation. The UX project manager works well for many teams, ensuring teams without direct design and research support have a better experience, and improving the effectiveness of teams with design and research support. The UX champion makes sure the key activities that need to happen do, and does so by making sure that someone is responsible for each activity and reporting status up through management. UI developers will be trained in the new Expression-based development tools as well as the asset libraries and principles of how to put the blocks together in the most effective manner. UI testers will be trained in how to best use personas and scenarios to frame the questions they ask during testing, in the bug classification scheme, and in design heuristics.

Motivate

Motivation within an organization begins with defining metrics that will be tracked and that matter to the organization. The model within the vision suggests that satisfaction is at the heart of what we want to measure. One step is to evangelize a consistent measurement and to drive broad adoption. We have helped drive a standard for this metric. It is often collected by sampling the user population as they use the released application, often by using user panels, so the value is in motivating release over release improvement. The goal is to build the metric into the system in a way that ensures it is exposed in the standard dashboards used throughout the management chain and is discussed during strategic and tactical review sessions.

The next step is to increase the visibility of the metric across the management chain. That alone is usually enough to stimulate action. No team wants to have a yellow or even red box around user satisfaction next to their project. There is an opportunity, therefore, to drive more activity around satisfaction by building user satisfaction into these goals. For more senior management, the goals would include either achieving specific target levels or achieving some percent increase year over year. For people closer to the frontline, the goals might include either target levels for usefulness and ease of use or operationally equivalent performance-oriented goals.

A satisfaction metric alone does not provide enough guidance about how to make improvements. It needs to be supplemented by more diagnostic tools. Typically the satisfaction metric is collected as part of a larger study, and if we can define an appropriate framework that deconstructs the experience along the lines of the vision model into components that are meaningful to the user, we can identify the degree to which each impacts overall satisfaction and therefore business value. Furthermore, if we can drive a consistent set of user feedback tools across the organization based on value, ease of use, and other factors, not only will managers have information about what is working and not working for users, but also they will be able to compare application experiences and make better decisions about the relative importance of various experiences and where to invest in improvements.

through design patents, internal and external publications, professional certification, and support for participation in industry research consortiums provides a good platform for their individual growth.

Adapt your management style to reduce disconnects between changes in company growth objectives and department workload demands. As the manager, you have fiscal, functional, intellectual property, and personnel management tasks that can conflict with unexpected changes in company direction for senior staff. Recognize your personal tolerance for risk taking and supporting unpopular policies and positions, and develop your interpersonal communication and interaction styles knowing your limitations, preferences, and strategies for growing the team. This needs to be done by keeping cognizant of your personal career goals and objectives (see Figure 5.9).

In summary, setting a management strategy and adapting the strategy to drive changes within the organization is an ongoing process, especially in today's volatile markets. The five dimensions in Figure 5.9 provide a platform to anchor the manager's strategic plan.

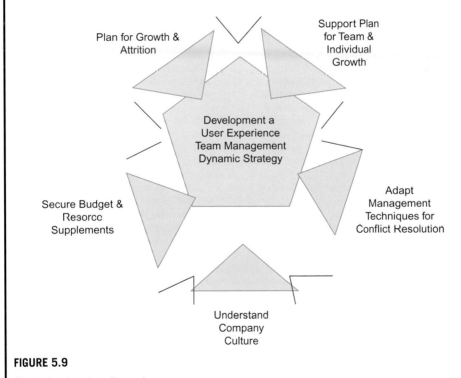

FIGURE 5.9

Strategic planning dimensions.

5.2 LESSONS LEARNED IN MANAGING A UX CONSULTANCY

By Simo Säde, PhD, CEO, Etnoteam Finland, Helsinki, Finland

I am sharing these practical-level thoughts and experiences from the point of view of a manager of an independent user experience consulting company. Our UX team has grown over the years, and most of the development of our activities has happened without a preexisting framework or guiding company policies. Below, I will describe some of the challenges we have faced in organizing our work and in developing our business. We have succeeded in some of the issues below and learned some of them the hard way. With many of these, we just need to keep on working.

The consultant firm environment is very different compared to an in-house UX team in a large corporation. The projects we work on are typically shorter than in-house development projects. Forecasting the project situation in the future is far more difficult and the time span of a reliable forecast is short. The importance of sales is more directly related to the team's everyday life.

Challenge of sizing the team to meet the market need

In consulting, usability and user experience projects are often short, as we typically participate only in a certain part of the overall customer project. Also, our sales cycle is short. It is common that the projects do not fall into our calendar nicely and evenly. There may be high peaks in workload and periods of quietness after that. The projects in a consultancy firm are often gained through bidding competition, and it may happen that there are several bids in at the same time. Winning or losing several bids at the same time may mean either a serious lack of resources or serious oversupply of them. Furthermore, the won projects are often confirmed just days before kickoff, so the reaction time is short.

High variation in the level of workload means problems in sizing the team. One solution is to have a core team supplemented with consultants under hour-based contracts. Normally this flexible resource consists of junior specialists, such as students, who work part time. This model may cause problems with communication and project quality. It requires more hands-on management tasks from the senior staff and more hours used for familiarization in the projects, which causes inefficiency. There is also the risk of not meeting the normal quality standards. Once an hour-based consultant has been in the company for some time and has gained experience, these problems eventually disappear. For the manager, this situation may cause an additional challenge. It may be difficult to keep the hour-based consultants happy, if they would like to be nominated to permanent full-time positions but growth does not allow it.

Another better, but more fundamental, solution is aiming at a large, widely spread clientele that can provide an even workload. Growing with dependence on one industry or on one or two main customers is risky in this sense. A recession hitting the industrial field in question or some sudden strategic change in the main customer may mean that outside consultants are no longer needed.

From individual to shared competencies

When a small team of experts begins to grow — outside a well-regulated environment of a large corporation — it is easy to realize too late how important it is to document the way the work is done and the best practices. When a small number of colleagues work together they know what each of them are doing and they develop the methods, processes, and skills together. With a bit of growth, when there begins to be several parallel projects and separate project teams, it is important to document and communicate. Mentoring a younger colleague informally, or sharing the lessons learned in corridors and on coffee breaks works for some time, but soon alternative, competing ways of doing the same thing start to appear, causing confusion, inefficiency, and uncertainty.

Written procedures and processes, checklists, and instructions not only make it easier for the newest team member to get in and start working effectively, but they also allow the whole team be efficient. As a very basic example, all the document templates needed in the team must be consistent and easily available. But even if they are, it is common practice to create a document by modifying an existing one. This way various, slightly different versions start to bloom and lead to an inconsistent, error-prone way of working.

Having lessons-learned sessions may serve also as team building effort. When team members discuss the successes and failures in a finished project, it grows the feeling of being in the same boat. Also, when a team member is training one's colleagues on a subject she knows better than even the more senior colleagues, it increases respect for her professional capabilities, and affects the team member's self-esteem in a positive way.

Shared knowledge means safety for the business and flexibility in reacting to new situations. In case of a sudden sick leave or a quick new important assignment of a key person in a project, her colleagues can step in and cover for her. The basic skills and processes in the company should be shared by everyone, but it is important to try to identify the special skills and experience each individual has. The team should ensure that this information can be found somewhere, when the person is not available. The difficulty here is that these pieces of knowledge may be subtle, tacit knowledge, and continuously evolving.

One longer term way of spreading the skills and experiences inside the company is the rotation of jobs, where the employee switches from her own position to another for a period of time. This enforces collaborative learning. On the one hand, in the consulting business this is easier to arrange than elsewhere because of the relatively short projects and the variation of the contents from project to project. So, one learns new skills by working on new kinds of projects, typically with a colleague with previous experience on the topic. On the other hand, however, our customers usually do not want us to change the trusted consultants they are used to working with. This is because of the learning curve, of course. In long-term cooperation, however, consultant rotation would be in the customer's best interest, as it increases the number of available capable resources.

Roles, responsibilities, and delegation

When a small team grows, it is important for the manager to delegate responsibilities to get things done. The manager, as a domain specialist, usually works in projects together with her colleagues. At first, most things outside actual project work can be handled by the manager. Once the team and the workload have grown a bit, more and more of the manager's time will be dedicated to managerial tasks, which at some point leads to stepping out of project work. Leaving the "real work" behind may be a hard decision for a specialist. This new setup works for some time, but when the growth of the team continues, the manager inevitably becomes an obstacle to efficient function, unless she starts to delegate the managerial responsibilities and decision-making powers to her colleagues. Delegation of responsibilities also releases the powers of others, leading to better usage of all the talent in the team. It is also a good motivational boost for the other team members to have new responsibilities and freedom in decision making. It doesn't necessarily require a formal higher position.

The delegation of tasks and responsibilities is closely related to the question of clarity in roles and responsibilities. The roles and responsibilities should be clearly defined and not overlapping to avoid ambiguity. At first, it may be reasonable to keep the economic, business, and budget responsibilities in the hands of the manager. For instance, when the team is divided into new smaller teams some people from the team need to be nominated as team leaders, as the direct supervisors of the other team members. They may be responsible for allocating resources into projects and for handling HR issues, but it may not be necessary to immediately make them responsible for the budget of the team, revenues, and costs such as salaries. In general, the delegated tasks should come with decision-making power and some budget, so that the newly nominated person has the tools and the authority for performing the tasks.

Freedom and control, targets, and communication

When delegating, the manager needs to give freedom, but keep control. It is human for anyone to overvalue the issues you get to be in charge of. If your job is to take care of employees' training and tools, you probably want the company to invest in those areas, instead of, for example, marketing — and the other way round. There may be a lot of good development ideas and very reasonable investment targets that are certainly important for the company, and it is the manager's responsibility to control and prioritize actions if you can't have it all.

The selection of actions taken should come from the company strategy, which is manifested in a road map. Employees want to have freedom, but they want the company to have a clear vision, which gives the direction for everyone to go. Everyday decision making should be based on the road map. This may sound easier than it is, in a changing environment. It is important for the practical everyday life of the team to first establish the strategy, but also to review it in new situations and to communicate it. One thing we have learned is that the strategy, the directions chosen, and even the practical-level decisions made cannot be communicated only once — even if there are no changes in them. They must be communicated clearly in the first place, then repeated, and then repeated again. If that is not done, even the people involved in decision making may soon lose focus, question the strategy, and start to ask the same questions again.

5.3 BUILDING AN INTEGRATED INFORMATION ARCHITECTURE PRACTICE AT SAPIENT DURING THE DOT-COM BOOM[3]

By Lillian E. Svec, Program Coordinator and Instructor, Web Design Program, UCSC Extension in Silicon Valley, Santa Clara, CA

Approved by Sapient 11/4/10

Sapient, a business and technology consulting company, acquired Studio Archetype and Adjacency, two Web design-consulting firms, during 1998–1999. In the summer of 1999, Sapient embarked on merging the competencies of the three original companies into one fully integrated offering. To accomplish this, the integration team looked across the joined companies for groups with analogous work practices. Project team members were reorganized into disciplines including Creative, Strategy, and Technology. The Creative Discipline was further organized into specializations or practices. At this time, the Sapient Information Architecture (IA) Practice was born.

Three groups that had been responsible for developing the information architecture and interaction design for Web sites or application interfaces were joined: the User Interface Group at legacy Sapient, which had existed for three years and had its roots in designing client server applications; the Information Design practice from Studio Archetype, which had existed for seven years and was originally more content design oriented; and the Information Architecture team from Adjacency, which had existed for six months and was more Web application oriented. The outcome was that there were about 60 designers spread throughout five offices who were now Sapient IAs.

The problem was that the work practices of the different groups were similar but they were *not* the same. Team members were frequently staffed on projects based in offices other than their home office. In San Francisco, we had members of all three legacy organizations working in the same office. IAs from different legacy offices had different terms and techniques. It was confusing for teams not knowing which "flavor" of IA they were going to be working with. It was confusing for the individual IAs, especially when IAs from different legacy organizations worked together on the same project team.

[3] Bibliography: Sapient Information Architecture: Practice Definition and Process Framework. March 6, 2000, Version 1.0.
Svec, L. (2000). Building an integrated Information Architecture Practice at Sapient. Handout and presentation of the same name, AIGA Advance for Design Summit, Telluride, CO.
Svec, L. (2001). Building and Expanding an Integrated Information Architecture Practice. Presentation, ASIS&T IA Summit conference, San Francisco, CA, February 2001.
Morrogh, E. (2003). *Information architecture: An emerging 21st century profession* (pp. 119–121). Upper Saddle River, NJ: Prentice Hall.

This situation made it difficult to answer the question "What is Information Architecture at Sapient?" It was impossible to ensure quality and consistency, it was unpredictable for teams and clients, and it was hard to bring new people into the practice and to train them. This was a serious problem because we knew that in the coming year we would be tasked with expanding the practice 50–100% and doubling to tripling the number of offices.

The leaders of the legacy IA recognized that they needed to agree on a definition of the practice, a process model, and nomenclature for tasks and deliverables. In the fall, as the newly appointed Global IA Practice Lead, I realized that if any one legacy felt their point of view had not been taken into consideration, we would fail both to get their buy-in and to gain from the value of their experience.

During the integration process three different levels of expertise within the IA practice were recognized. My strategy was to bring together the twelve most experienced IAs — IA Directors — from throughout the company for a four-day offsite. Our high-level objectives were to learn about the work that each office had done, to craft a common IA Practice definition and process model, and to forge a leadership team across the company. I was fortunate that the Creative Discipline's executives saw the value in this effort and were willing to allocate budget for it.

In early December, at the offsite, the IA Directors from each office presented the IA process followed in that office and showed "best practice" examples of their deliverables. Using a workshop approach similar to how we worked with clients, we worked as a team, in real time, to develop a detailed IA process model. As each director presented, we used different colored Post-its® for that office's deliverables and placed them within Sapient's five-stage process model, which was drawn on a whiteboard. Once all offices had presented, the participants used a variation of the affinity diagramming technique to group the Post-its® into higher level tasks or deliverables and labeled them. Using multiple whiteboards, the group iterated on the emerging model. We identified critical path activities, sub-tasks, deliverables, and entry and exit criteria for each high-level activity and added these to an evolving diagram. At the end of four days and many iterations, we had drafted a comprehensive IA process model, identified "best practice examples" of deliverables, defined the communication vehicles for documenting our work, identified key next steps, and assigned sub-teams to finish the work.

In follow-up work, we wrote a practice definition; defined terms; refined the model and designed a detailed diagram representing it; and created a 122-page, spiral-bound book to document our work. The book included step-by-step best practices guides keyed to the diagram and pointers to examples of deliverables, which were available electronically. Benefiting from a slowdown in our consulting work at the end of 1999 due to the business world's preoccupation with Y2K information technology fixes, we used the time to conduct these practice development efforts.

As consultants, we recognized that adapting to the needs of each project and to emmerging technologies was crucial. Thus, we were leery of this work being used rigidly and inhibiting flexibility and innovation. For this reason, the work was named the Sapient Information Architecture Framework 1.0. We rolled it out to the IA team members as a guide, not an operating standard, and recognized that it would need to evolve over time.

What we accomplished was an example of the whole being greater than the sum of its parts. We found that the variations in practices between the offices, when synthesized, made for a more comprehensive process than any one office was following.

The Sapient IA practice grew to approximately 100 members in 18 offices worldwide in the next year. The IA Framework was an invaluable aid in this effort and was the foundation we used to develop a weeklong IA training program for new IA hires and cross-training other team members.

Since 1999, the Internet consulting industry and Sapient have changed in countless ways. The company has adopted different organizational structures, work processes, and roles. The Information Architecture role continues to be an important part of the Creative group at SapientNitro, a division of Sapient. The pioneering effort that established this role in the company remains a valuable example of company process integration and codification (see Figure 5.10).

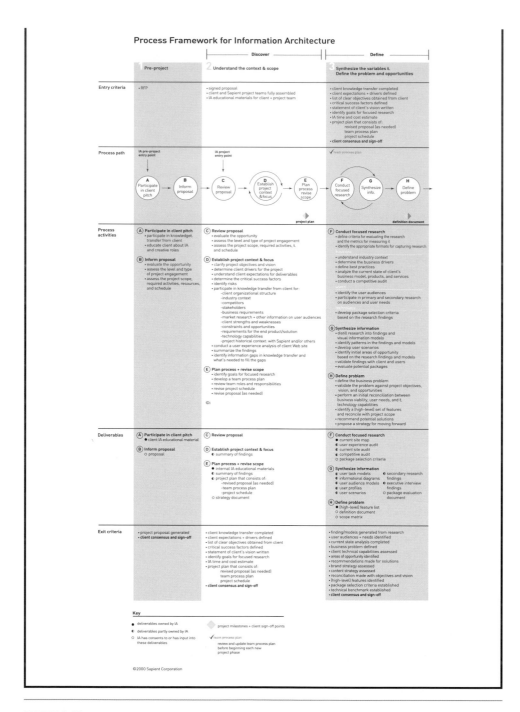

FIGURE 5.10

Sapient IA process framework.*

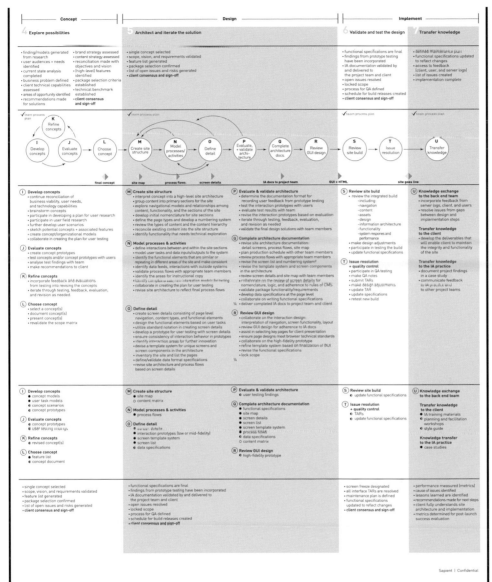

Concept	Design		Implement	

4 Explore possibilities — **5 Architect and iterate the solution** — **6 Validate and test the design** — **7 Transfer knowledge**

4 Explore possibilities
- finding/models generated from research
- user audiences + needs identified
- current state analysis completed
- business problem defined
- client technical capabilities assessed
- areas of opportunity identified
- recommendations made for solutions
- brand strategy assessed
- content strategy assessed
- reconciliation made with objectives and vision
- (high-level) features identified
- package selection criteria established
- technical benchmark established
- **client consensus and sign-off**

5 Architect and iterate the solution
- single concept selected
- scope, vision, and requirements validated
- feature list generated
- package selection confirmed
- list of open issues and risks generated
- **client consensus and sign-off**

6 Validate and test the design
- functional specifications are final
- findings from prototype testing have been incorporated
- IA documentation validated by and delivered to the project team and client
- open issues resolved
- locked scope
- process for QA defined
- schedule for build releases created
- **client consensus and sign-off**

7 Transfer knowledge
- defined maintenance plan
- functional specifications updated to reflect changes
- access to feedback (client, user, and server logs)
- list of issues created
- implementation complete

Develop concepts (I)
- continue reconciliation of business viability, user needs, and technology capabilities
- brainstorm concepts
- participate in developing a plan for user research
- participate in user field research
- further develop user scenarios
- sketch potential concepts + associated features
- create concept/organizational models
- collaborate in creating the plan for user testing

Evaluate concepts (J)
- create concept prototypes
- test concepts and/or concept prototypes with users
- analyse test findings with team
- make recommendations to client

Refine concepts (K)
- incorporate feedback and evaluations from testing into revising the concepts
- iterate through testing, feedback, evaluation, and revision as needed.

Choose concept (L)
- select a concept(s)
- document concept(s)
- present concept(s)
- revalidate the scope matrix

Create site structure (M)
- interpret concept into a high-level site architecture
- group content into primary sections for the site
- explore navigational models and relationships among content, functionality, and the sections of the site
- develop initial nomenclature for site sections
- define the page types and develop a numbering system
- review the types of content and the content hierarchy
- reconcile existing content into the site structure
- identify functionality that needs technical exploration

Model processes & activities (N)
- define interactions between and within the site sections
- model user tasks and data inputs/outputs to the site
- identify the functional elements that are similar or repeating in different areas of the site and make consistent
- identify data feeds, interactions with outside systems
- validate process flows with appropriate team members
- identify the areas for instructional copy
- identify complex or key interaction models for testing
- collaborate in creating the plan for user testing
- revise site architecture to reflect final process flows

Define detail (O)
- create screen details consisting of page level navigation, content types, and functional elements
- design the functional elements based on user tasks
- utilize standard notation in creating screen details
- develop a prototype for user testing with screen details
- ensure consistency of interaction behavior in prototypes
- identify interaction areas for further innovation
- devise a template system for unique screens and screen components in the architecture
- inventory the site and list the pages
- define/validate data format specifications
- revise site architecture and process flows based on screen details

Evaluate & validate architecture (P)
- determine the documentation format for recording user feedback from prototype testing
- test the interaction prototypes with users
- evaluate test results with team
- revise the interaction prototypes based on evaluation
- iterate through testing, feedback, evaluation, and revision as needed
- validate the final design solutions with team members

Complete architecture documentation (Q)
- revise site architecture documentation: detail screens, process flows, site map
- plan production schedule with other team members
- review process flows with appropriate team members
- revise the screen list and numbering system?
- revise the template system and screen components in the architecture
- review screen details and site map with team members
- refine/iterate on the review of screen details for nomenclature, logic, and adherence to rules of CMS
- validate package functionality/requirements
- develop data specifications at the page level
- collaborate on writing functional specifications
- deliver complete IA docs to project team and client

Review GUI design (R)
- collaborate on the interaction design: interpretation of navigation, screen functionality, layout
- review GUI design for adherence to IA docs
- assist in selecting key pages for client presentation
- ensure page designs meet browser technical standards
- collaborate on the high-fidelity prototype
- refine template system based on finalization of GUI
- revise the functional specifications
- lock scope

Review site build (S)
- review the integrated build
  - including:
    - navigation
    - content
    - assets
    - design
    - information architecture
    - functionality
    - system-response and performance
- make design adjustments
- participate in testing the build
- update functional specifications

Issue resolution (T)
- quality control
- participate in QA testing
- make QA notes
- submit TARs
- make design adjustments
- update TAR
- update specifications
- retest new build

Knowledge exchange to the back end team (U)
- incorporate feedback from server logs, client, and users
- resolve issues from gaps between design and implementation steps

Transfer knowledge to the client
- develop the deliverables that will enable client to maintain the integrity and functionality of the site

Transfer knowledge to the IA practice
- document project findings in a case study
- communicate feedback to IA practice and to other project teams

---

Develop concepts (I)
● concept models
● user task models
● concept scenarios
○ concept prototypes

Evaluate concepts (J)
○ concept prototypes
○ user testing findings

Refine concepts (K)
○ revised concept(s)

Choose concept (L)
● feature list
○ concept document

Create site structure (M)
● site map
○ content matrix

Model processes & activities (N)
● process flows

Define detail (O)
● screen details
● interaction prototypes (low or mid-fidelity)
● screen template system
● screen list
● data specifications

Evaluate & validate architecture (P)
○ user testing findings

Complete architecture documentation (Q)
● functional specifications
○ site map
○ screen details
○ screen list
○ screen template system
○ process flows
○ data specifications
○ content matrix

Review GUI design (R)
○ high-fidelity prototype

Review site build (S)
○ update functional specifications

Issue resolution (T)
- quality control
○ TARs
○ update functional specifications

Knowledge exchange to the back end team (U)

Transfer knowledge to the client
○ IA training materials
○ planning and facilitation workshops
○ style guide

Knowledge transfer to the IA practice
● case studies

- single concept selected
- scope, vision, and requirements validated
- feature list generated
- package selection confirmed
- list of open issues and risks generated
- **client consensus and sign-off**

- functional specifications are final
- findings from prototype testing have been incorporated
- IA documentation validated by and delivered to the project team and client
- open issues resolved
- locked scope
- process for QA defined
- schedule for build releases created
- **client consensus and sign-off**

- screen freeze designated
- all interface TARs are resolved
- maintenance plan is defined
- functional specifications updated to reflect changes
- **client consensus and sign-off**

- performance measured (metrics)
- cause of issues identified
- lessons learned are identified
- recommendations made for next steps
- client fully understands site architecture and implementation
- metrics determined for post-launch success evaluation

Sapient | Confidential

Sapient IA Process Framework Credits: Initiative Leader and Global IA Practice Lead: Lillian Svec; IA Process Workshop Planning Committee Chair: Darian Hendricks; IA Process Framework Model Committee Chair: Joanne Mendel; IA Universal Deliverable Definitions and Glossary Committee Chair: Isabel Ancona; IA Practice Definition Committee Chair: Page Ikeda; Initiative Collaborators: Isabel Ancona, David Garner, Shuli Goodman, Darian Hendricks, Page Ikeda, Steve McGrew, Joanne Mendel, Rob Manson-Pollard, Mark Stockwell, Lillian Svec, Miwa Wang, Jen Wolf, and Alder Yarrow.

Creating a High Performance Team

Great teamwork is the only way we create the breakthroughs that define our careers.

Pat Riley

Research at IBM showed that 25% of the variance in their business results can be attributed directly to variations in the climate and its impact on satisfaction, creativity, motivation, and retention (Nair, 2006). They concluded from various surveys conducted within IBM that the climate is responsible for attracting and retaining talent and improving productivity, effectiveness, and creativity. This productivity translates into results such as growth in sales and earnings, return on sales, and lower employee turnover. Other research showed that a positive work climate can account for nearly 30% improvement in financial results (Creating, 2002; Goleman, 2000). The argument is that a positive climate increases the extra effort that people give above and beyond the formal job expectations. People who are highly motivated are willing to take on the big challenges, innovate, and take risks. Those who are demotivated not only do not do the extra work, but they can also act as anchors pulling the team down. This is supported by a Gallup survey studying employees in 2,500 business units and 24 companies throughout the United States (Buckingham & Coffman, 1999).

The Hay Group defined climate along six dimensions: clarity, standards, responsibility, flexibility, rewards, and team commitment (Fig. 6.1; Nair, 2006). This climate includes everything that impacts a group's ability to perform better. According to Goleman (2001), "An analysis of data on 3,781 executives, correlated with data from climate surveys filled out by those who worked for them suggests that 50 to 70 percent of employees' perceptions of working climate is linked to the characteristics of the leader." Stringer (2002) argued that the manager's behavior is what drives climate, and Watkins (2000) argued that leaders have it in their power to create a climate that motivates, grows, and retains the talent on their teams.

most important project we had. The lead for the team was the person who had been on it almost from the beginning, but some of the people hired and now working on the team had as much if not more experience in design. Not too surprisingly they were deep in the storming phase of team development. I sat down with the facilitator on a couch we found, she took her shoes off and twisted around, faced me, looked in my eyes, and leaned forward. I definitely felt her attention.

I shared the challenge and she asked a series of questions to explore the context. She had all the right attributes for a good field researcher. She then shared something called the Stafford Beer Model of management. Stafford introduced management cybernetics in the 1950s based on a theory of communications and control (Rosenhead, 2006). According to the model, there are three components to shaping a successful team: managing the present, creating the future, and creating identity. Managing the present is the implementation and optimization done to deliver on the bread and butter UX responsibilities that satisfy most of what those who fund us are looking for. Creating the future is a component that sets the vision of where we want to go. This is the UX leadership we can provide on teams. There is the vision of where we want UX to be within the organization, the vision of the experiences we are trying to create in general, and the vision for the individual projects. We had most of the processes and tools in place for managing the present, and people were executing very successfully. We also had a clear vision of where we were heading, and a strategy for how we were creating the future.

The third component needed to create a highly functioning team was creating identity, which ensures that everyone on the team has shared purpose, values, and behavior. In other words, it is about creating a team culture that bonds people, and shapes the way they see the world and see each other. It is about ensuring that everyone has an answer to the question of why we are here and why it matters to each individual that we are part of the group. It is also about the symbols and tools we share that signal who we are.

Once she pointed it out, it was clear that when my teams perform at their highest levels, they have an identity. When I was at Ameritech, the experience of having the corporation become design centered and focus on our work drove the identity. The branding on the Web site around our lab and user-centered approach (represented in Fig. 6.2, and shown on the corporate Web site and through our ads) became a visible reminder of who we were and what we stood for.

One high-level technique the facilitator shared that worked well was to have my team sort themselves into the four corners of the room based on whether they had no idea what the identity of the team was, some sense of the identity but did not know how much of it they shared, a clear sense of the identity of the team but had not fully bought in, or a clear sense of the identity and had fully bought in. Then as a facilitator I randomly selected people from the groups to talk about why they felt as they did, and what it would take to move to the higher level. The sharing helped us understand each other better. The distribution really gave me a feel for where the team was. In listening to each other, some at lower states of buy-in and understanding edged a little higher, and we all got a better idea of what it would take to

FIGURE 6.2

Ameritech's user experience test town.

continue to move the team. This technique also worked well for assessing where people were in buying into the vision and mission, and could even be used to see how people were feeling in general about the climate. With this information I now had the insight needed to grow the team's identity.

Recently a climate poll was taken, and we discovered that the new funding model imposed upon us resulted in a big hit to the morale scores. Besides my own surveying of people and discussions with the team, I brought in another organizational consultant and had her do an independent set of interviews and root cause analysis. It turned out that people felt like they were working alone. They felt like there was very little collaboration, and that others on the team would not cover their backs if necessary. They felt like they were not part of a team, or that they would not be rewarded for team behavior. Unfortunately, the new funding model destroyed the team identity.

Knowing this, I worked with my management chain to ensure that we would operate not as a service organization but as a team focused on a common theme. We would still provide some support for individual projects funding us, but focus as a team on a common set of experiences to drive across the projects. Everyone was in this together. I explicitly worked toward identifying each individual's challenges with those they support, and then brought others to bear to help address the challenges. And when people jumped in to help out, I leveraged an internal awards system to make sure that everyone knew how much I valued this cross-team collaboration. This resulted in a strengthened identity. Clearly, creating identity is one component that needs to be monitored and continually nourished.

TAKING THE TEAM PULSE

In the mid-1990s there was a wave of corporate downsizing (*aka* layoffs) going on around the United States and many user experience teams were targeted. There certainly seemed to be an air of doom and gloom in the conferences. Since Ameritech was going through its own process there was also a vibe in the air that was working against the creative energy that was necessary for us to be successful.

Many of the companies conducted work climate surveys. These are usually questions about the local organizational effectiveness, the effectiveness of the more global organization, senior management and the strategic direction, job satisfaction, compensation, diversity, and other topics that Human Resources is concerned about and that are relevant to the culture the company is trying to drive. Experience shows that people often rate their own team as being great, but they have more doubts about their sibling organizations, and people in different parts of the company are seen as ruining the company. It seems that the further away others are organizationally the less positive people are about them.

I concluded that the survey questions conducted at Ameritech were not getting at the factors that I sensed were important for my user experience team's attitude about their work climate. As I result, I developed my own survey within the R&D organization and customized it for my own team (Lund, 1996a). I then monitored changes in the results quarterly to drive tactical activity around creating a better climate, and to understand how events in the larger organization were impacting my team's attitude. I also ran the survey on another segment of the user experience of the community to compare attitudes of my team to the larger external professional community.

The survey was intended to measure several factors. The first factor and the one that accounted for the greatest amount of variance was "Conditions for Excellence." It consisted of items like "I am fully using my skills to benefit my company. I am growing in my job. I am challenged by my work." This factor is basically at the heart of what is needed to create a flow state (Csikszentmihalyi, 1982) — where a person's skill is roughly matched by the challenge they face, and both increase over time. When you are *really* enjoying your job, you are in that state and time flies by, the work is creative and insightful, and everyone is energized. Other studies have shown that having the right work is one of if not *the* most important factors in job satisfaction. I have found that when I get up in the morning and I am not excited by the work that lies ahead, I start thinking about the next gig. As a manager, therefore, one of the things you should continually try to work on with your team is to get the best match possible between what the business needs and what excites the individual — you are trying to achieve a portfolio of projects that balance individual excitement with your strategy.

The second factor was "Work Valued." It had items like "My creativity is valued. My work is respected by my management." The UX twist on this factor is clear, and since management includes management above the UX manager it also reflects a desire to be respected within what may be an engineering organization. This is a factor that the manager can actively influence. You are one of the most important people in showing what is valued and how to interact with each person on your team from day to day. You also have the ability to make people's work visible to management higher in the chain (and to let people know you have done it).

The third factor was called "Stress Manageable," although more recently it is positioned as work-life balance. It includes the items "I am not stressed excessively. My job does not interfere with my home life. I am not overworked. I am 'in control' of my work situation." The last item recognized the literature that much of stress (e.g., during times of change) is feeling that things are out of control. You may be bothered by the hours you are putting in for a deadline, but if at some level you feel that what is happening is because you have chosen it, you can handle it better than if you are feeling randomized from managers in the clouds.

The fourth factor was related to work valued, but recognizes the unique relationship we have in UX if we are centralized. It is called "Partnership," and includes "I feel in contact with the organizations that use my work. The organizations that use my work value my contributions highly. I feel personal 'ownership' for ensuring the success of the organizations that use my work." To ensure you are meeting the needs of your partners, evaluation of your team's performance should be through 360 feedback from the teams. Are they MVPs on the teams they support? This is only half of the information you need as a manager to help ensure that the entire system works effectively. The other half is understanding what your team members are feeling as they work with others on a project. If your team feels they have no impact with teams, and that the work is not being recognized and used by those they are doing it for, it strikes at the heart of their feelings of self-worth. If a manager finds an issue here, it is critical that you get deep into the root cause analysis and address it.

I have mentioned elsewhere that at Ameritech we had a wonderful lab. Any physical resources we needed seemed to be there. Yet I would sometimes get feedback that something was missing. So the fifth factor, "Resources", attempted to address the issue with statements like "I have the resources (e.g., hardware, software, and lab) to fulfill my responsibilities. I have the information I need to fulfill my responsibilities. I know how to use my role in the company to fulfill my responsibilities." What matters most to people is whether they feel they are in control of their careers and daily work lives, and a key element in that is whether they have the information they need (especially from upper management), and whether they feel like they understand the rules of the game and how to play it to get things done. Issues in this area often are tied to having a trusted, candid relationship with the team, and knowing what information to share, how to share it, and when. It is also about leveraging the team to share best practices and to help each other in navigating the company to get the job done.

A final factor was truly a check on the pulse of the organization. It was about "Motivation" and included "My bias is toward 'making it happen,' in spite of obstacles. My work is important. My work is important to me personally. I am committed to helping the teammates with whom I work excel." It was another angle on the first factor, getting at the fundamentals of how people view their work and how it motivates them as well as working in a bit of motivation around team identity and collaboration.

The Gallup Organization created a standardized instrument called the Q12 that was used by many companies to assess climate (see http://gmj.gallup.com/content/811/Feedback-Real.aspx). It is a survey of 12 questions that identifies how engaged employees are based on a large number of focus groups and thousands of interviews, and correlates highly with superior job performance. Many of the questions touch on the same categories found in the Ameritech study. They address clarity of expectations and support for growth, availability of resources, recognition and the value placed on work, and other issues.

WHAT PEOPLE WANT

Reviewing the literature, the factors that other people have identified match well with what I found in the survey I derived from my team. There was an article in the January 28, 2008, *Christian Science Monitor* (2008) titled "Seven Things Employees Want Most to be Happy at Work." It noted that researchers are increasingly finding that it is the intangible aspects of the job such as respect, trust, and fairness that are important to people. Another study they report found that the top three things people want are interesting work, being appreciated for their work, and a sense of being a part of what is going on. The seven intangibles they list in the article are

- Appreciation
- Respect
- Trust
- Individual growth
- A good boss
- Compatible co-workers
- A sense of purpose

Joy and pride in the work and the exercise of our profession is at the heart of what matters to people, and it is tied to the path we chose for our lives. Most of us want to have impact. We entered the field because we want to make a difference in people's lives; we want our work to change technology so that the world is getting better in some way. That means we want whatever we do, whether it is ideation, exploratory design, uncovering new needs, design and development, or evaluating existing products to find its way into what is created by the companies in which we are working.

We also want to be respected and rewarded for the work we do. As other studies have shown, it is not necessarily the money, it is recognition for the importance and uniqueness of what we do and knowing that it is indeed valuable for the business and for users. As a manager, one of the roles you play is trying to paint that road more explicitly and clearly. You can make it a point in team meetings, one-on-ones, and even in broadcasting status notes to try to draw out those connections. Certainly it is important to work hard at taking the extra steps to recognize good work. When you see good work that is not getting praised, encourage the clients to say something nice about the work. Make sure people know about the praise you are receiving about them. When I get praise about people, I try to share it with senior management as well as to draw out the business impact of the excellent work.

Praise that feels specific and detailed means more than a general "Way to go!" I received a copy of one note, for example, from a general manager in the business and that person's boss (a vice president) about how wonderful it was that we had done a particular usability test (conducted and reported by one of my researchers, Alexander), and how vital it was to listen to the users. I forwarded that to my boss, his boss, and even his boss. The most senior executive in turn circulated it with his praise about the importance of the work to every manager in the IT organization. That communicated a message of recognition not just to Alexander but to my entire team, and served to strengthen the UX brand across the entire IT organization.

At a more local level, one of my new employees, Sindhia, bought several small inexpensive items from a store: a lantern, a Rubik's cube, and a football. She then started a process where every few weeks at one of our staff meetings whoever had an object would present it to someone else on the team for something good they did. The lantern was for a good idea, the cube was for help in solving a tough problem, and the football was for going the extra mile. Every month the person who had received an award would then pass it with the appropriate specific praise to another person. This is a fabulous and light way to recognize people, and it contributes to team identity.

There are the usual corporate reward programs, and you should leverage whatever tools you have available. Sometimes the corporate awards are bigger formal awards, and sometimes it is possible to get money for "light" awards like gift certificates that can be handed out when you or others catch someone doing something special. Another activity that can be powerful is to make it a point to reward or recognize those who are friends of user experience. As they move up in the company and prosper they may have even more influence in creating a great work environment for user experience people and helping you prosper. Remember it is not just the big formal award; it can be just as powerful to take a moment to say a sincere thanks and to be explicit about what we are thankful for that makes a difference. I have to say that I have been fortunate to have had members of my team over the years who even occasionally give me a pat on the back. During a recent round of organizational changes, for example, I was feeling some stress and was not my usual self. I cannot tell you how important it was to me when I came into my office and found a card on my desk from a member of my team with a word of encouragement.

What makes a great work environment for designers and user researchers? People certainly want growth and growth opportunities. In many engineering environments user experience people feel a glass ceiling that is hard to get through. They see paths for project managers and engineers all the way up to the highest levels in the corporation, but often they do not see the same path for user experience. Many go into management because they see that as the only way to continue to grow and reach higher levels of reward, or they may move into other disciplines such as project management where there seem to be more possibilities. Movement to grow skills in new areas of interest is great, and it is a wonderful way to drive more design thinking through the entire corporation, but you would like to avoid having people move because they do not see any other opportunities. One of the values of having higher level user experience people at the VP and CEO levels is that it provides an example of what might be possible. You can help create an effective UX program by getting involved in shaping the rules used to evaluate performance and support growth.

MOVING THROUGH THE GROWTH CYCLE

A fairly common model of team formation is shown in Fig. 6.3. The first stage in the model is forming. This is when the team first comes together with your first hires, or when your team undergoes major changes (e.g., a reorganization or a rapid period of hiring). Everyone is a relative stranger (including the manager), and everyone's strengths and weaknesses are unknown. Everyone wants to make a great impression right away, wants to be assigned to work they will enjoy, and wants to start showing success. Some handle this by becoming hyper-conservative, and others handle it by becoming hyper-assertive. The team may feel more impersonal, people may be a little guarded and dependent, and some slowly feel their way into a situation while others jump in heedless of impact.

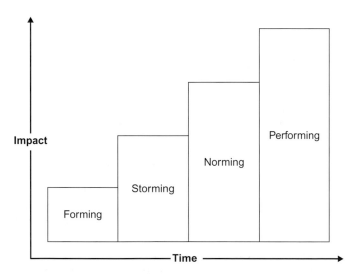

FIGURE 6.3

Team formation model.

Your role as the leader in these early days is to be more directive in leadership style, perhaps more than you are used to or are comfortable with. The idea is to clarify roles and responsibilities quickly, and assign who is doing what. Get everyone focused on a set of goals and objectives, and show progress toward those goals. Be more hands-on and keep up on what is happening and provide lots of guidance. Keep communication flowing. You do not know what everyone can do, so you want to learn as you work with team members and help them to learn from each other. Start to bring people together by building out the strategic framework, clarifying the common purpose and values of the team, establishing operational norms and policies, and working together to define your vision and mission.

Pretty quickly the team is likely to move into the storming stage. My experience is that as individuals start to get grounded in their space, they want to start really showing what they can do. Since the members of your team do not completely understand their peers yet, they get frustrated when others (who in turn are trying to establish themselves) do not yield to their will and seem to get in the way. They sometimes forget to share what is on their minds, so other team members see them as loose cannons. The team becomes like a dysfunctional family, confronting and blaming as communication breaks down. People may rebel against you and against each other, some may try to seize control from you or from each other, and others may simply react in an emotional counterproductive way.

The manager needs to become the therapist and provide a directive (to keep the team moving forward) and supportive style. I have found that if values of openness and communication were established up front, you can leverage those to bring people together; avoid assigning blame; and just get conflicts and disagreements out in the open with an attitude of "We're in this together. How do we move this forward?" It is important to give lots of feedback both on what you like and what you want to see happen. You want to give each member of the team a sense of where they are succeeding so they understand what success looks like, that they are getting the visibility and recognition that they desire, and that they are on the right track. But you also want to end the superstitious and counterproductive behaviors that cause misunderstanding and problems. This is probably not the time to overreach; instead it is the time to help team members become successful as they focus on the tasks at hand. Extra steps to connect people at a human level can be important during this time — morale events, time working on joint projects together as a team, and so on. This is a good time to get people laughing together.

The norming stage is when people are settled into their jobs and they begin to understand each other. I liken it to the time after I had been married for a few years or a friendship that is deepening. You understand what you like about the other people on the team and know how to work around what annoys you about them, and they understand your unique strengths and weaknesses and how to deal with them. You begin to understand what team members are going to do in different situations, and they understand what you are going to do. You have a personal connection with others on the team, and appreciate and enjoy much of its diversity. When conflicts happen, and they do, there is a habit of getting them resolved early rather than late, and it is relatively straightforward to get most resolved. At this stage people are clearer on their respective roles, and they are more open to feedback. The team has found ways to communicate reasonably effectively, and the team identity is starting to form — there is team cohesion.

As a UX manager or lead in this stage you can do more coaching and be less directive. You see who you can trust to really run with their jobs and who takes a little more engagement. You also see how the team is working, and are able to help them grow to independence as they build knowledge and skills. It is a time to refresh the strategic framework, and to start introducing some of those big bets and big challenges that further grow the team together and begin to really establish your unique brand — your unique mark on the organization. More and more leadership is delegated to members of the team, and you are able to drive your own initiatives while working on unblocking and supporting the team. You are providing a supportive leadership style.

The final stage (some models include a further excelling stage, but I see that as part of this final one) is called performing. A team that is performing is like a well-run professional kitchen or a sports team that is really clicking. Everyone has the same goal, but everyone knows their individual roles and responsibilities. They do their jobs, but are able to adapt as circumstances change and as others have to adjust to the circumstances. There are often multiple interdependencies, but nobody is dropping the ball, or if they do someone else is there to pick it up. The team is focused on the goal. They trust each other, they are committed to the team goals and each other, and they are open. They are interdependent and support one another, and you see real collaboration. Think about a design team that has been in this stage. The image is often a group huddled around whiteboards doing a lot of sketching, talking, and creating. There is always plenty of laughter. Ideas spontaneously pop up, and people pull together to make things happen.

This is the stage that brings the greatest joy for many managers, because now you can really challenge and grow the team. You are reinforcing what you like, but you are also moving the bar higher and engaging the team to collaborate in achieving the higher bar. You want to stay out of the way, but not disappear. The team is successful when you do not need to be there, but it is better when you are. You challenge individuals and the team as a whole. This is when you can drive big bets and the results inspire and transform organizations. Even better, members of the team on their own initiative are doing things that exceed your expectations but align with your dreams.

It is frustrating that whenever you go through a major change such as when people are added, an organizational change such as layoffs, or something else significant, the team can go all the way back to the forming stage. The good thing working in your favor is that at least some of the team has been through this before, so the rails are already laid to move more quickly through the stages. You probably need to harness your experienced people to help you help the new ones understand what they are experiencing and how to embrace it.

Managing Through Change

Everything is in a state of flux, including the status quo.

Robert Byrne

I have been through major changes at several points in my career. One of the most stressful was when I was at Ameritech and the first waves of layoffs were going through the industry. Many people who had assumed they would have life-time employment suddenly were finding themselves out of work. At one company a manager was shot and there were bomb threats at the job site. After the layoffs there was survivor's guilt, and while the company was completely reinventing itself the organization needed to adjust to missing people who had been part of the family. A milder change, but one that still added stress to the management role, was when my team moved to a new organization and doubled in size within a month, and then more recently moved again, had layoffs, grew again, and then completely changed in how it was funded. In our industry, the norm is change. Managing through change often requires you to go back to the forming stage in the growth cycle. Sometimes it is traumatic; sometimes it is exciting.

I have noticed that the best description of the emotions people tend to go through during change is well-represented by Elisabeth Kübler-Ross' (1969) grief cycle shown in Fig. 6.4.

This experience is typically triggered when the change is unexpected. A fair criticism — but one that it is hard to avoid — is that if people had known what was coming they might not experience the change in quite this way. Changes that the UX manager is driving can and should involve the team, and people can move through the stages very quickly. But changes that senior management is driving and

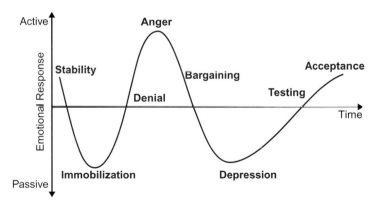

FIGURE 6.4

The grief cycle.

where decisions must be made without involving the team typically cause members of the team to experience most if not all the stages of the grief cycle.

When people feel the changes are hitting them unexpectedly, it is the unexpected nature that is the problem and they feel powerless. The core to helping people through the process is to help them regain a sense of structure, predictability, and control. Building on that structure, the goal is to re-engage people in a positive vision that will motivate them. To do that, one of the best techniques is to engage them in refreshing the vision and mission of the team. With my Windows Server System team, when we made the changes, we set up an offsite and began by explicitly presenting this grief cycle and recognizing that the feelings were normal. We then divided into the new teams, and the new teams began to work on reinventing their vision and mission statements and bonding around the leadership of their new managers. That approach seemed to work well. When my current team doubled in size, we began by gathering at an offsite and started to build out our strategic framework (especially identifying the shared values, roughing in the elements of a vision, and starting to build a mission statement).

As the changes at US West Advanced Technologies started during the acquisition by Qwest, the company leveraged guidance from change management consultants Price Pritchett and Ron Pound. They identified a variety of principles useful in helping people reacquire a sense of structure and control, and how to focus them on the future. These (fairly self-evident principles) include:

- Keep a positive attitude.
- Take charge.
- Set a clear agenda. Give your troops clear-cut marching orders. Focus on short-range objectives, and establish clear priorities. Nail down each person's job, roles, and responsibilities. Focus on hard results rather than intangibles.
- Pay attention to process.
- Promise change … and sell it (carefully).
- Get resistance to change out in the open.
- Raise the bar. Show a sense of urgency.
- Encourage risk taking and initiative. Motivate to the hilt.
- Create a supportive work environment. Spend freely with "soft currency."
- "Ride close herd" on transition and change. (I found this means spending more than the usual amount of time one-on-one with people listening and seeing where people are in the curve and supporting them.)
- Rebuild morale. (This is a good time to crank up the pats on the back.)
- "Beef up" communications efforts.
- Go looking for bad news.
- Re-recruit your good people.
- Take care of the "me" issues in a hurry. Play the role of managerial therapist.
- Reduce the level of job stress. (I found this means for the near-term, simplify the job.)

- Be supportive of higher management. (Do it by finding what you can support, and being candid and honest about your own feelings and how you are working through them.)
- Be more than a manager … be a LEADER.

Winning Loyalty

The secret of managing is to keep the guys who hate you away from the guys who are undecided.

Casey Stengel

Creating team loyalty begins with being a leader rather than a manager. The goal is to be the kind of person that people want to follow and to create loyalty, rather than just relying on the formal designation of manager. At a workshop on ROI at the Usability Professionals Association (UPA) one year, the representative from Intuit talked about loyalty as a metric. Customer loyalty is another step beyond customer satisfaction. It is satisfaction that is so great that the customer is willing to put their own reputation on the line by recommending the product or service to one of their friends. Employee loyalty is similar. It is a willingness to follow that is so great they are willing to recommend you and your team to their friends and colleagues. Your own employees are recruiting on your behalf everywhere they go and pulling others with them as they try to follow you.

To get at that kind of loyalty there are a few additional principles that build on the standard leadership principles. First, genuinely care about each individual. For myself, I try to explicitly and implicitly establish a kind of contract with each individual who joins my team. I do not expect people to work for me forever, and I will not hold them forever. I will "compete" to deserve their loyalty and their best efforts by working to grow them further than anyone else, to help them be successful, and to help them get rewarded to the maximum extent possible for their work. I will work to remove barriers for them and to do everything I can to create a great working environment. I will try to match their interests and passions with what I need to get done. In return I expect them to give their best while they work for me, just as I am giving my best to them. If the time comes when they have grown beyond the team and their role, or if someone has lured them away with a situation better than I can offer, then we will part friends and colleagues. Indeed, I will help them get there.

It is important to be genuine. A nice phrase is "listen hard, talk straight." There is also "practicing what you preach." Living the values you believe and express is the place to start. You want to be as honest and transparent as you can. There are times you cannot share everything because of the constraints you are under in a given situation, but try to share everything you think people will want and need to know. Also make it clear where the boundaries are on what you can answer and why.

Finally, make sure you are rewarding success and shaping the right behaviors. Catch people doing the right thing, and recognize and reward it. When something is happening that is clearly bad and going to hurt, catch those things early. Talk them through with the person and describe the behavior you want to see, then recognize and reward that person as they work to get there. In conditioning theories, punishment has a tendency to generate random behavior whereas positive reinforcement has the ability to focus behavior. I have found it works for teams in the workplace and not just in the laboratory.

IDENTIFY SHARED VALUES

Trust takes a lot of moxie and commitment to build. It takes a long time, and you can lose it overnight.

Max DePree

Values are the beliefs that are shared by the team. They are at the heart of the emerging culture of your team, and when articulated provide rules of collaboration to help resolve conflicts. Right after I doubled my team in size, we were back in the team formation stage. There was already feedback that people were reporting misunderstandings in their conversation, mistrust of motives, and other communication issues. Worse, people were struggling with how they could resolve the issues. A lot of people were coming to me to "fix" the problem with the other person (by implication, to whip them into shape). I laid the groundwork for dealing with this by getting everyone on the same page about the values we all agreed on and what we wanted as the rules of engaging one another. This was one of the techniques I adapted from the Sapient culture. At Sapient we used it to get workshops off on the right foot.

I set the workshop up simply as wanting to identify the shared values we wanted to use as we interacted with each other and the teams with whom we work. We began by throwing out individual words and thoughts. Some of the words stimulated people to talk about things that mattered to them such as what it means to grow in trust of another, what respect means, and so on. After collecting all the words and phrases, we clustered them to find the key words that captured the big thoughts. We eventually got to a list that we all agreed were the shared values. After the offsite, I then started thinking about how we could represent the core ideas that we were talking about and how we wanted to work together as a team. I wanted to avoid the traditional sports metaphors, and thought back to successful team building experiences. One, which I describe in the section describing morale events (Chapter 7), was the experience in a gourmet kitchen. I found a picture of such a kitchen and created a poster (Fig. 6.5). We posted them around the team spaces.

FIGURE 6.5

Team values.

In subsequent one-on-ones and sessions working with team members struggling with how to work together we were able to draw on the shared values. I could point to the values that we all agreed on, and begin with the understanding of the common goals. We could then brainstorm about solutions to the conflicts that were consistent with exercising the values. I was also able to set up metrics and goals in terms of the values, and to build growth in relevant values within the team commitments.

CLARITY IN ROLES AND RESPONSIBILITIES
RACI

One of the common themes woven throughout the discussions of how to put an effective user experience team together, how to resolve conflict, how to manage through change, and how to collaborate across discipline boundaries is to reach clarity on roles and responsibilities. There are a variety of tools to do this. Within my current organization, the tool of choice is the RACI matrix, also known as the Responsibility Assignment Matrix or the Linear Responsibility Chart. There are variations on the classic RACI based on additional roles to be assigned and there are variations on the approach (e.g., the OARP, the owner, accountable, responsible and participant).

In our organization, the R in RACI is the person who is responsible. People who fall into this category do the work to achieve the task. In some organizations there is only one R, and others assist in supporting roles; in other organizations there can be many Rs taking responsibility for different portions of the overall project. The A is the person who is accountable. There should only be one person who is on the line to make sure the task or deliverable is completed. This may be the person who signs off that the work that the R person or persons have done is complete and acceptable, or it may be a person who is both the A and the R for a project. There are also C people. These people are consulted and their opinions are sought. They do not have veto power. Their input is not mandatory, but it is carefully considered and incorporated. It is a good practice to ensure that they understand how their input was used (or not) and why. Finally, there are the people who are kept informed. This is typically just one-way communication.

RACI is just a tool to add clarity. An RACI can be defined for how various disciplines and organizations should work together through the course of a software development project (see Fig. 6.6). It lists all the deliverables that make up a typical project, and assigns the appropriate roles to each person for each deliverable. When I joined the IT organization, one of the early projects I was part of included going through the existing process, integrating user-centered design into it, and then redefining the RACI to include user experience.

Project Phase and Task	CMG (Corporate Marketing Group)			Global Owners	IT Engineering		
	Marketing	Prod Mgmt	Design		Site Mgmt	UX	ProgMgmt
Business Strategy							
Define Vision/Strategy	RA	C	C	C	I	I	I
Communicate Production Process	RA	C		I	C		I
New Site Experience Envisioning	A	C	RA		C	C	C
Storyboard	C	C	R		C	R	C
Competitive Audit	C	C	C		C	RA	C
Brand Ownership							
Define Business Requirements	C	RA	C	R	C	I	I
Define Scenarios	C	RA	C	C	C	C	C
Define Business Objectives	RA	C	C	R	I	I	I
Define Brand Style Guide	C	A	R	I	I	C	I
Define Header/Footer Requirements	RA	C	C	C	C	C	I
Application User Experience Development							
Create UX Mock-ups	C	C	C		R	RA	C
Storyboard Experience	C	C	C		I	RA	C
Create Hi Fi UX Prototypes	I	C	C		I	RA	C
Information Architecture	C	C	C		I	RA	C
Usability Testing	C	C	C		I	RA	C
UI Text Creation	C	I	I		I	RA	C
UI Bug Triage and Resolutions	I	C	C			R	RA

R = Responsible
A = Accountable
C = Consulted
I = Informed

FIGURE 6.6

RACI example.

Another way we have used RACI is to resolve interorganizational conflict between collaborating UX teams. There is a user experience team in corporate marketing responsible for branding, which supports the marketing organization in its definition of the design direction they would like key areas of the corporation to head. My team, on the other hand, is responsible for the detailed design of many of these areas, and is in the organization creating the platform and common design patterns across the site. We negotiated an RACI to help clarify how we will work together across our respective organizations and through the process. Starting the project by laying out the principles and getting senior management sign-off, and then drawing out the implications within the RACI, has made it easier to collaborate effectively. When our respective designers bump up against each other, we both can pull out the RACI as a way of resolving the differences. The third way we have used this tool is to clarify roles and responsibilities within the user experience team itself, especially where there are several people working together on a project (and indeed when there are several people leading different aspects of the project such as research, design, and overall planning).

6.1 MENTORING AND APPRENTICESHIP MODELS

By Gavin S. Lew, Managing Director, User Centric, Inc., Chicago, IL

How do you train someone to be a user researcher or designer? In most cases it starts with formal education. Professors usually do a good job teaching information architecture, design, and user research principles. But in the end, that's all theory. In reality, much of what we do cannot be learned in school. Success in the user experience field depends on understanding subtleties and perspectives that are very hard to teach, yet make the difference between a good researcher and a great one. At times researchers may do something in a way that goes against personal logic, but makes sense with an understanding of overriding priorities, the client's greater objectives, or our relationship with the client. The challenge comes in figuring out how to teach those nuances to individuals on a team. This is why we have implemented a mentoring/apprenticeship model.

When a person joins our team, he or she is assigned a mentor. The mentor's first role is showing the ropes to a new person, answering administrative questions, and generally helping that individual become acclimated. As the new person begins working alongside a mentor on projects, he or she begins picking up on the important subtleties of user research. The mentor provides anything from general guidance to help with specific tasks, and may give input regarding performance and career advancement. The mentor pairs have quarterly lunches to talk about progress and personal development. The mentor also gives feedback to management, so we're aware of where consultants may need help, and can determine how to place consultants on projects where they need more experience (or have a special area of interest).

Most mentor relationships continue for at least a year, and mentors may change on a yearly basis. But our feeling is that no one ever really outgrows the need for a mentor. Even our senior people have said they need mentors to keep growing. This tells me the system works, and is valuable. Forging these kinds of cooperative relationships with the support of upper management strengthens the whole team. Everyone becomes better in an environment where they can openly share their expertise and readily learn from others. Mentorship fosters just this kind of cooperative interaction and continuing growth.

The mentoring program is also an attractive selling point in recruiting new researchers and designers. I emphasize to applicants that we don't expect them to know everything. We want them to come in with a willingness to learn how to apply what they already know, and to fill in gaps in their knowledge as they work alongside more experienced consultants. This fosters organic growth, which is always best in an organization. When you can bring people in with the right background, then give them the growth opportunities they need, the whole organization will be stronger as they take more responsibility and move forward in their careers. Mentorship is one of the keys to making this happen.

Organic growth is also made possible through internships and apprenticeships. Many of our senior and management staff began as interns or apprentices. Bringing someone in for a three-month commitment enables us to learn whether they have the intellect and the capacity to do what we need them to do. In turn, they can learn about our work and whether they like it here. If it's a mutually good fit, we may hire them. We've found great success with this model; half of our company has been built on organic growth. Some people who've come in through internships during graduate school have risen to director positions within ten years.

However, there are only certain economies that will support apprenticeships and internships. When the market is booming and demand is high, people may not want to take the risk of quitting one job to take a three-month contract. On the other hand, when the market is poor and there is less opportunity, there's much less risk involved and short-term opportunities become more attractive. There are times and places for different practices. Often, we find ourselves locked into a practice. Adapting to the changing workplace will ensure that you have the most appropriate positions to secure top talent.

Finding and training the right people is never easy, but internships, apprenticeships, and a good mentor program have made a big difference for our company. We're able to hire the right people, train them in more effective ways, and enable everyone to benefit as they learn from each other's strengths and grow together.

6.2 TRAINING ORGANIZATIONS

By Natalia Kirillova, Managing Partner, Business Development Director, UIDesign Group, Moscow, Russia

My company was founded in 2003 when there was still no usability market in Russia. One of the main problems we faced was that nobody knew what usability was and why customers would need our services. We have carried out a major effort to establish the market, to educate it and to move it forward. Eventually, when the business started to grow, we encountered another problem that was even more difficult to solve. There were no trained professionals around. Today there are still no educational programs in usability, user experience, user centered or interactive design in Russia. Lacking qualified resources is even more painful because the market is growing.

The only solution is training the staff ourselves. My story will look very familiar to companies in young UX markets. Mature markets have similar issues. Our discipline is complex, dynamic and developing. A good UX consultant should be equipped with knowledge, experience and skills related to how technology works, and how to talk to users and elicit requirements. This person has to know user research techniques and when each of them is to be applied. He or she needs to have a good grasp of visual design, as well as decent communication and prototyping skills. They should be a broad-minded person who can consult onsite. Today UX services come together with search engine optimization, marketing, web analytics and other areas. How do you obtain these "golden" brains and hands?

We started training and teaching in 2004, when we decided to assign a mentor to every new employee in the project. The particular feature of this method is that the mentors assign tasks and then do not leave the trainees alone for a long time. The trainees are supposed to work under the direction of their mentors in order to learn how the professionals deal with different issues. To track the progress in mastering new skills and acquiring experience, it is good to have a list of personal competencies for every trainee, and to regularly update the record with the types of projects and work completed. Learning from a user experience mentor reminds me of other professional fields where creativity plays a significant role, like painting, cooking or any other art or handicraft. To obtain the full skills of a chef, an apprentice has to observe the master's work for a long time. That is how a new master can be created.

Though practice means a lot, it is not enough. Practice should be supported by the theory. There are several ways to train professional skills and advance knowledge. They should be offered in an appropriate combination for the individual (defined by a mentor depending on a trainee's personality):

1. Internal and external seminars and workshops provide a chance to apply theory and sometimes include practice.
2. Books and articles give fundamental theory.
3. Authentic blogs and news help to keep a trainee up to date.
4. Activities such as conferences and participation in professional societies provide the state of the art.

The careful application of these activities gives an opportunity not only to learn, but also to discuss and exchange opinions with colleagues. It helps them to develop a personal opinion on different issues and to broaden their horizons. This is crucial for a mature consultant. Besides professional knowledge and experience, working in the user experience field requires accuracy, curiosity, self-discipline, creativity and many others. Some of them, such as creativity, are possible to train, but it takes a lot of time. I belong to those who believe that creativity is a skill and is not simply an inborn talent. Everybody can become a creative thinker when trained using techniques such as brainstorming, brain writing, mind mapping, and storyboarding.

6.3 BOOMERS, GEN X, AND GEN Y DIFFERENCES IN THE WORKPLACE

By Gavin S. Lew, Managing Director, User Centric, Inc., Chicago, IL

If a team is going to be highly productive and functional, leaders need to understand the dynamic presented by having different generations working alongside one another. Even though our company's two principles are a Baby Boomer and a Generation X-er, our company was recently named one of the Top 50 Generation Y Employers in Chicago. Why? We recognize that Generation Y has different needs, and we try to understand and adapt to them, rather than succumbing to the irritation and aggravation that can prevail in multigenerational work environments.

One way to understand the differences in these groups is by looking at advancement. Baby Boomers came of age in a work environment where if you stayed with a company a certain length of time, you would be promoted. This was accepted, and even if someone excelled at work, there was an understanding of "doing one's time." The Boomer generation shared a set of ideals, rules formed around those ideals, and people followed the rules.

Generation X came along, and while they focused more on relationships and their personal rights and skills in the workplace, they understood the legacy of the Baby Boomers. The ideals and rules, while not embraced by the Gen X-ers, were (perhaps grudgingly) accepted. This group was more individualistic, and while they might have looked for ways to have more control over their career advancement, they still played by the rules the Boomers had laid out.

Generation Y, on the other hand, grew up in a high-tech world, and they expect things to happen at a different pace than the Boomers or Gen X. Short attention spans may have started with Generation X, but they became a given with Gen Y. The Boomers' mentality of "Wait seven years and something good will happen" will not fly with Gen Y. They need something happening — whether it's advancement, a title change, or some kind of ego boost — every 18 months. Gen Y-ers also feel entitled to praise — they were, after all, raised in an era where everyone on a team got a trophy. They need to feel valued and sense that they're moving forward. Rather than facing this as a frustration, the wise employer will recognize that Generation Y is a smart, technology wise, and flexible generation. If we're willing to re-tool our approach, we can better capitalize on their strengths.

Successfully working with Generation Y also requires a different way of communicating than Boomers and Gen X-ers are used to. Gen Y individuals need to be given very explicit directions and descriptions. Here's an example (which actually happened at our company): An urgent matter arose late one afternoon, and the Baby Boomer said, "I need help with this; it needs to be done as soon as possible." The Generation X employee buckled down immediately and worked late. The Generation Y employee left at 5:00 p.m., without notifying anyone. He had plans that night, and figured that getting the project done in the morning would be "as soon as possible." This wasn't negligence, but rather was a reflection of the Gen Y employee's need for a clear definition of the time frame. (He also needed to be told to check in before leaving, something a Boomer would think was second nature. Not so with Generation Y.)

Generation Y doesn't understand the definitions and principles and ideals that Boomers take for granted (and Generation X picked up on due to proximity). This doesn't mean there's anything wrong with any of these groups. They just work and communicate differently, with different expectations. Managers need to recognize this fact and adapt to it, because it's reality. Struggling with it will cause unnecessary frustration, but handling the differences with wisdom and understanding can catapult a team to new levels of productivity and success.

6.4 USING DISC PROFILES TO GET NEW TEAMS TALKING

By Tharon W. Howard, Director, Clemson Usability Testing Facility, Clemson University, Clemson, SC

I like to think of the "stuff" my teams create as a by-product of good communication between members. The real *product* of a team is communication; anything else the team creates — like a new interface design or a research study — is just gravy. So if communication is the *sine qua non* of team building, then my job as a team manager is creating the conditions that allow members to communicate with each other as successfully as possible. However, the problem with a new team or a new member on a team is that people have different communication needs and different styles of communicating, and when new members don't understand those needs or styles, miscommunication, misunderstandings, and dissent can occur.

One technique I've used successfully to deal with this is to use DISC profiling with new teams. Based on the work of William Moulton Marston and his 1928 book, *The Emotions of Normal People*, DISC was one of the earliest psychometric instruments created, and like the famous Myers-Briggs personality type indicator, DISC classifies people's psychological traits using four different quadrants and scores them based on how people respond to a series of statements and word associations. DISC is an acronym that describes each quadrant.

D = Dominance: People who score high "D" tend to communicate very directly and forcefully; they value visionary thinking and problem solving, but don't like a lot of details and can get annoyed when people don't get directly to the point.

I = Influence: People who score high in this area are almost the opposite of Ds. Their communication focuses on others' feelings and emotions and they are quick to put people's attitudes before facts.

S = Steadiness: People who score high in this area value stability and loyalty. They dislike communication that will "rock the boat" and are annoyed by "mission creep." They often have to be drawn into a discussion and prefer to listen carefully and then find points of agreement.

C = Conscientiousness: People who score high in this quadrant value logical presentation, accuracy, and clarity of expectations. They are annoyed by communication that is overly emotional and doesn't "stick to the rules" or pay close attention to protocol.

The way I use DISC with new teams is to contract with Inscape Publishing or one of the several vendors who offer online versions of the DISC instrument and then have all the members take the test and obtain their reports. Then we meet as a group in a comfortable location and we talk about what we've each learned about our own communication styles and needs. In order to keep this from becoming too personal or to keep people from focusing entirely on the negative aspects of the different communication styles, we start off by having the team brainstorm about famous leaders who fit each category — Gandhi was probably an "S," Jimmy Carter was probably an "I," and so on. Basically, I try to generate a list of people the team respects who exemplify each DISC quadrant so that members recognize that each style offers value as well as limitations. However, asking the team to figure out whether Teddy Roosevelt was a D or an I makes it possible to talk about how people have elements of all four quadrants, and no one should be "pigeon-holed" as a D. This is an important point to make with your team because one of the dangers I've discovered with using this approach is that people will often try to use the information in their DISC profile reports to attempt to excuse inappropriate behaviors. They'll say, for example, "You just have to deal with the fact that I'm a C, and we're gonna play by the rules here."

I try to teach my teams that they can't allow themselves to make this sort of statement since, ultimately, the goal is to realize that "playing by the rules" is a blind spot for both Ss and Cs. It's a crutch they use when they're under pressure, but what they need to do in order to become more successful communicators is to find ways to build up their D and I qualities. Their DISC profile is not a clinical measure of who they are and always will be; rather, it's merely a description of their particular communication tendencies at that moment. However, those tendencies can change.

I have to confess that I've had mixed success at getting everyone on a team to buy into the idea that they have blind spots and that they weren't born a D and can't change who they are. It's also a technique that only works well one or two times since repeating the DISC profile with the same members gets stale after the third time. Nevertheless, I can report that using DISC with new teams certainly does get them sharing information about their communication styles and needs, and it does make them more tolerant of their differences. Naturally, they still get annoyed with one another, but they do communicate with each other faster and more effectively, and since my job is to facilitate that communication, that's a positive result I can accept.

6.5 HR POLICIES AND RATIONALE

By Gavin S. Lew, Managing Director, User Centric, Inc., Chicago, IL

As the person who's in charge of personnel at our small company, I noticed that many of our human resources policies — which are intended to solve or prevent problems — were actually causing more confusion. After our office manager would implement a new HR policy, I would end up spending an inordinate amount of time answering questions.

As a solution, we began issuing a statement of rationale along with each new human resources policy. Since every policy emerges because of some rationale, we decided it made sense to give people the rationale along with the policy. When given the reasons — from a business perspective — for a policy, most people understand the rationale and fall in line. Of course there will always be individuals who just don't like rules, but even they do better with this system, because they get the thinking behind it, rather than just having a rule laid on them. If someone has ideas about approaching a matter differently, we're open to their suggestions. We make it known that we'll listen to anyone's input as long as his or her proposed solution considers our rationale.

Since explaining the reason behind policy decisions is so important, we actually spend more time on the underlying principle than the rule when introducing a new policy. This is more difficult than it seems as it requires discipline to provide rationale as new employees come on board. Thus, documenting is essential. We also continue reminding people of the rationale as time goes on. This has alleviated many issues by empowering people to think through things themselves. When questions come up about defining sick time, working from home, etc., there's no need to quote a rule. People who understand the rationale will make better judgments and come to sound conclusions on their own without being held to the rule of law. When coupled with a mentor or apprenticeship program as described [insert citation], communication can be extremely clear and create a community that supports policies.

As an example, let's look at our Work From Home (WFH) policy. At User Centric, we recognize that the need for flexibility is paramount to having a well-functioning and productive team, but this is nothing new. Flexibility is different from a permanent WFH schedule that individual employees negotiate. This policy is for those instances where we need to support life's everyday challenges or to make employees more productive while working on a specific project. So, we made a special WFH option to be used by request.

We thought this policy made sense. Employees found it to be very useful. We asked that employees e-mail at least 24 hours in advance to WFH and that they had sufficient work to do. In our history, we never turned a WFH request down, but then we started to get requests that appeared to be somewhat suspicious. In one example, one employee made a request in the late afternoon for WFH the following day. Basically, the workload to be performed at home was to catch up on e-mail and expenses. We thought that these activities tended to not fill a full business day, so we asked questions and quickly realized that the request was due to a lack of transportation that was known about a week prior.

Our subsequent discussion focused on the fact that the transportation issue was known well in advance and the workload did not represent a full day's work. The employee said that there was not much work to do, so working from home seemed to make sense. Our response was that had we been aware of the issue, we could have assigned work to be performed. The rationale behind the WFH policy is to allow flexibility but to also allow a full day's work to be performed, or personal time if warranted. If there is nothing to do then we would like employees to speak up, as there are areas where more effort is needed or fellow team members could use support.

Issuing rationale statements also helps smooth the implementation of new policies by mitigating fears about something new. It may answer questions before they even arise, and assure staff that things are happening for good, well-thought-out reasons. Our intention is to provide for independence and allow for flexibility. We need to improve communication between HR management and individual work effort. While putting new human resource policies in place can be a minefield, we've found that simply being up front with a sound, clearly communicated rationale prevents problems, saves time answering unnecessary questions, and fosters better communication overall.

6.6 MANAGING A FAST-GROWING UX TEAM AND MAINTAINING QUALITY

By Tim Bosenick, Managing Director, SirValUse Consulting GmbH, Hamburg, Germany

In the year 2000, when I founded SirValUse in Hamburg, Germany, it was my aim to build a small but effective UX research and testing company in 10 years with approximately 12 employees. This clearly failed. Since the beginning of 2010 the SirValUse-Group employs approximately

100 people, and is one of the largest UX research and testing companies in Europe, and I am more tied up in "managing" than anything else.

One of the biggest challenges in this growth process was, and still is, to maintain the quality of our work. Especially between the years 2003 to 2006, when we doubled our sales yearly, many new colleagues started to work at SirValUse with little experience in the relevant areas. This is all tied up with the fact that UX/UCD is a relatively young discipline in Germany and only a few universities offer a relevant education, especially in the fields of "research" and "testing."

So in 2004 it was our task to incorporate as many new colleagues as fast as possible, but our clients expected our accustomed quality. "Quality" was and will be important to us on two different levels: on one hand it means "quality of process," and on the other it means "quality of results." An important aspect of process quality for us was to get the new colleagues familiarized with the standard processes so they would be able to carry out those standard processes independently. These processes concern all phases of a project, from preparing a screener for recruitement and the session guide and performing the session itself, to the analysis of data and the report. The quality of results build on the analysis of the test object and the contents of the screener and the session guide, as well as depth of analysis, arrangement and presentation of the report, and the development of recommendations.

In a first step to help as we added new colleagues, a group of experienced members of the team defined the standards and guidelines for process and performance quality. This process wasn't that easy because of different practices even between teams. During many meetings and sometimes contentious debates we defined these standards and were finally able to document them in a binding agreement. This process took place from the end of 2003 until early 2004. Afterwards the team worked out a teaching and qualification plan to bring the new colleagues closer to the developed quality standards. The quality measures were coordinated with the management and the HR departments. To make this happen one of the most experienced colleagues was freed from project work to work exclusively on this task.

The training and qualification plan consisted of the following components:

1. Support of exchange in connection of concrete project work
2. Formal qualification measures
3. Accompanied project coaching measures

1. Support of exchange in connection of concrete project work
   To support the exchange between colleagues, two approaches were taken.: The complete company was divided into three (later four) teams based on SirValUse relevant branches. The result was that members of one team can work on similar themes and questions and acquire experience in these sectors. One approach to exchanging information is that all team members meet weekly for approximately one hour to discuss projects and discuss methods and results. Problems from one project can be avoided on other future projects.

   Another approach to exchanging information is that after the weekly company meeting a project member presents a fascinating 30-minute project from the last 3 months. The focus is mainly on an exciting "best practice" aspect of this project, both methodological and in terms of results. The aim of the event is to transfer learning across the teams and to discuss measures and examples, making it clear how they drive the quality of results.
2. Formal qualification measures
   We have determined the following themes as formal qualifications:
   * Communication with clients
   * Project kickoff, proposal, calculation, briefing
   * Project organization
   * Running international projects
   * Creating moderator's guides

- Moderate sessions
- Documentation of sessions
- Analysis and interpretation of data
- Creating the report
- Documentation of projects
- Usability and user experience basics
- Usability and user experience methods
- Cross-cultural usability and user experience testing

3. Accompanied project coaching measures

   In the middle of 2006 we invented accompanying project measures. Our quality manager collaborated with the personnel manager to develop a coaching plan. The coaching plan included general aspects that repeat and/or sharpen single items of formal qualification measures. All this is broken down into the specific coaching needs of single colleagues.

   The essential idea of coaching is to coach in conjunction with real projects, thereby concrete problems of colleagues are adopted and one can learn on the job. With the high involvement of the colleagues we achieved a deeper awareness of learning.

Finally, internal qualification measures were completed with external quality guidelines. For example, at least once a year our external service providers run through a quality feedback. Within our international network UXa (user experience alliance; www.uxalliance.com) occurs mutual feedback after every project and our clients are asked for concrete project feedback regularly. All of the external feedback has in turn influenced internal qualification measures planned for next year.

I am pretty happy and proud in retrospect that we created this "quality offensive" from both direct and indirect acknowledgments from our clients. Also our colleagues are more motivated by the feedback and time the company provides for quality measures.

6.7 THE 4 STAGES OF TEAM DEVELOPMENT

By Tharon W. Howard, Director, Clemson Usability Testing Facility, Clemson University, Clemson, SC

Teams have life cycles; like people, they go through stages of development. I've found that when members don't understand those stages and then encounter misunderstandings and dissention the result is that the team shuts down and stops functioning. To avoid this problem, I train my teams to use Bruce Tuchman's theory of team development to talk to each other about where they are as a team.

Tuchman was a social psychologist who worked for the U.S. Navy. His job was to try to identify what characteristics of small group dynamics would lead to successful unit performance. To investigate this question, Tuchman conducted a meta-analysis of 50 different research studies that psychoanalyzed small groups. His research identified four distinctive phases.

- **Forming:** During this initial phase, team members obey social protocols of polite behavior in order to communicate with each other. They try to use social conventions in order to minimize conflicts and to get along with one another until they learn more about other team members and their roles in the group.
- **Storming:** This is an extremely important and *necessary* phase of a team's development, and it's the point where differences in interpretations of the team's mission, the scope of the project, means of measuring successful completion criteria, descriptions of each member's role on the team, and other disputable issues emerge. The term "storming" doesn't mean that teams have

to suffer acrimonious and agonistic debates, but it does mean that there are questions and issues that have to be resolved before the team can move to the next phase.

- **Norming:** The group reaches some form of agreement about issues raised during the storming phase and begins working out practices and procedures for functioning together and for making collective decisions. During this phase, teams agree on the "rules of the game" and how they will collaborate.
- **Performing:** During this phase, team members share a common vision and understanding of what constitutes success. They have shared protocols and procedures to which they all adhere, and because they have learned to trust each other, they are able to function autonomously and without overt supervision.

One of the things I try to communicate to my staff about Tuchman's model is that it's an iterative model, which is to say that a team can get knocked out of the performing stage and sent back to the storming phase at any time. A new team member, changes in upper management, funding reallocations, new technologies, and many other factors can require that a team renegotiate all of its understandings. More importantly, however, I try to help my staff understand that "storming" isn't a bad thing and that they avoid storming at their peril. High-performing teams often need to go through long periods of storming to learn to trust each other and to become successful.

Nurturing the Team

THE CRITIQUE

One of the best techniques for driving up quality while taking advantage of the power of a centralized UX team is the design (or for that matter the research) critique. Creativity comes from a cycle of exploration and convergence. The richest exploration comes with a diversity of perspectives collaborating and uncovering areas to explore. Design may begin with a charrette focused on the design problem, but the exploration continues and is refined through a series of critiques. The critique is a gathering of those diverse design and research skills to focus on early ideas and to explore them, and eventually to refine them.

My Tablet team gathered each Monday in a team room we created from an old conference room. We arranged comfortable chairs in a semicircle around a projection screen we had set up at one end of the room, and the walls were covered with floor to ceiling whiteboards. Standing by the projector was one of my designers who had been sketching alternative approaches to represent the passing of time as a digital pen was pressed against a screen. Gathered in the room and in various states of comfort around the chairs were my designers and my researchers as well as the project manager and a couple of the developers who were working on the feature. The designer presented each idea and we discussed how it worked as a design. We talked through what users needed and how they think about time. We brainstormed other alternatives and variations, and sketched on the whiteboard. We compared the ideas based on how well they delivered on the needs identified. Over time, as one Monday passed to the next, and as more and more lattes were consumed, we moved from the traditional metaphor of the hourglass to something that looked like a clock to a more abstract design like a bar sweeping in a circle. To enable targeting, we decided to remove the center, and something that looked more like a donut emerged with a moving comet of light passing around the circular path; it entered the vocabulary of Windows design and from there has propagated through the industry. The process began with a very functional need to show as a pen pressed to a Tablet that time was passing and the user needed to be induced to wait until a menu became available. The critique resulted in an even more flexible indicator that could be applied to many situations and carried an aesthetic that fit within the design language that had been developed for the operating system.

In addition to the obvious benefits for improving the innovation, quality, and effectiveness of the design, there were other benefits as well. The process of bringing the team together for charrettes and critiques drove more consistency across the team's design, and grounded it in common user assumptions. It helped unite the team in how it thought about all of our designs. It bonded the team as a team, and reinforced the values that were common to the team. It also educated stakeholders by exposing the design process to them, and indeed giving them experience in being a part of the process and exercising their own design-thinking skills. It made the design a creative collaboration.

GROWING PERFORMANCE AND CAREERS

> Coaching is unlocking a person's potential to maximize his or her own performance. It is helping him or her to learn rather than teaching them.
>
> **Timothy Gallwey**

You have several tools as a manager or lead that you can use to raise the level of individual performance and to grow performance and impact growing careers. Much of the year you are working with individuals one-on-one, or as part of a team to motivate, guide, and support them. You have the portfolio of recognition tools available in your organization and that you have created. You have career discussions and various feedback tools that can be used to refine performance. And of course you have formal and informal performance reviews that build on the other interactions. Together they are all aspects of the coaching function of leadership — the growing of the individual talent on your team that results in growing your overall team.

Setting Commitments

Next to understanding what motivates the individual, the most important thing you can do with each individual is to have clarity around your expectations, the goals the person is working toward, and how they will be measured. Companies take different approaches to how the goals or objectives are framed. At Ameritech the objectives were to be aligned along a golden thread, where an individual's objectives mapped to their boss' objectives, which mapped to their boss' objectives and so on, up to the business model for the organization. Each individual's activities should clearly be aligned with how value is delivered. At other companies the commitments are more focused on the impact the individual plans to have, and as a manager your job is to ensure that the various commitments across the team allow

HINTS FROM EXPERIENCED MANAGERS

Encourage every day. Thank people for their hard work. Be sincere. Don't be serious all the time; save that for when things are really serious and it will have more impact.

Listen always. Open door, means an open door (as much as possible). My job is to be interrupted.

Robert M. Schumacher, PhD, Managing Director, User Centric, Inc., Oakbrook Terrace, IL

1. Encourage and support your staff to be creative in their use of methods and approaches. This field can get very dry and routine (depending on industry/role) and as a result, the output of the work can become "canned" and people lose the energy they had at the start. I look for ways to reward people for innovating new methods and approaches to answering important research questions better.
2. Just because someone isn't complaining about something doesn't mean you can assume everything is fine or just ignore their situation. Many of the better performers do not like to be the "squeaky wheel" and many managers believe that if someone doesn't squeak, they don't have problems. It's important to look at what everyone is doing and evaluate how they are feeling. Asking them is a good idea too!
3. Only as the exception share information differently among your staff because you have a relationship with someone or they are someone that asks lots of questions. You don't want others to get wind of this and you also don't want to put your staff into a position where they have to hide information from their peers. This develops a level of distrust that is difficult to fix.

Ross Teague, PhD, Partner and Director of Research, Insight, Raleigh, NC

A great article and concept of "Everyone gets a trophy" is how many new employees have been raised and brought up. The need to appreciate all efforts rather than single out stellar individuals can have a large impact on the psyche of today's youth.

Gavin S. Lew, Managing Director, User Centric, Inc., Chicago, IL

you to achieve the strategic objectives for the UX team. The commitments may be coordinated with those of the teams you support as well.

For each commitment specific activities undertaken should be defined, and the metrics used to measure whether the commitment was met should be described. Metrics ideally should not be just about doing the activity, but should be defined in terms of impact. UX does not design or study users for the sake of the activity; it creates great products that matter to users. For some projects and organizations this process can be fairly straightforward. For others, your visibility may be limited to a few months if projects frequently change and the demands on the UX team vary based on the immediate context. In that case you are trying to work with the individual to create a framework for measuring success that can handle the changes in the project over time, and that lets you update as needed. When performance reviews include both the concept of meeting expectations and exceeding expectations, it can be useful to negotiate a description of what exceeding expectations looks and feels like with the members of your team.

At one point I took a class on risk taking. They made the point that there are actually three states you can be in. Many people gravitate to the safe end of risk. They only take on things they know they can succeed at. They set commitments low, and may claim big results and want big rewards at the end. They typically never fail, not because of extraordinary abilities but because they have not pushed themselves enough. At the other end are those who gravitate toward taking on extraordinary challenges where they are almost guaranteed to fail. This was a new insight for me. These are people who are like the first group, however, because they *know* they are likely to fail, but failure does not hurt. It again often means they are not pushing themselves all that hard, but they will talk a lot about how impossible the task is and how heroic they are in tackling it. In between these two extremes is what the class called the zone of optimal development. This is the zone that appeared in my climate survey, and this is where flow happens. It is the area where the tasks are sufficiently challenging that there is a probability of failure (and some failure may happen), but with careful planning, hard work, and applying talent and experience usually there is success, and you learn and get better from the experience. This is where you want your team.

The goal is to have very clear commitments, but commitments that challenge appropriately. When at the right level there should be some failure, but success should be more frequent and the impact should justify the occasional individual failure. As a manager you can use your UX team to ensure that failure does not result in failure for the larger organization you are supporting.

Fruitful Coaching

You are a manager and a leader because you cannot do everything yourself, and your impact is going to increase dramatically as you work through your team. The process of achieving impact through others and increasing that leverage by growing the ability of others to execute and add to the direction you are providing is called coaching. It is about providing direction and empowerment without doing the job yourself.

Coaching takes time, but it is critical to creating a high performance team and accomplishing your user experience vision. I have found that when I have a half a dozen reports or less, I can do the weekly one-on-ones and have the frequent casual conversations that enable me to feel like a coach. As my direct reports go up from there, administrative and other management overhead tends to go up and the opportunities for deep coaching get fewer and fewer (and my team gets more and more frustrated that they have less and less time with me). In my current job I have had to manage the nine direct reports and manage contractors and vendors. In addition, the expectation is that I should be leading other major projects and virtual teams composed primarily of engineers. This hurts the ability to coach as effectively as I would like to coach. In this situation part of what I am working on is trying to find ways to work around the barriers to success. One obvious step is to build in another layer of management. As it happens, there are larger organizational constraints that are not letting this happen, so the best I can do is to leverage one of my senior people as a business manager to help with the coaching. Then I must find ways to reward her for the management role she is undertaking without a management title (a further limitation placed by human resources policies within the organization).

It is probably not too surprising that research suggests that one of the most important reasons that people do not do what we want them to is that they do not actually

Pam deserves a round of applause!!!!
Great job Pam, your effort are appreciated by all!

YAY Pam! Thanks for your authentic work —
and for always sharing the true spirit of UX!

FIGURE 7.1

Evana's praise of her colleague Pam for leading a team. (Artwork used by permission from Evana Gerstman.)

review process they immediately go to the "growth areas" list, the rank ordering section, and the money. In recent years, even when the review feedback is largely positive, raises have been so small my best people often are disappointed with the compensation. But doing performance review is part of the job, and how you do it impacts the climate within your team and your ability to motivate individuals.

I remember one of the reviews early in my career when my manager announced we would do my review in the car while she went to pick up drapes. The review was very important to me, and I still remember how I felt when it seemed like drapes were more critical than I was. As a result, I believe it is important to give it my best on behalf of each member of the team whether they recognize it or not. At one company they had wisely forced a separation between the performance review and the career discussion, and I think that made each more productive.

Much of the performance review work is hidden. For the UX manager, if the ranking part of the process is against the rest of the engineering organization, you find yourself not only arguing on behalf of the individual but your hidden agenda will be arguing on behalf of user experience. For each individual, therefore, I begin by collecting the praises and compliments about each person that I have received and saved over the course of the year. I try to summarize the impact they have had, and to do it in terms that are likely to be similar to those used by the engineering managers about their teams. I collect 360 feedback from the people each person works with to add richness to the descriptions, and tell compelling stories about their impact. When I know of other user experience teams working in a similar space, I meet with the managers of those teams to calibrate across the teams to make sure I am using similar criteria. I also go through the various skills lists the employees should be demonstrating at their levels of experience to identify where I think they are, their strengths, and where they should be growing. Often I have had to complete a spreadsheet with the ratings on various dimensions. I also put together briefs about each of my direct reports to make sure I have thought through the points I want to raise when I defend my ratings in the calibration process. When I have managers reporting to me, I ask them to do something similar in anticipation of the calibration process we will hold; if the particular organizational structure does not allow them to do this, then I use their input when preparing my ratings and briefs and as a reality check on my analyses.

I remember the first time I was in a performance review calibration meeting at Bell Labs as a manager. The department was probably between 20 and 30 people. We had to rank order each person in the department and there could be no ties. There was an additional factor that was in all of our minds in that the manager's rating partially depended on where their people fell in the overall stack, so each manager was arguing on behalf of their own performance. It was kind of ridiculous in practice since the position of one person versus another ended up only driving a hundred dollars or so in compensation. In this particular session you saw all the political games at work. I remember one person wanted to negotiate a deal. They wanted to say "If you put person A here, you can put person B there." But when they offered it up, everyone jumped on it with "Okay, we'll accept putting person B there, but we'll see about A later." The calibration went on all night, and at one point a physical scuffle broke out between a couple of the managers. I am sure none of the people who have worked for me even came close to imagining how intense some of these sessions can be. Fortunately, while often intense, the calibration sessions since then have been far more civilized. Being well prepared, having good relationships with the other managers, and the skills and preparation of the person leading the calibration make all the difference.

In general, across the various companies I have been at the employees document their accomplishments and their own analysis of how they did. I then use the material I have collected, the feedback from the people with whom they work (the 360 feedback), and craft my comments. I spend a lot of time on this. Employees argue, correctly, that at some level — no matter what the company says — the process is subjective. Yes you can argue whether or not an objective was met, but often for user experience the objectives frequently evolve during the course of the year and how one is ranked often turns on what was done, how it was done, and more subtle aspects of how much impact the employee has had. So for me the 360 process where you hear from those with whom an individual works provides very important data. Since we are about impact and driving user experience into the organizations in which we find ourselves, the data of interest are how those organizations see us. The 360 process, the collection of strengths, areas of growth, and perceptions of impact that come from those with whom we team and who are impacted by our work as well as from those up and down the management chain, are in fact the metrics that speak to team impact and individual performance.

I apply my own experience and evaluation as well, and that of managers working for me, but I have found that my analysis aligns well with that of the organization (as it should, if I have been effectively working with each person). The organization's feedback is the most persuasive and least subjective from the employee's perspective. They understand and can cope with the ratings a little more when they come from the people they are working with every day.

When I was at Ameritech, they introduced a 360 process where managers and leads would get input from anyone who worked for them, all employees would get input from their peers and people they worked with, and everyone would get input from their managers. The questions that were asked included "What should the person continue doing? What should they do less of? What should they do more of?" When the company has no such tool, or when an employee just wants to get feedback, I add "What is this person's strengths?" and "What other feedback would you like to share with this person?" I also sometimes add a few Likert items for skills that are identified in their growth plans and identified as strategically important for UX to be effective in the organization. The Likert ratings provide numbers that can sometimes be used as part of the discussion, especially when they are informed by the verbatim feedback.

When I write a review I try to stay fact based but use the facts to speak to broader themes. I try to avoid the situation where the employee and I fight over whether a particular fact happened as it was reported, but rather use it with others that I have in my pocket to speak to what the impact was and how it was perceived and experienced. I use anonymous quotes to give texture to the write-up. In general, I structure the write-ups by starting with the overall positive impact and strengths, highlighting a few growth areas, and then summarizing with the vision for the next year and how leveraging the strengths and growing in a few areas should result in even more impact. In some cases I describe how the feedback aligns with attributes in the career ladder that correspond to the employee's level.

I try to identify roughly three growth areas for the person to concentrate on over the next year. For the best people, that is sometimes a challenge and is a discipline for me to make sure I am really looking hard and working with them closely to make them as good as they can be. For the people with the most issues, I do not want to discourage them by laying out all their issues. My attitude is if each year we could make progress on just a couple of areas they would be growing in important ways; often that growth will improve their skills in other growth areas.

One principle is that the review feedback should not be a surprise to the individual. That can be hard if it is their first review, or if they have not worked with you very long. I often find that it takes between 3 to 6 months for me to really get a handle on an individual's growth areas, since most of us have developed strategies to try to work around, compensate for, or hide our growth areas. I have personally been surprised by feedback I have received at performance review, so clearly preventing surprises is not easy. After a recent layoff where people at various places in the team stack rank were let go some of the people remaining were surprised with where they ended up in the rank order since the layoff happened just a couple of months before the review period. Ideally, it should not be a surprise. Strengths and growth areas should have been discussed as situations arose during the year highlighting each. Some people keep tickler files on each employee to track the incidents that illustrate the good and not so good.

Most managers I have had only share the review during the review discussion, and the idea is that I will go away and come back with questions before I actually sign it. Others share it in the meeting and want an immediate signature that the meeting took place. I have sometimes shared the review write-up before the meeting so people can process it before coming to the meeting. There is no strong difference between sharing it early and sharing it in the meeting in terms of how the meeting actually goes.

At the review discussion I welcome the person and try to settle them in. There is usually less small talk than in normal one-on-ones, but there is some. I then lay out the agenda for the discussion so they know what to expect. This typically involves my talking through an overview of the year's accomplishments as we both look at copies of the write-up. I provide my commentary on what I thought went well and what did not go quite as I had hoped (and I recognize circumstances that may have been important in the success or failure as well). I then move to what I saw as the strengths the person demonstrated during the year, and to areas where I feel if they grow more skills they will have more impact. This often is where there is a fair amount of Q&A ranging from the particular incident that led to the comment to comparing where the person is to others at the same level. I try to not select growth areas that only have a single incident behind them (one of my biggest gripes with some of the managers I have had). Then I share the ratings and typically the compensation changes. I invite any final questions and we talk more generally depending on what is on the person's mind. Finally, I describe any next steps (e.g., when the form has to be signed by, any process for them to offer a rebuttal, etc.). This has been a fairly consistent process with each of the teams I have managed.

The biggest challenge is not getting caught up in point-by-point defenses. If the process is done right, the strengths and growth areas clearly are major themes of how the person performed over the year, and the impact is the impact experienced by teams and that could be compared across the team. Some individuals, often those at the lower end of the scale, will approach the discussion more like a checklist and will be trying to argue each check on the list. In situations like this, as with conflict resolution, I try to get them to focus on the future, and get them to understand that it is not about how they see themselves as much as how they are seen by others, and that the data I am sharing represent broader themes. I also try to keep them from trying to speculate on which individual was the source of a particular comment (since hopefully it came from more than one). The general recommendation is to get them to share what their own needs and goals are, and to get *them* to generate plans that address the themes highlighted that will move them toward satisfying those needs and goals. Having clear commitments and speaking to evidence as it relates to skills in the career ladder helps.

Another perspective on this was described by the managers participating in the Adaptive Path workshop as they discussed how to effectively review (Adaptive Path, 2008) their team members. They began by pointing out that you need to communicate clear expectations. Factor in the person's career and other personal goals (e.g., building on work-life balance discussions). They also recommended what I have found as well — leverage peer and client feedback. Have a consistent scoring system that you can use across your team that your team understands. As discussed earlier, the objection is often that performance reviews and coaching are subjective, and to some extent they are, but you want to build the confidence that you are working from the facts; you want people to understand the rules they are planning by so they can act accordingly. Track the results over time, and give feedback on an ongoing basis. The goal is that neither of you are surprised when you get to the big performance review. This may be a challenge if you are in an organization that does an end-of-year calibration and a forced distribution of ratings, but if you can avoid surprises it is more likely this process will turn into something useful. Finally, at those formal feedback times, deliver the news with compassion, be prepared and fact based, and focus on positive steps that can be taken.

After the process I usually go home, have a glass of wine, and get hugs from my family.

Encouraging Professional Activity

Professional activity can be a reward, can be part of career development, and can enhance the quality of your team's work. It can be an important tool as you coach and define tactics to implement your strategy.

When I was still early in my career at Bell Labs and was working for Judy Olson, the ACM SIGCHI conference was held at Gaithersburg, MD. I remember us all loading onto a train in New Jersey to head down to Gaithersburg. Someone in the group had smuggled on various alcoholic libations and food, and as you can imagine we had a wonderful time bonding and building team identity. At least the rest of the train could identify us based on the laughter filling the car. At the conference, I remember hearing John Gould's paper on user-centered design, and the research and intense discussion on whether scrolling a window should scroll the

---

HINTS FROM EXPERIENCED MANAGERS

Encourage Economical Professional Development

Especially in tough economic times it is easy to get caught up in the daily and weekly project deliverables and to neglect investing in personal and team development. There are many ways to develop individuals and the team without a huge investment. Here are some suggestions:

- **Reading clubs:** Over lunch or morning coffee, bring the team together.
- **Member-led workshops:** Identify experience topics that the team (and individual team members) are keen to learn more about and set a goal for one (or more) of the team members to become an expert in that topic and to lead a workshop instructing the rest of the team about it.
- **Vendor workshops:** Invite your favorite vendors to teach the team some of their tools and techniques. They'll likely be honored and offer these workshops at an economical price.
- **Open office hours:** To develop more junior members of your team or to interface with experience experts in other parts of the organization, hold open office hours where they can come to you to discuss research plans or designs in progress. Be sure to include your strongest designers/researchers in these sessions.
- **Team-led design reviews:** To encourage creative design and to develop best practices, establish team-led design reviews. Be careful that these discussions do not devolve into "opinionating" about design (often signaled by "well, I like this ..." or "I think ..."); instead, help the team grow in providing grounded design rationale (e.g., is there research to suggest, what are tangible/measurable impacts of design alternatives, are there alternatives that warrant testing with users?).
- **Usability lessons learned**: Because experience researchers/designers are often working on their own projects it is likely difficult for them to individually monitor and integrate important user research, usability evaluation, and metrics findings. Help the team grow their expertise by tasking one or more team members to periodically synthesize the lessons learned across the various research and metrics projects. Ask them to host an interactive readout for the team as well as to create a summary report. Consider doing this for your strategic partners and stakeholders throughout the organization as well.

Marilyn Salzman, User Experience Strategist, Salzman Consulting, LLC, Louisville, CO

---

content past the window or scroll the window past the content. I remember coming away both with new ideas about how to think about my work and new friends. These have been friends and colleagues that I have maintained over the years and have continued to draw on for insights about various management and design problems I have faced. I also came away with a sense that one could approach anything they were doing from a bigger perspective, thinking about the larger issues that transcend a specific design in a given situation. Since then I have continued to find stimulation at SIGCHI and HFES conferences, and at UPA, CSCW, and other conferences that I have attended. I found even more ways to derive benefit not only for myself, but for my team, and for my company. But personally, and perhaps as important, I felt that professional activity has been a way for me to give back to the profession a little of all that I have received from it — a small return for the great life it has enabled me to have.

When I was managing the Tablet and mobile computing user experience team one of my managers, while supportive in theory (at least he paid for my trips), periodically would ask "Why do you do this?" He did not resonate with all my answers, but in responding I came up with a series of benefits. Professional activity contributes to the business by:

- Providing continuing education for the UX professionals.
- Providing leadership experiences for UX professionals.
- Providing support for recruiting great talent (from interns; to new grads; to mid-career professionals; to seasoned, senior professionals with whom relationships are being built).
- Inspiring innovative ideas that apply to corporate projects.
- Encouraging UX people to derive general principles from their work that apply across projects.
- Recognizing and rewarding excellent UX work.
- Adding to the user-centered brand of the team's company and products.
- Enabling the UX team to influence the direction of research and the industry.
- Protecting the company's innovations when patents are not appropriate, by making it public.
- Increasing the satisfaction of the team by building relationships.
- Improving the quality of the UX team's work by engaging external critiques.

There are many types of professional activity. There are excellent conferences, and most of the larger societies also have local chapters in or near major cities. There are workshops and symposia on special topics. There are events sponsored by various groups or combinations of groups like World Usability Day and National Ergonomics Month. For these activities, you can attend, present, sponsor (and have your company's logo plastered on lots of visible places), and can get involved in running them and shaping the program. Even getting into a position reviewing content for the program is an excellent opportunity to get on the inside track of emerging ideas and get a sense of what is happening, and to get a better sense of what excellence in user experience looks and feels like. There are even opportunities to get involved in the sponsoring societies themselves. Your team can become members, and get benefits such as journals and access to libraries such as ACM's digital library. Some societies have competitions and there is recognition that comes by winning that can aid recruiting. Team members may want to get into leadership positions and influence policy. There are publications sponsored by the societies and other publishers, and turning work into articles is a great way to get people to think more generally and come up with the big ideas that can really make a difference in a company. You can also get a position on the editorial board, and while reviewing for conferences there is a chance to get early insights into emerging work before it becomes available to others.

I consider customer interactions as a kind of professional activity, since it leverages many of the same skills. I had a chance to visit several major customers and share some of our best practices around building user experience labs, and to speak at a briefing center to major customers who wanted to learn more about our emerging design practices. We have also gone to industry conferences such as one of the major developer conferences where we talked about design patterns for natural user interfaces. Other places where your team can reach out are the various social networking sites and list servers that we all use. An area that is sometimes under-appreciated is working on national or international standards. Many large corporations are willing to fund their employees to have an active presence there, and you may be able to find funding and develop work outside of your immediate organization that you can leverage to increase the guidelines activity within your team. Working on the first US HCI standard (sponsored by HFES, and now an ANSI standard) and with the CIF and CIF-R efforts (feeding the ISO standards), I have not only had a chance to take a direct hand in shaping the standards of our field but have made many new friends and developed close colleagues. Standards work gives you a chance to represent your company, and also to get an early read for your company on emerging standards. It is a forcing function to get you to read the literature on a specific topic and develop expertise in it.

There are many other ways to grow your team professionally. In addition to people sharing what they have learned from conferences, you can have them share what they have learned from interesting books and articles. Several teams have had book clubs for discussing new HCI publications. People can regularly gather to share their critiques of Web sites or user experience technology research, or even talk about topics that are more general than the specific work they are doing at the moment. When people discover an online training event, either internal or external, or online access to a special speaker, they can arrange for a broadcast to the team and discussion afterwards.

Finally, there is the opportunity to work with universities. I have had several opportunities to teach, and through the teaching to bring great students into the companies for whom I have worked. Teaching gives me a chance to represent my companies to the students who in turn take that understanding and perspective with them. I have sponsored industry-shaping research at various universities, and collaborated with university researchers on projects that provided insights we could not get in any other way. Universities are also a great source of interns, and the front end of the pipeline for bringing new talent into your team.

Even assuming you give flexibility for individuals within your team to choose activities in which to participate, and assuming the activity fits within your budget and corporate policies, some of your people are likely to participate but many will just concentrate on their jobs. You, however, can encourage and potentially reward activities that meet your strategic goals. A framework that can be used to prioritize your involvement might look like the one illustrated in Fig. 7.2.

Each of the major categories of professional activity in which a UX team, or individual team members, may participate is listed. The major benefits that each activity might provide are also highlighted. Finally, you can prioritize the benefits with respect to the needs of your organization. The result is guidance on where it might make sense to invest team effort and an organizational budget. This can be refined by attempting to weight each category by the importance of the benefits for your UX program.

If you think about the potential resources you may have to invest, it obviously begins with the motivations of the individuals (which are influenced by what and

	Education	Recruiting	Recognition	Branding	Innovation	Influence	IP Protection	Thinking	Relationships
Importance	H	H	H	M	M	M	M	L	L
Conferences	■	■	■	■	■		■	■	■
Social Networking	■	■	■	■		■			■
Societies	■		■		■	■			■
University Relations		■	■	■			■	■	■
Publications			■	■	■	■	■	■	
Customer Visits			■	■	■	■			
Standards			■	■		■	■		■

FIGURE 7.2

Professional activity model.

how you reward the activity). For most of my career professional activity and broader research has at best been tolerated and has occasionally been punished, so recognizing and rewarding forward-looking research, generic research, and professional activity has largely been up to me as a manager. Another resource is your own budget. There is usually training and travel budget you can draw on, and budget may be provided for professional memberships (and possibly for subscriptions and books). You may also have a recruiting budget that you can apply, and your recruiting organization may have a budget you can draw on. These are often great budgets to drive sponsorships, which in turn can result in free conference registrations for your team. If you have a centralized user experience team or a research organization, you can sometimes find budget for professional activity.

Another place to look is marketing (or market research budgets) for funding can be justified by conducting research at a conference.

By looking at the nature of the budgets that are available against prioritization, you can develop a specific action plan that drives the most value out of your professional activity. If you tie business-relevant metrics to these activities (e.g., number of recruiting contacts made, interns brought in, publications, etc.), you are even more likely to be able to grow professional activity over time.

There is one logistical detail that should not be neglected. External presentations or publication of work can have legal implications. At Bell Labs, we needed to have peers in an organization outside of our own review material we wanted to publish, and an executive needed to pass on its suitability for external publication (i.e., that it would not compromise AT&T's proprietary information or violate customer privacy). At other times, I needed to submit content to the legal department with a rationale for why it was appropriate to publish it. More recently it has been my responsibility (or my boss' responsibility) to determine that content was appropriate for external release, and if legal issues eventually occurred, the consequences would also be my responsibility. It was my job to use judgment about when to bring in legal people for a review. If your team is new, you may need to work with your management team and the legal support for your organization to define an appropriate policy.

MANAGING CONFLICT

> Stellar teams are invariably made up of quirky individuals who typically rub each other raw, but they figure out — with the spiritual help of a gifted leader (such as Phil Jackson at Chicago or Los Angeles) — how to be their peculiar selves and how to win championships as a team . . . at the same time.
>
> **Tom Peters**

There are studies that suggest an estimated 20% of a manager's time is spent resolving interpersonal conflicts. I do not think it is quite that much of my time (meetings and e-mails are another matter), but it is true that people in conflict do take up a tremendous amount of energy and time. Conflict can get in the way of delivering the great experiences we want to deliver, and the clashes between people can cause all kinds of personal cost in emotional well-being and psychological (and physical) health. That being said, conflict is probably inherent in the people gathered by external forces (a hiring process) and placed together and told to get a job done, especially creative, right-brained people who have to function in the middle of a left-brained engineering culture. Bringing smart, assertive, and confident people together to solve problems that have more than one solution or path to solution is virtually guaranteed to cause conflict. Indeed, the conflict can be the seed for creative solutions and can drive innovation, almost as easily as it can hurt projects or even cause them to fail. Being a manager, therefore, is not so much about avoiding conflict as it is about managing it. Being a user experience manager should in part be about managing conflict to advance the user experience agenda and vision within the organization.

I remember one time as a new manager at Bell Labs when I was sitting happily in my office going over budget numbers or another administrative task, trying my best to pay attention to the mundane while a part of my head was working on a project problem. Suddenly the door of my office slammed open and another manager stormed in with a "What the hell do you think you are doing? How could you let this happen?" If anyone had been walking by and looked into my office at that moment they would have seen the notorious deer in the headlights look. I had absolutely no idea what she was talking about. The first thing I needed to do was calm her down so we could talk. I got her to sit down, and started through the process talking a little slower and soothingly to get her to do the same while projecting a concerned and problem-solving attitude. Inside, of course, both flight and fight reactions were going on. I knew that if I actually expressed either the situation would escalate.

I once took an interesting variation on the Myers-Briggs questionnaire. It assessed interpersonal style under normal situations, and then profiled one's style in conflict situations. While normally I have more of an analytical style (which goes with being a conceptualizer) and lean toward introversion, in conflict situations I have more of an assertive style. While I prefer to deal with problem solving analytically, I also recognize that internally I am hypersensitive emotionally to conflict situations. I tend to project what, in the Northwest culture I grew up in, is seen as a stereotypical Scandinavian coolness (as in "That was so hilarious it took everything I had to keep from laughing."). As a problem is building, therefore, I may seem to be ignoring it. Inside it is building to an exploding point. When it reaches that point, then my inclination is to gird myself up, confront it, and resolve it. In resolving it, the place I typically come from is "Hey, we are two human beings. This is just a job, not life and death. Let's just work this out." That is how I approached the situation with my colleague at Bell Labs. While this situation resolved amicably, I find it difficult to teach my team to resolve conflict; it is just one of those skills I am not very good at passing on to others.

On the other hand, I have known several people who are good at it. At Ameritech I had a contractor working as a usability researcher, and it turned out that on the side she had been formally trained in conflict resolution. Time and again I could pull her in and she had a process to drive resolution that worked for all kinds of conflicts that arose in the course of our projects. More recently I have had some teams where individuals within the team seemed to go through periods of clashing with each other. Usually they are attributing some hostile intent to the other person, when in fact it is usually because the participants have somewhat different goals and are simply not communicating well with each other. One of the senior people on my team, Karen, is excellent at listening to each of the conflicting individuals to get their points of view, sitting them down together and getting them to listen to each other, and finding actionable win-win ways to move forward.

In general, when I work with my team as conflicts are starting to arise I first ask them whether they have talked to the other person directly about what they have heard and what they are feeling, and whether they have attempted to deal with the conflict directly. I believe the manager is not the first step in conflict resolution, but rather an escalation point partly because effectively dealing with conflict is a sign of growing as a professional. There is an interesting article by Gatlin et al. (2009) that argued there are eight causes of conflict. Conflict comes from conflicting needs, it comes from conflicting styles and conflicting perceptions, it can come from conflicting goals or conflicting pressures, it can come from conflicting roles, and it can come from conflicting values and policies. These sources, I find, often lead to conflict because of breakdowns in communication.

When you work with team members there are a variety of ways to deal with conflict, and as with situational management styles there are times when it may be appropriate to move between them. Each team member may have their own preferred style and will often become more effective as their toolkit becomes richer. One style is confrontational. This is often where conflict starts and it is typically highly emotional. There are times when it can get things done that need to be done, but you have to be careful to not win the battle and lose the war. Another style is compromise. In this case each person may need to give something up to reach a settlement. Here the danger is that the solution reached is not right for the business even though it deals with the conflict. Collaboration is a third style, and is sometimes known as driving win-win solutions. In a sense this can be thought of as win-win-win, as the solution may be more than just the least painful, a compromise, and may actually represent a new and better perspective on the problem. A fourth style is accommodation where someone just gives in. The key here is to realize that some problems are not worth fighting for, and accommodating at one point may mean someone will accommodate in the future when you want something. This may even be a little like sacrificing a pawn when playing chess in order to end up being in a better position. Finally, there is avoidance. Avoidance when there is a real problem can be bad. But avoidance in the early stages when you can steer around a problem — avoiding someone's hot button by being aware of what is needed in order to make progress and achieve a goal — may be appropriate.

There are a variety of principles that are used by people who are trained in conflict resolution that can be adapted to work situations. At the risk of stereotyping, user experience people frequently approach problems with a lot of passion. Many of these techniques are particularly good at reframing the problem to make it more tractable. These techniques include:

- As a manager, create a fair process that assures everyone will be heard, that models the focus on solving problems, and gets away from winners and losers. Insist that everyone be treated with respect, and that all share responsibility to achieve a solution. Recognize that each side typically feels wronged and/or threatened and is hurting. As a manager, practice emotional intelligence and look for what people are feeling.

- Define the conflict objectively, rather than subjectively. Move beyond feeling to thinking. If each side can clearly understand the objective facts of the conflict it can be easier to resolve.
- It should not be about one person against another person; it should be about solving the problem. It is after all just a job. Focusing on the problem itself allows each person's perspectives to become elements in the solution rather than choices where one is right and one is wrong.
- Find the shared goals. If you can find out what each person wants you may be able to find a way to satisfy both. The question is what does each really want, and what are their priorities? What are they willing to give up in order to achieve higher order goals?
- Conflict often begins with miscommunication, so resolution needs to be grounded in creating communication. Communication begins with active listening. As a manager, use neutral language.
- Create a neutral ground for the parties to come together. This is often the manager's office when it has escalated in that direction. When I personally have stepped out to resolve a conflict, I make it a point to go to their place of comfort or to find a neutral place like going out to lunch together or talking over coffee.
- Drive to actionable steps that make progress. Begin with what is doable. Get each party to express what specific actions they would like to see the other party take. As the manager you may actually take away some of the action items.
- Forgive, forget, and keep things in perspective. There are always more significant problems in the world than those we face at work. We are working with other human beings, and as user experience people we should care about them in the way we care about our users.
- Realize that often there is a richer context and the conflicting parties are probably impacting others. Resolve the conflict in the most effective way possible and take the pulse of others who might be impacted and be sensitive to their healing as well. Make sure they are not being randomized, and instead are focused on their work. Make sure they are feeling supported, but also that they see you as fair and just and that you are modeling how you want them to approach their jobs. What you do with the conflicting parties will teach them how they should deal with conflict.

Focusing less on the past and more on the goal is important. Avoid getting caught in resolving "facts" that cannot be verified and that are interpreted differently by each individual. Still, I have seen value in just getting each person's perspective out on the table. Find out what happened in the context of each perspective and the feelings it caused. Each person's perspective has validity and should be heard. The sharing can potentially help each person understand the richer context of where the other is coming from.

A controversial area is whether or not the manager should bring the conflicting people together. One article says to never interview the participating parties together, and to ask them not to communicate to each other about the issues or with co-workers. I suspect this advice is more about the conflict that arises due to a hostile workplace. I am not dealing with conflict in this area, and my clear advice on that kind of conflict is for the manager to go directly to their Human Resources representative as soon as they learn of it and take the guidance of their HR person on how to handle it. Each company should have very clear steps that they want the manager to follow, and anything in the "hostile workplace" area is very serious and should be handled in close partnership with your local HR person.

CREATING WORK-LIFE BALANCE

Clearly work-life balance is important for each member of the UX team, as well as for the entire team so everyone can be as vibrant and creative as possible. The right balance also provides a willingness on the part of the team to bear down for the short term because they know in general they are being treated well. Obviously we all know from the research that stress shortens one's life, and many of us have seen it impact health and the quality of performance. It often comes from within, however, as a way of avoiding the guilt of not attaining a bar we have set for ourselves. Being responsible is about actively managing your load and activity, and achieving the level of healthy stress that keeps us energized. Just as people should be mostly doing work that they find exciting and where they can have a meaningful impact, they are only really successful when achieving both professional and personal goals. They need to manage their own lives not just day to day, but toward the future as well (just as the group is being managed). They need to make sure there is time each day to take a breath and think about where they are at the moment, where they are heading, and to adjust their course.

This is one of the toughest problems I have faced over the years. I hire people and try to match them to jobs they have a passion for. I hire people because of their passion and desire to produce excellent results, and their commitment to taking responsibility for the quality of their work. I try to create an environment where they get into the flow and time disappears. I also reward them for their impact. That can mean that even when the project is scaled properly on paper (and often it is too ambiguous to scope cleanly), my best people will work their butts off to deliver something that makes them proud, but they often work too hard.

Unfortunately when the annual corporate climate survey is taken and they see the item on work-life balance they typically rate it as "Terrible." Yet in general, I have given them the power to say "No!" to requests (including to me) and I will support them. I tell them I would rather know up front because I typically can find another way to get the job done if they do not have the capacity, or I can help them reprioritize and negotiate with their clients if necessary. The only time the issue appears during performance review is when someone is not as productive as someone else at a comparable level. It is usually only the most mature of my team who have learned the skill of managing their own workloads to ensure they are able to do their best work on the most important tasks and still have work-life balance.

One lesson I have learned over the years is that I cannot create work-life balance for people. I can do my best at balancing workloads, I can define policies, I can be consistent with my words, and I can try to model work-life balance, but I cannot force people into work-life balance. At least not when I am managing them as a higher performing person where I am trusting them to run their own work. The best I can do is to continue to message my goal for them to have the balance they want, coach them when I see behaviors that I think are going to hurt them in the end, intervene in extreme cases, and to regularly explicitly create a situation where we can have a heart-to-heart about how the work-life balance is going. I can check in regularly with them one-on-one, and take the kind of team pulse that helps me decide whether I need to more aggressively intervene.

I have also accumulated tools to support the discussion. While they are proprietary, the general concepts are what you would expect them to be and similar tools could be created within any team. One nice set consists of a checklist to help the manager and the employee prepare for a discussion about work-life balance, a script to help both the employee and the manager to have a fruitful discussion, tips for the manager to help in the discussion, and a warning to managers about being a good example.

The checklist includes a manager section and an employee section. The manager section reminds the manager to be explicit about making it clear that this is an important discussion, and to ensure that there is sufficient time to be candid. It reminds the manager to review the background material on both why a good work-life balance is important and how to be supportive. It suggests that the manager makes sure he thinks back through the past history of conversations and situations where this has been important, and encourages the manager to draw on his own mentoring and other resources in preparing for the discussion. The checklist reminds the manager to think ahead about what it might mean if the employee really is serious about reducing their workload. What can be dropped? What will need to be made up elsewhere, and how will that happen? What will need to change? The checklist sets the stage by having managers be ready to project openness, clarity, and their position on the topic, and the context. The goal is to find something actionable that both the manager and the employee can agree on, with a clear understanding of implications, time lines, and metrics.

For employees, the checklist also reminds them to prepare for the meeting with the materials provided, advice from their mentors, and other information available. It makes it clear that they need to be drivers, but they also need to be aware of potential implications and be ready to accept them. They should talk to friends, family, and colleagues, and think through questions and bring well-proposed solutions. They should also think through the implications for potential actions, time lines, and metrics. They are reminded to be open, and how to engage in this sensitive topic with their manager.

The script sets up an assessment stage where employees are encouraged to figure out where they are on the "I am satisfied with the balance" to the "I want to change something" dimension. It encourages them to be explicit about their personal life priorities around physical health and mental health; their spiritual, self-realization, and values goals; their family and social goals; and their career aspirations. It also encourages thinking about the relative importance of each. People need to be realistic. They may need to understand it is going to be hard to be rated as the very best in the team if they are choosing to only work part time, but that the right balance point is theirs to determine.

The second step is for the employee to explore with the manager who or what is inhibiting the right work-life balance. Those challenges could come from work, family, friends, personal style, health, or other sources. The script also suggests thinking more deeply about personal drivers (e.g., desire to please, perfectionism, fear of authority, etc.). Then it goes on to suggest they can also think about where they have support in achieving the right balance. With this information, the encouragement is to brainstorm specific personal steps that the employee can take that would help achieve a better balance.

For those steps, the two of you can discuss what is needed and who would provide it. Talk about how to harness the support structure to implement the ideas, and about likely outcomes and implications (and as with most things in life, there are probably pros and cons). Out of that discussion you can identify the most promising steps. The final step is to formalize an agreement about which actions will be taken and by whom with milestones and clear accountabilities to know when they were accomplished and (as with any good user experience activity) an evaluation of whether the desired result was achieved, and if not why not. This agreement is typically not an "official record," but rather a working agreement between you and the employee; although both of you could decide that some activities are represented in formal objectives.

A section on discussion tips consists of tips that are usual in the UX field, but that are probably worth noting as a reminder. There are suggestions about active listening, and the attributes the discussion should have (honesty, openness, action and solution oriented, clarity, staying focused, etc.). It encourages thinking through pros and cons honestly and candidly, and to be explicit about the feelings that typically float around the various situations that lead to the discussion. The discussion tips document suggests open-ended questions and thinking about the future to get the context out, and then more precision questioning and closed-ended questions to bring the discussion to concrete action. There is clearly a sense that the employee should leave feeling like he owns the action plan, that it came from him and that he believes it will achieve his goals. I would encourage that there should also be a sense of balancing the personal and strategic goals and tactical responsibilities of the team. It is about trying to get at the optimal match that the UX manager is after to put together the most creative and impactful environment. Impact, as we know, is not so much about working more hours; it is about working on the right problems and bringing the solutions that no one else can produce in a way that generates big value for users and the business.

HINTS FROM EXPERIENCED MANAGERS

Relax and give things some time; wisdom doesn't come overnight. Build hypotheses, then test them using metrics and by asking for others' views. Be careful when tracking things; sometimes there's more volatility than you'd like, or the data will be inconclusive — but don't let that stop you from trying.

David Bishop, Director, Human Sciences Group and Senior Interaction Designer, MAYA Design, Inc., Pittsburgh, PA

LEVERAGING MORALE EVENTS (FUN WITH A PURPOSE)

Michael Wiklund (1994), in his book *Usability in Practice: How Companies Develop User-Friendly Products*, does an excellent job of describing one of the key challenges managers face.

> . . . there are ever-present threats to our good time. The fun drains away rapidly when usability specialists have to fight for respect, opportunity, and resources to do the job their employers hired them to do. Many usability specialists complain about the incessant need to sell usability, as if one were peddling snake oil. They also get frustrated when their role on a design effort is reduced to polishing up nearly finished designs, rather than getting involved earlier on when major user interface decisions are made. Also many usability groups seem chronically understaffed and underfunded, which makes everything more of a struggle. Hence usability specialists end up performing triage on the product line — helping the most needy products that are likely to make it to market, rather than aspiring to design excellence across the board. (p. 19)

Part of identity is just shared experiences, especially shared experiences that are unique to the team. These might be formal morale events such as the gourmet cooking class illustrated in Figure 7.3, or they might be more casual shared experiences. When I started with Sapient in Denver, they had just moved into a new space in the LoDo area. The space was open with large rooms, lots of whiteboards, and long walls of windows looking out on either the Rockies or the city. It also had an incredible deck area off to one side, cleverly wired at the time with ethernet and power so you could work outside. The space was enlivened by the game room, which got regular use, late night parties when projects were running long, regular BBQs on the deck, and other events. The social times were part of what bonded us as an office, and that bonding in turn was behind the effective operation of teams working out of the office. When people got together for morning stand-up scrum meetings and looked each other in the eye to talk about who was doing what, whether it would be delivered on time, dependencies, and other project-related topics, that conversation built on a history of personal relationship and friendship.

For each team I have managed we found time to get together for lunches and occasional social activities. At one point in Chicago, for example, I held a beer and sausage tasting party at my house that brings back fond memories (and we did not forget the mustard tasting either). I am sensitive to the fact that some people are reluctant to invest non-work time in work relationships (and that may be part of how they maintain a work-life balance), so I avoid too much outside activity that might be interpreted as mandatory. But new-hire lunches, birthday lunches and celebrations, farewell lunches, and so on all provide a calorie-based mechanism for helping the team to bond and develop identity. There is nothing like breaking bread together to support a relationship. Sometimes people pay for themselves, and sometimes I have budget for the group that I can use. Who pays does not seem to matter, especially when the group already has good morale. (If the team is bitter about

FIGURE 7.3

A gourmet morale event.

something the company is doing, making them pay for themselves for a "mandatory" lunch could feel like rubbing salt in a wound and the conversation might not go in the direction intended.)

It struck me a few months ago as we were sitting in a grill restaurant in Issaquah, WA, how important this is. Jak's is one of those grill and brew houses that remind me of my college days. It has lots of dark wood, oversized tables and benches, and forgettable art on the walls. Some people ordered iced tea and some beer. Most ordered some sort of gigantic meat sandwich dripping in BBQ sauce, but the vegetarians were able to find pasta and salads. Over the course of the lunch, conversation let us find out more about each other, our hobbies, and our lives. We talked about interesting books one or the other of us had read, and learned more about how each of us thinks. We were able to get a deeper appreciation of the diversity of the team, a team from a variety of countries, from a variety of life experiences, and from a variety of user experience backgrounds. There was some natural conversation about things going on with projects and in the company. The nice thing was that it could be light and candid, and we could work through some of the thoughts and feelings people were having about the work. While it was specifically a time where we did not want to dwell on work topics, I could insert a few light issues into the conversation here and there that I thought were worth fitting into that sharing discussion.

In addition to these ongoing casual gathering opportunities, in most companies I have worked at there have also been official "morale events." Many teams use these events purely for fun and that is okay. It can be worth it to get away occasionally, and again, there is nothing wrong with having shared enjoyable experiences. My teams have certainly had some of those events. At US West Advanced Technologies we went to Dave and Busters, a kind of arcade for grownups. I paid for food and beer (there is clearly a theme here) and tokens. We all ran around in various combinations competing on the games. The arcade had a virtual reality flight simulator that was wonderful. For each game, you received tickets that could be traded in for cheap prizes. What we did was combine all of our tickets and we picked out a giant stuffed rabbit as the team prize. The rabbit became a team mascot; a mascot can be one of those objects that contributes to identity.

There have also been morale events that we have held that taught something, stimulated ideas, or reinforced a user experience principle. In Chicago we all went out to a firing range. In case you are wondering, we already had good morale at this point. Part of what was interesting was to see how much fun some members of the team had who had never even thought of using a gun. What was really fascinating for everyone was when we tossed marshmallows into the pond and tried to shoot them. It was a very visible example of the importance of feedback in becoming more accurate in a targeting task. When you eventually hit one, they jump 10 feet in the air emerging from the splash. I should point out that some HR departments might frown on the safety issues associated with a team building activity like this. Also in Chicago, we went down to a new virtual reality-based gaming center. We played, which was fun, but we also had a chance to experience the technology and what could be done with it. We were starting to explore interactive television at the time and it led to lots of brainstorming around entertainment possibilities in the new digital environment. It also eventually led to the design of a project we installed in the Chicago Museum of Science and Industry. We managed to get time with the head of the company and had a great conversation about potential projects we could work on together.

The best morale events have been those that intentionally pulled the team together in unique ways, and that were also fun and rewarding. I mentioned earlier that Dick Notebaert was brought in as a change agent at Ameritech. One of the steps he took was that he looked at all of the purely entertainment-oriented morale events taking place across the company and concluded that all money being spent on those events could achieve the same goals but with more return. He argued that what people needed was to get closer to the users of their services, and that the brand should be more about projecting that Ameritech cares. He mandated that every team have two morale activities a year, and that each of those activities consist of an activity working with a non-profit. I remember tutoring kids at an inner-city school, and handing out groceries at a food kitchen in Michigan. Dick arranged for a database to be created with potential activities throughout the region that any team could access and materials were put together around the activity to help get the most value out of it. We gathered and talked through the lessons that we hoped to learn and the experiences we wanted to have during the event, we met with the non-profit contacts who set up the goals, did the event, and then finished off with a debriefing and casual time to explore what happened during the activity.

My favorite projects were those with Habitat for Humanity. At these projects there was a chance to talk with the users — the people who were going to live in the houses — because they were participating as part of the crew. You knew you were doing something good, and for many of us that is why we got into the user experience area in the first place. We were building something to a design. We were, in essence, the developers putting together a user experience. Sometimes we were undoing what previous crews had done badly and redoing it. That is not too different from fixing bugs, and like bugs, the more that had been done before the problem was discovered the more effort it took to fix the problem. Many learned new skills, but we also saw people in new ways as the context changed.

I recall one house where our vice president, who was an engineer, and a few general managers were supposed to put siding on a house. They were measuring and leveling and measuring and leveling, trying to get each piece of siding perfect. They covered about two or three rows as they worked on their part of the house, while the site supervisor did the wall on the other side of the house. There was a sense that sometimes good enough is good enough. Different team members also had a chance to step into new roles. I had a great user experience person working for me named David. He was normally pretty quiet and mostly led through his tremendous competence. At one point in his life, he had built his own house. In the Habitat for Humanity project he was clearly the lead as he worked with the site manager and directed us here and there on what we should do. It changed everyone's mental model about David, and expanded our appreciation of each other and our various hidden talents; people directly experienced that each of us has many competencies that potentially can be mined in different situations.

HINTS FROM EXPERIENCED MANAGERS

Listen. The very best manager I ever had never directly offered me a word of advice on the project from hell. I would spend my one-on-ones explaining the difficulties I was having, she would listen and understand, then ask "what would you like me to do about this?" (often offering to intervene). I would almost immediately propose my own solutions. Listen more, act only when asked.

Susan Boyce, Principal UX Lead, Microsoft, Mountain View, CA

These really apply to any field: your team is only as strong as your weakest link. If you have a poor performer, take care of it (training, firing, re-positioning). Your team will respect you for it and their overall performance will improve. The longer you wait, the weaker you and your team are. Be passionate about growing the strengths of your people. Their success = your success.

Julie Jensen, Principal User Research Manager, Microsoft, Redmond, WA

Here in Seattle we had a very different morale event. You can take your team to a restaurant called Kaspars where they take you back in the kitchen and organize you into smaller teams. Each team creates a course of a gourmet meal. Everyone wears chef's clothing, and we ran around in the industrial kitchen, squeezed around each other, and shared the equipment and resources to pull the meal together. The chef moved from team to team and taught each of us a little of what we needed to know to create the course. During this event there is lots of laughter, but also lots of concentration as we taste and season and get our hands in the food. Again, it is about creating a user experience from a design (the recipes), but it is also about reusable patterns (sauces, etc.) that are used in different ways. When we were about two-thirds of the way done, we all went out into the dining room. It was a beautiful space with a view of the Olympic Mountains. Crystal and china and silver were everywhere, and there was ample wine. The sub-team that created the first course went back, suited up again, finished off their course with help from the chef; and then they served it. We all sat and ate and talked about the experience. Then the next sub-team would go back and do the same thing. The ample wine clearly greased the conversation and the sharing. Finally, the chef came out and went through the menu with us, talking about how with the basic patterns of each course, you could vary this ingredient or that ingredient and create a whole variety of experiences. Through this event another way of experiencing teamwork was demonstrated. The kitchen was a kind of dance. The resulting experience touched nearly every sense. The richness of this morale event served as a context for the way my current team framed its shared values, and how we want to operate as a team.

TAKING CARE OF YOURSELF

The person who beats the drum must also sing the song.

African Proverb

Clearly one of the most important influences on the organization's climate is the manager. This is especially true for a UX team where the leader and the team often feel out of sync with the engineering culture around them. I have found that my teams are often tuned in to what I am feeling, and to how senior management is relating to us. If my boss is largely absent from the team and they have no sense of what he or she is feeling about their work, or if my boss is either hostile or a randomizer, the team feels it and responds to it. As a manager I am often caught in between — on the one hand with a trust bond with my team that dictates that I should be as candid as I can be, but on the other hand with a responsibility as a manager doing my best to represent the company and its management chain. I have repeatedly found that building loyalty to a bad senior management team unfortunately can have a backlash effect on how I am seen as a manager; and if the senior managers really are not the best, it is clear who will take the beating if the UX team is not happy.

One of my managers, who was particularly astute and a mentor in guiding me through the organizational politics, had a piece of interesting advice. He noticed how loyal I felt about my team, and he argued there should be a limit to that loyalty. Just as I try to create an environment where each person on the team gets up in the morning and is excited about the day ahead, he argued that I should be feeling that as well. If I do not, if the prospects in the organization will not let me achieve the team vision, and if what I do achieve will not be recognized and contribute to my own growth, it may be time to move on. He argued that the team will take care of itself. Some of the best will follow, and others will move into their own new opportunities. This is even true in situations where everything is going reasonably well but the excitement of the job is no longer there. Some people start a job and are there for years and years. Some people receive the most stimulation during startup phases, others from big challenges or big problems, others from periodic new experiences, and others from implementing and optimizing. Just as with your team, it is important to know yourself.

The team definitely picks up the vibe from the manager. When you are excited about the job and the prospects for the team, when you believe in the vision and the mission, and when you are having fun and enjoy working with the team they will feel it and respond to it. At one of the management courses I attended, they strongly encouraged scheduling a regular time to just get outside of the office and think a bit. They had us practice taking daily time to check in on ourselves, to explore what is and is not going well, and to sort the chaos into more concrete steps to address making things better both personally as well as for the team and the work program. The course encouraged thinking about what is happening right now, what you are doing, what you are feeling, and what you have been thinking about. They suggested working through what you are trying to achieve and what you may be doing that is getting in the way of achieving your goal. They then encouraged brainstorming alternatives and thinking about what you might change, and what you should keep doing or what you should do more.

I found over the years that having a personal mentor or mentors can have a similar function. Early in my career I looked for people who struck me as being particularly successful in areas of the business where I wanted to grow, and I asked them if they would be willing to serve as mentors. Even now, it is clear that there are many smart people out there with life experiences that I will never have. I have been fortunate to have several people I consider both friends and mentors. I always feel privileged to get together with them periodically to pick their brains on whatever issue it is that I am working through.

I have been lucky on several of my teams to have key people on the team with high emotional IQs who are especially attuned to my state. They will leave a card or a note or a book or something else often at a time when I am stressed. When I get something like that it is a wake-up call. Not too surprisingly, when I find myself in that situation I often realize that I have not taken time off for a while. The other day, for example, I suddenly discovered I was only half way through the year and had somehow accumulated an entire month of vacation time. No wonder stress was building. I know I need to give myself the same advice I give my team, take time off. If I am not taking time off and if I am sending e-mails in the middle of the night and all weekend, the team will feel that they need to do it as well. This makes it even harder to get them to the work-life balance that makes them the most creative and productive.

For myself, there are other things that add spice to the job and that make it more interesting. I enjoy my own research and working on tough problems. I like to get in the flow of inventing something new. Professional activity provides a chance for stimulation, for growth, and for networking. I personally enjoy teaching as well and working with students on research and sharing my experiences with research, design, and management.

Hal Hendrick (2010), a luminary in the human factors and ergonomics area, has recently published *It All Begins with Self: How to Become a More Effective and Happier You!* based on a course that he has taught over the last 19 years. His book covers several important areas for growing as a leader, drawing in part on his own experience in the user experience field. He addresses becoming more self-aware, improving communication and influencing others, reducing your stress, moving toward conceptual maturity, and leadership.

The lesson is make sure to take care of yourself. If you are doing your job, taking time off will not hurt the team; in fact it will give members of your team a chance to grow their own leadership skills. Take a break and keep your own work-life balance in check, and model the right behaviors for your team. Find the things that energize you and make sure they are present in your job. Check in on yourself periodically to make sure you are not falling into a rut, but are taking risks and staying in your own zone of optimal development.

Improving as a Manager

No one knows everything. There is always something to learn. Early in my career as a manager I began running my own 360 process to see how I was being perceived by those around me and to identify areas where I should improve. When I was at Ameritech, they actually had a version of this process. The Ameritech questionnaire asked "What is the person doing that is working well? What should the person do more of? What should the person do less of?" I typically add "What other feedback would you like to provide to the person?" when I run this kind of feedback. I either try to find a neutral tool with which people can provide the feedback, or I find an administrative assistant or someone who is willing to accept the input and make it anonymous. I have found over my career that while there are common growth areas I have had to work at across my entire career, there are others that come and go as I find myself in different contexts with different challenges. Alas, I rarely find myself clicking on every cylinder at once. As I concentrate on one set of problems, some skills just simply get neglected. Ongoing feedback is a great way to bring them back up to par.

The Adaptive Path workshop on management topics in 2008 (Adaptive Path, 2008) nicely summarized principles that I find are important both to receive good feedback and to get people to invest in you as a leader (knowing that their commitment, their investment, will pay returns to them over time). The key principles include:

- Be clear about your goal in getting feedback; I would add that you value it and embrace it as a gift.
- Show that you are listening to the feedback, and again, that you want to understand it (not explain it away).
- Make yourself accountable by publically committing to take action and being concrete about the actions you are taking.
- Track your performance and provide feedback on progress back to the team.

Besides improving yourself, you are modeling what you want others to do. If you live what you ask of others, career coaching and performance feedback become much easier.

The Adaptive Path workshop also reinforced the value of mentors. They can help in brainstorming effective ways to grow your skills. Team members can help as well. If you have people on your team who are mature and trusted they can be powerful not only in giving you candid feedback in how you are showing up in these areas, but they can also be independent voices to the team and tell them that you are working at being a better manager.

Rosenberg (2007), in his introduction to the *Interactions* special business issue, noted that as the appreciation for user experience in companies has grown over the recent decade, opportunities for user experience managers to move up the organizational structure have also increased. He said he knows of at least a dozen UX VP positions, with several at the senior vice president level. When I started my career such a role was virtually unheard of. However, in the last year I have had headhunters calling every couple of months with positions at this level. If only there was one in the city where my family wanted to live … well, that is another story and fits in the work-life balance discussion. Rosenberg noted that the trend mirrors the growth of the design discipline as it moved from a largely consultancy-based practice to a well-defined, corporate function during the 1970s and 1980s. A key to personal growth, however, is the development of a new range of skills. He argued that to move up into these levels, people need to have a general business background. This kind of background is not typically taught in the behavioral science, human-computer interaction, and design programs many of us have come through. It needs to be acquired independently.

The self-improvement that comes from professional activity that makes sense for members of your team also makes sense for you as a manager. This is especially important when you are at a company where there is no large user experience community where you can find and learn from colleagues and peers. Society activities such as conferences become the place to meet other managers and share experiences, problems, and solutions. Stay up to date on the state of the art in UX design and research, and continue to grow your understanding of the skills of your team and your ability to exercise some of those skills. Conferences provide an efficient way to do this.

Another source of growth that many managers have been taking advantage of is the Design Management Institute (DMI). DMI has a series of seminars and webinars designed to support design managers and managers who are concerned with design. There is training on managing a creative staff, learning to lead and how to articulate the value of design, how to increase innovation, integrating design and technology, brand topics, and more. Books and formal training are another way to update your skills but demand more time. Taking on responsibilities that let you grow and practice your UX skills also helps you grow. Growing your own skills will help you manage more effectively, and will earn the respect of your team and can increase their loyalty. It is yet another form of modeling for your team.

7.1 PERFORMANCE REVIEWS

By Barry L. Lively, Manager of the User Interface Design Group (retired), Lucent Technologies Consumer Products

Performance/salary review has its own unique problems and I don't know how to solve them. Someone new to management wasn't considered to be a real manager until they had been through this at least once. It is a kind of initiation ceremony. We tried many different methods but the most common involved the managers in the departments under one director getting together and rank ordering everyone in their groups at the MTS (or other) level. I present my candidate, you present yours, and other managers present theirs. Questions are asked and then all the managers vote. Hardware designers were being compared with software people, physical designers, human factors people, and whoever else was at the MTS level. The heart of the problem was the question: How does this hardware designer's contribution compare with the contribution of this other hardware designer from another group, a software designer, and a human factors engineer? You can see the problem. The human factors contribution tends to be abstract in the sense that you can't measure it in dB, amount of code, or sophistication of the circuitry. In fact, the better human factors contribution might come at the expense of more code or more circuitry. And when you win a position for one of your people in the standings, don't count on getting the next position too. One year I kept track of the success of a manager getting slots that were one above the other (e.g., slots 23 and 24), two removed (slots 23 and 25), three removed (slots 23 and 26), etc. The probability of getting two slots improved the farther apart they were in the rankings. The likelihood of getting adjacent slots was almost zero. Salary increases were then determined largely on the basis of ranking and years of experience. Our group did pretty well and as I said we tried many methods, but I still don't know how to do performance/salary review.

7.2 RALLYING THE TROOPS

By Barry L. Lively, Manager of the User Interface Design Group (retired), Lucent Technologies Consumer Products

"Once more unto the breach, dear friends, once more," or rallying the troops.

Let's face it. Sometimes, as a manager, you are going to be standing between the dog and the fireplug. You will have to deliver unwelcome news. Upper management has a penchant for not understanding problems at your level and your job will be pretty unpalatable sometimes because you have to deliver upper management's message. This of course is not limited to the first level of management. An executive director (next step up from director) used to come to Indianapolis from time to time and go drinking with people he had worked with over the years. He would moan and complain that nobody ever told him anything, he had too much to do, etc. In other words he sang the same song the rest of us sing from time to time. All I can say is this is one of those times when the reputation you have with your people will have a lot to do with how they ultimately accept bad news from you. The best way I found to handle this was to be as honest as possible with your people all the time. Note the balancing act between "as honest as possible" and "all the time." We can't always say everything we know. A great example of the kind of message that creates great dissatisfaction is "we have to work smarter with fewer resources." The response to that could well be "We've done that six times in the last three years, you want more?" There is the time to deliver the message and there is the time to work on implementing the response. They are often separated by hours or days but seldom do we have the luxury to take weeks. This is another one of those opportunities to be creative. If you have nurtured a creative environment and your people trust you, you stand a chance at coming up with a good response to unwelcome news.

7.3 UX TEAM LUNCHES: CREATING TEAM TRADITIONS

By Lillian E. Svec, Program Coordinator and Instructor, Web Design Program, UCSC Extension in Silicon Valley, Santa Clara, CA

The genesis of a workgroup ritual presented itself my first week at Walmart.com in Brisbane, California, just south of San Francisco. I was hired as the first permanent Director of User Experience. Peter Merholz of Adaptive Path had been consulting as the acting director. He and three or four members of the fledgling User Experience team took me out for lunch to welcome me to the company. We went to a Burmese restaurant. It was an exotic choice for me, given I had never even seen a Burmese restaurant before. Once there, we sat at around a Chinese restaurant-style table with a lazy Susan turntable in the middle. Then, the group went into action. There were particular dishes they always got and shared. One person ran through the choices, someone checked in with me to make sure I was OK with their selections before placing the order. Then we shared a delicious meal.

I was charged with expanding the information architecture team to seven and hiring two user research leads. In time, the content strategy team also became a part of the UX group I led. Over the next several months, welcoming new members to the group was a regular occurrence. Each time someone new joined us, I invited the whole team out to our favorite lunch spot for an initiation lunch. I did the same for departures. We consciously developed a set of rules around our ritual: who was the keeper of the customary menu selections, how we tried new dishes and retired others, who calculated the tab. We had our own nicknames for some of the favorite dishes. The guest of honor got to suggest something new, then we reached agreement on whether or not it was added for future meals. It was a model of consensus decision making. I didn't have budget to treat the whole team to lunch regularly, so we made that part of the ritual. The guest-of-honor's tab was on the company, but the rest of us split the bill. After all — we joked — we worked for a company famous for its thriftiness.

We didn't usually talk shop at these lunches. I had a deck of conversation starter cards that I kept in my purse to pull out when we needed a jumpstart, but usually it wasn't necessary. The team really looked forward to these jaunts. It helped that the food was delicious and unique, but we also took pride in our ritualized way of having lunch together. UX team members used to report that when they took other people to the restaurant and tried to suggest the communal approach, they just didn't get it.

In December, after the online shipping cut-off date, when our work slowed down before the holiday, I established a special version of this UX lunch. By this time, there was a good rapport within the group. We did a white elephant gift exchange and a special round of shoptalk. With the end of the year approaching, I asked each team member to tell the group which project or initiative he or she was the most proud of from the past year and why. I was last to talk. After reporting on one of my projects, I concluded by saying that as the leader of the team, what made me the most proud was all of the above, everything *they* all had accomplished over the year.

7.4 GROWING PERFORMANCE AND CAREERS

By Robert M. Schumacher PhD, Managing Director, User Centric, Inc., Oakbrook Terrace, IL

People want to feel fulfilled in their jobs. While managers aren't the only ones responsible for making this happen, there are certain things I can do to enhance my employees' performance, and help them get where they want to go in their careers.

Part of growing performance is helping people understand the importance of what they do. Fortunately, user experience research tends to be a field where people feel very passionate about their work, know they're contributing to something that matters, and believe they're making a difference. But as with any job, it can be easy to lose sight of the bigger picture when caught up in everyday details and decisions. So every now and then, I take the opportunity to find information or work up numbers that remind employees of the impact of our projects. This information gives us a sense of the magnitude of our work. For example, once we were testing a mobile device. We looked at the number of units sold, and calculated how many times a day each user would likely use their phone. Changes we recommended impact users millions of times a day. And it's not an overstatement to say that sometimes the things we do will be life changing — in the medical field, for example. Taking the time and effort to highlight and celebrate the significance of our work can go a long way to foster job satisfaction. The result is a sense of pride whereby our consultants pour themselves into projects a little more seriously, and approach their work with renewed vigor. We work on so many different projects that it's important to help everyone understand what's at stake when we make changes or recommendations to even a single product.

Another key is making sure that I, as a manager, understand what each person on the team wants out of his or her career, now and in the future. Where do they want to be pushed? Where do they *not* want to be pushed? What skills do they want to gain? Do they want to become managers or leaders? All people have different goals and skills, and meeting face to face is the most important thing we can do to learn about them. Our organization is quite flat and makes it possible to meet twice a year with employees to discuss their performance, skills, and desires. Once we understand what someone's goals are, we may be able to adjust the business to give them the opportunities they're looking for, or find places to put them so they're stretched a bit. We aim to keep people challenged in a way that's not too much for them, but enough that they're learning, growing, and staying interested. As a consulting firm, we have the opportunity to let people work on a variety of projects, giving them the chance to see how skills and knowledge gained in one area can be transferred to another. Developing and using knowledge across varying domains helps keep us sharper, makes us think more broadly about the world in general, and prevents us from compartmentalizing what we know.

Another way we like to stretch people is by providing opportunities to attend conferences. While there, we encourage our team to see presentations about things with which they're not familiar. By doing this, we learn about new methods, about new ways of thinking and doing things, and can then bring those ideas back to what we do in traditional user research. Part of this profession is making the group smarter by what one learns. Going to conferences is an important way to make this happen. It also gives our researchers knowledge to share with our customers, and further builds their own set of abilities.

By helping employees understand the impact of their work, being attentive to their personal goals, and encouraging them to learn things outside their realm of experience, managers are much more likely to have employees who are fulfilled, and therefore more likely to be a genuine asset to the company.

Transforming the Organization

8

Software design is an art as well as a science. Designing products that meet the needs of customers requires insight, creativity, knowledge, skill, and discipline. It is a complex process that is almost always done in the context of organizations. An organization can do much to support the process and to help ensure success. By the same token, the organization can impede the design process, stifle creativity, and damn a project to the software hell of producing a product that is unfit for customer use.

Laura De Young

Laura De Young (1996), in her chapter on organizational support for software design in Winnograd's *Bringing Design to Software*, identifies what she believes are the three most important objectives in organizational support for design. One is setting and maintaining clear goals, the second is focusing on customers, and the third is empowering designers. She argues that one of the biggest challenges that a designer has in creating great design within an organization is to get everyone aligned on what they are trying to achieve. Most managers (and project managers) claim they have clear goals, but the history of failed projects shows something different. One of the major sources of project failure is scope, which changes through the development process and the lack of clarity around goals and requirements (e.g., see the Standish Group and related research on the sources of IT project failure). Focusing everyone on the same vision, clarifying what is meant through the co-creation of prototypes, and centering on a clear description of user goals and context can help. De Young points out that organization after organization claims to be focused on their customers, but the work to really design based on what customers need (as opposed to what they think they want at the moment) is hard and much rarer. We found that scenario-based design helps when those scenarios are based on a deep user understanding that comes from contextualized research. The empowerment of designers is often the most challenging. It is partly about tools and environment, but it is also about the process and the culture of the organization.

It is about getting the organization to understand that designs do not just drop out of the sky on demand, but take hard, thoughtful work, work that includes creative exploration and divergent as well as convergent thinking.

One model for how to change organizational culture through your strategy was presented in Chapter 5, Focusing the Team. Janice Rohn (2007) expressed many of the same themes. She suggested you need to start by understanding the business, culture, and stakeholders within the company, and then integrate those goals into the user experience plan. Each organization has its own formal processes (and informal processes), and user experience needs to embed its activities in those processes. You want to harness customers to serve as user experience champions. Much of what user experience needs to do is done through influencing others. Positioning the team within the organization is critical to success.

Eric Schaffer (2004), in his book on institutionalizing usability, suggested four deep changes. One is to shift the focus away from features and toward user-centered development. One is redirecting the recent tendency toward "cool" or "impressive" technology to truly usable software — software that is simple, practical, and useful. A third change is evangelizing executives and project managers to focus on the value of usability. And finally, the fourth is to follow a systematic process for institutionalizing usability and, more broadly, great user experiences. This kind of change does not happen quickly. Schaffer suggested that it could take two years before the full implementation is in place, and I have found that in many cases that can be optimistic (especially as the size of the organization to be changed grows).

A different perspective is offered by Andreas Hauser (2007). He provided several ideas about how to institutionalize the kind of collaborative process you want to create — the shared ownership of the design. Indeed he argued that only the user experience team can lead the process of institutionalizing user-centered design within a company, and that it is critical as a user experience leader to be visible and sell user-centered design within the organization. Furthermore, you not only are the mid wife of organizational transformation, but you are the nanny nurturing and supporting its growth. His hints (and a few variations) include:

- Everyone needs to work as a virtual team and share the same goals on a project.
- The process and deliverables should be clear, so people know what to expect and can take dependencies.
- There should be clear roles and responsibilities on the projects (and across organizational boundaries).
- Understand the needs of each member of the team.
- Engage them in the process (of understanding users and in design).
- Involve developers early in the process to enroll them in the user understanding. There are definite benefits of engaging Test as well since their quality control role is important to ensuring the targeted scenarios are delivered.
- Provide training and coaching for the team (see the section Training Others later in this chapter).

- Leverage use cases as mandatory product management deliverables, prioritize them, and focus the user experience work on the most critical ones. Build these off of the scenarios that capture the more contextualized user goals

In Eric Schaffer's book (2004), Janice Nall echoed several of these ideas as she described steps that she has followed to institutionalize usability within the federal government. She has presented and engaged people in testing to show the differences between usable and non-usable sites. She works to use the language of the leaders within the government. Her team has driven training through the organization and provided supplemental tools. They have built an internal panel of stakeholders and people committed to their initiative that they communicate with and through about the value of usability.

ROI

Given the adoption model that has been discussed and both the direct metrics that are optimized such as efficiency and effectiveness and the indirect metrics such as satisfaction (and perhaps brand promise, expectation, and loyalty), it would be surprising if user experience work did not have direct business value. The only question is how effectively they can be measured and how they can be expressed in a way in which audiences find compelling, and which advances your influence goals.

The list of potential areas where user experience brings value to companies is long. It is difficult if not impossible to attribute the benefits to only the work of user experience. The experience is typically a shared responsibility, although in many cases you can demonstrate through user research the specific impact of design changes if they are implemented. But as noted in the following discussion, the kinds of tactical improvements typically are not what matter most to senior management. It often makes more sense to point to the areas that would be expected to be impacted by improvements in usefulness, ease of use and lowering cost, and driving the right emotional connection; then connect the dots to how user experience activities contribute to the end goal. If you can use the kinds of arguments that typically drive many executive decisions you can pass the red-faced test and have credibility. If you have data that show a direct linkage, that is even better. Areas that have worked well in management presentations include:

- Increase revenue
- Strengthen the brand, and fulfill the delivery of the brand promise
- Improve customer or user satisfaction and loyalty
- Drive customer or user adoption
- Improve user effectiveness, user decision making, and other outcomes
- Improve user efficiency and productivity
- Improve the rate at which users obtain value

- Reduce total cost of ownership
- Reduce training costs
- Reduce support costs
- Enable integration of applications (creating experiences that are better together)
- Reduce the cost of wasted development and reduce project risk
- Reduce the costs of rework and repair
- Improve business agility
- Increase the likelihood of delivering the business value justifying the project (increase the rate of achieving ROI)
- Improve data quality
- Improve the efficiency and effectiveness of processes and user work flow
- Reduce the cost of development (through reuse and standards)
- Showcase corporate solutions
- Increase traffic to sites, the value of return visits, and the revenue per visit
- Create more partners selling on behalf of the company
- Improve the effectiveness of advertising
- Improve the quality and user value of documentation
- Reduce administrative costs

Traditional Perspective

Clare-Marie Karat and I contributed to a volume on *Cost-Justifying Usability*, by Bias and Mayhew (Karat & Lund, 2005) that is worth reading. Their book, *Cost-Justifying Usability: An Update for the Internet Age,* is an excellent summary of current thinking on the topic. In it, Deborah Mayhew and Marilyn Tremaine (2005) offer a basic framework as well as a variety of examples. In one instance they laid out a step-by-step example of how an analysis is done. They started with a usability engineering plan that identifies everything that needs to be done over the course of the project. This list varies from project to project. They also established the specific parameters for the costs and the predicted benefits based on the nature of the project. These parameters might include the expected number of end users, their loaded wages and work days, the ratio of expected early versus late bug fixes, the transactions per day, and so on. They then calculated the cost of each of the tasks in the Usability Plan. For example, they worked through the costs of creating a user profile, the cost of a contextual task analysis, the costs of defining usability goals and doing an analysis of the technical constraints and capabilities, the costs associated with performing the information architecture work and defining a conceptual model, usability testing costs, and the costs of a variety of design activities. These costs are calculated to take into account usability engineering and designer hours, developer hours, manager hours, and user hours.

On the other side of the equation, they selected the relevant benefit categories for the project. As noted earlier, there can be many categories to choose from. They are especially looking for those that can be monetized such as increased productivity, decreased errors, decreased training, and decreased late design changes. Using the specific parameters for the project identified earlier, they then predicted the value of the benefits. In their example, they used figures like a 5-second per transaction improvement in productivity, a decrease in 1 error per day, 10 hours saved in training that normally takes a week, and catching 20 changes that would have otherwise been late and costly and fixing them earlier in the development cycle. By using these data for number of users, number of transactions per day, cost of time, and so on, it is simple math to turn these figures into projected benefit. They pointed out that for some analyses you may need to draw on existing case studies or research to rough in the estimates for the benefits that will be realized.

While their example projected the potential benefit of applying usability work to a project, a similar approach can be used to estimate the benefits that were realized after the fact. These methods are not that different from the way many business plans are created, where assumptions are made such as "If an additional 10% of the current traffic to the site clicks through an ad, we'll be able to increase sales by 2%." When arguing with these kinds of numbers, it can be effective to convert the numbers into the kinds of metrics used by your organization. At several of the companies I have been at, for example, this was net present value (NPV). NPV represents the present value of the future cash flows (benefit minus cost) over some period of time, discounted by the cost of the investment. NPV uses the shareholders' expected value as a basis of comparison, and recognizes inflation in the calculation. In the companies I was in they were typically focused on a five-year investment horizon. By comparing the NPVs of different places where they could place their money, shareholders could pick the best investments. It was useful, therefore, to compare the NPV of an investment in UX versus other places where they might invest.

Rethinking the Argument

Dan Rosenberg (then vice president at Oracle) wrote a very influential article called "The Myths of Usability ROI" in 2004. His core proposition was that the way ROI has been discussed traditionally is misguided. He noted that he had never been asked in his career to defend the ROI of his work, and he argued that at the senior levels of major software companies ROI arguments are largely irrelevant. Traditional ROI arguments are at best tactical. In the body of the article he goes on to argue against what he refers to as myths (often based in implicit assumptions or failures in critical thought) such as:

- There is plenty of empirical data supporting the ROI claims for usability.
- ROI calculation from the producer's perspective is sufficient.
- ROI claims can ignore other contributing factors and overgeneralize.
- Comparisons to analogous domains are not required.
- Executives can be fooled by voodoo economics.
- Decision makers will be so impressed by usability ROI that they will not weigh it against other investments.

What executives care about, Rosenberg argued, are revenue and strategic issues, and value arguments need to be framed in those terms. He proposed a focus on customer total cost of ownership, which includes the life cycle activities of field-testing, production deployment, installation, configuration, administration, training, internal as well as external support, and other operational costs.

While some of us have been pressed at various points in our careers for ROI justifications for further investment in user experience work, I definitely agree with much of what Rosenberg argued. When pressed, it is often by lower level managers who are indeed making tactical decisions about their budgets, and are making trade-offs and want dollar-based arguments to justify user experience budget asks. Senior managers are (and should be) more interested in moving the business. It is the senior managers who seem to resonate the most with the adoption arguments I have made, the impact on customer satisfaction, the impact on total cost of ownership (as Rosenberg suggests), and similar arguments. New user experience managers, however, may find themselves being pressured for ROI arguments, which is probably part of what fuels some of the debate on this topic.

A related ask that I get is couched in positioning user experience in the same productivity context as other disciplines. Here ROI is not so much about justifying the work; it is about identifying metrics that are tied to value and demonstrating productivity improvement. At Ameritech, this was known as the golden thread. There was a corporate business model that described the way the corporation wanted to generate shareholder value and grow its business. Each part of the corporation had to create a model that described how it contributed to the corporate model, and identify the metrics that could be used to manage their area of the business. This continued all the way down to frontline management teams where each had to define the metrics that measured their team as it contributed to the organizational model, and set goals for productivity improvement around those metrics. In my current organization there is a rhythm of monthly business reviews to discuss the status of all the projects in the organization. These reviews focus on where projects are in the development cycle, bugs found and how quickly they are being closed, build metrics, and so on. Management wants UX represented in a similar manner, but delivering deliverables to committed milestones and the status of bugs found during usability testing are not treated in quite the same way as the engineering metrics, and any discussion of the quality of the experience itself feels too soft for these discussions.

A Strategy Perspective

In general, I tend to reframe the ROI justification as strategic justification, and tend to build many of my cases around the adoption model that I described in Chapter 5. My advice is that you have to be flexible and fit your arguments to the needs of your audience. ROI, in that sense, is defined from the perspective of the audience. Several of these alternative approaches were discussed as part of a UPA workshop in 2006 (later documented in a special issue of *User Experience Magazine*; see Lund, 2007).

In my presentation and in this article I described how what mattered to management at each company was different. When I was at AT&T, we performed some analyses that fit the traditional ROI approach that were not to justify usability but rather the entire company was focused on being as efficient as possible. We also were motivated by understanding what quality meant to users, and made sure we were delivering on that quality. At Ameritech, with the arrival of the new CEO, we were focused on how we fit within the larger business model for the corporation. There we were interested in the NPV argument, and also the impact of user experiences on the dimensions of ease of use, usefulness, and user satisfaction. We were trying to measure our work and discuss it in terms of delivering on the brand promise. When I was at US West Advanced Technologies, the highest value seemed to be in the intellectual property we were generating. Other places I have been focused on satisfaction, and executive compensation was in part driven by the customer satisfaction numbers. Lessons learned at these companies include:

- The ROI is in the eye of the beholder. People "get" our value when we can tie it directly to what matters to them.
- The value is less in justifying our existence than it is in positioning our work to have maximum impact for the business and the user.
- A test of whether we are focused on returning business and user value is whether it is sufficiently under control to be improved systematically over time.

At CHI 2002, Gitte Lindgaard and Nicola Millard held a workshop called The Business Value of HCI: How Can We Do Better? (Lindgaard & Millard, 2002). Lindgaard noted a story similar to the one I mentioned in the argument about sponsors and champions. In her story a successful HCI program at Australian Telstra was scrapped once a top manager, who was a friend of human factors on the board of directors, left the company, and the company decided to outsource all its software development. This was despite producing traditional ROI figures to the tune of $30M per year for the program. They pointed out that often the tangible costs of developing systems are accounted for with little attention to subsequent costs once the project is launched. Their workshop explored different ways teams have found to sell their role and value (e.g., in terms of preventing usability failures and the cost of those failures), and whether the value can be realized at the Internet speed at which many development teams are working.

In the workshop Making the Business Our Business: One Path to Value-added HCI, Lindgaard described two studies that demonstrated that focusing on what the business is looking for may result in different methodological decisions that actually return more business value. She described one classic study that applied GOMS to a Toll and Assistance Operator workstation, and compared it with an approach that decomposed Directory Assistance calls to determine where time could be reduced without increasing an operator's workload (Lindgaard, 2004). She suggested a different approach might get closer to the business value that motivated the original project. In another example, she compared a study that started out as a competitive analysis of two technologies being considered for a large warehouse with a simple time and motion approach. She concluded by arguing "by enlarging the focus to the business itself, we give ourselves and others more freedom to define problems, address them correctly, and provide novel solutions rather than merely 'doing as we are told.'"

While the numbers are great, in some ways the purpose of these kinds of arguments is not the numbers, since it is indeed rare for a real business case to be created around user experience; rather the purpose is similar to others making cases for alternative investment directions for the business. It is about influence. In some cases that requires numbers that have the same kind of weight to them as those used in the arguments (in other words, in some cases it is okay if the numbers are soft, as long as they are no softer than the other numbers), and in other cases it is more about logical argument.

A variation on the traditional perspective, but with a nod to the concerns expressed by Rosenberg, is expressed in the article I wrote for *Interactions* (Lund, 1997a). In this article I reported Ameritech's shift to a focus on its own value model and the requirement that each manager identify how their work fit within that value model. For Ameritech, it was about creating cash flow that could be used to invest in new businesses, which in turn raised the value of its stock (and that in turn contributed to the ability to raise more cash). They set a shared commitment through the management chain of continuing year over year productivity increases to reduce costs, increase profits, and drive more cash. For some areas of the business, they modeled their contribution in terms of efficiency — getting more done faster and with less resources. This is closer to the traditional ROI argument. Productivity was conceived in terms of rate of output of activities.

I explored a variety of models to find out where my UX team generated the most value and how, which included looking at these traditional productivity measures. Running more users through usability tests, running more usability tests, producing more screen designs — none of these have much of an impact in the big picture and a year over year productivity increase did not seem sustainable with this kind of model. Getting involved earlier did have an impact, especially in two areas. One way it impacted was when we uncovered new business opportunities such as major new sources of revenue or cost savings that would not otherwise have been discovered. The other way was when we were able to increase the usefulness of what was being created, which happens during the earliest stages of designing and architecting the product. I have described the fundamental adoption model that has framed our thinking, and this is how it connected with the value proposition for Ameritech. The nature of the impact was to increase the net present value of the products on which we were working. In the article I was able to tie the model of how we increased value to the price of Ameritech's stock. In other words, I could clearly state the impact of UX in the business terms that mattered to the executives. Yes, there are many other factors that influence stock, but the cash generation that we were able to influence contributed to stock price in a way that was similar to the justification for other potential investments. We were speaking the language of the business.

POSITIONING IN THE UX PROCESS MATURITY MODEL

Almost all of the problems with modern software user interface design originate from well-intentioned, intelligent and capable people focusing on the wrong things. Instead of technology and tasks, we must focus our gaze on the goals toward which users strive, even if they themselves are sometimes unaware of them.

Alan Cooper

The default process that most teams tend to use is still some variation of waterfall. User-centered design fits nicely within a waterfall model. More recently there has been more discussion of Agile methods, and many teams have been trying to figure out what user-centered design means within that Agile method and how methods need to evolve to fit. This evolution will continue, especially as new people come out of schools and bring the tools they are using to function in school (e.g., social networking applications) to their jobs. Furthermore, each team you work with is likely to have their own flavor of how they implement a particular type of process for their team, given their own needs and their unique team culture. The ideal approaches to user-centered design in waterfall and Agile processes are covered well in the literature (see Chapter 5 for a version I have used), but it is worth taking a look at the process of customizing how your team works to the organization in which you are functioning.

Virtually every process has something equivalent to the planning phase. This is normally when analysts uncover new opportunities to drive business value and where strategies are turned into tactical implications. These are the business goals of the projects. At AT&T this is when the project description is created. Once the business case is created and the project is defined, the requirements of what is going to be built need to be identified. Usually it includes business requirements, technical requirements (e.g., a preliminary view of existing architectures, systems, and capabilities that are assumed), and user requirements; the document may also organize these requirements into features. This is the description of the various needs that must be satisfied to achieve the business goals. At Bell Labs, our systems engineering team created these requirements.

The next step can be called the design stage, which is when the requirements are taken and turned into the blueprint of what is going to be built. Most of the companies I have worked at refer to the output of this phase as the specifications, and the specifications are frequently primarily owned by the project managers, architects, and developers. At Bell Labs, we would pass our requirements to the development team who would then handle the creation of specifications. A frequent point of contention is when design is included in the requirements, as opposed to being generated as part of specifications. When there are design teams embedded in each of these phases conflict is almost inevitable.

Once the blueprint is created, then the developers actually start building the project and testing what is built to make sure it meets the specifications and the requirements. Finally, there is deployment, support, and maintenance. Within the telephone companies, the code would move to the network for implementation and ongoing sales and support activities. This last phase is where the activity shifts from the developers to the operations people, with the exception of potential priority fixes that need to be made before the next product or application release. Many of the alternative development processes primarily address changes to the requirements, design, and development phases and attempt to make them more efficient, or raise the quality bar during the phases, or otherwise improve them.

Within Bell Labs, there was a user experience team within the operations organization who tended to work closely with the marketing organization as they framed proposals for new work, feeding them issues that were identified in the field. In the systems engineering organization, my team worked on more forward-looking opportunities that might not have been otherwise identified, as well as working on the creation of the requirements. There was also a user experience team within the development team, working on the detailed design, and driving design standards for the developers. Finally, there was a small user experience team in the enterprise-wide architecture team that attempted to drive overall UI guidance that we all worked within. For Bell Labs, therefore, each of us defined what we did in the context of where we fit within the process. Because each team contained designers and researchers, and each felt they personally had the best creative vision for what was being built, there were regular points of conflict between the teams. Companies that centralize UX to provide support throughout the entire process avoid this. Without centralization, defining very clear roles and responsibilities, and ensuring the manager of each team appropriately focuses their team on their area and trusts the other teams to do their jobs are critical.

A new manager starting a team is often going to have the opportunity to define how the team wants to be seen. Their role can be described in many different ways and can put the stake in the sand around the best practices they want to establish in the organization. If the organization does not already have people who have experienced UX this is a great place to be. However, in practice, the forces that motivated the building of a UX team are usually more tactical.

Often it is clear that the developers are simply not implementing usable software, which causes complaints from users. The organization knows this and brings in professional designers who might help things look nicer to be able to pick up tasks done by the developers and do them better (from a design perspective). They probably justified some of the budget as coming from the development budget, figuring that designers are just another type of developer. The organization has probably heard about usability, and know their problems are being called usability problems. They may want to hire a usability expert, and the organization assumes the researcher's role will immediately be to start identifying and prioritizing the problems so that the designers and developers can fix them. In other words, they think of the usability people much like they think about their testers and quality assurance effort. These stereotypes are what leads managers to push for production metrics analogous to those used for Development and Test so they can manage user experience in the same way.

You can remove all the bugs from the design and still have a failed product. If you want to make a big difference in the success of your products, move your team's impact upstream in the development process. You can make the biggest impact on the corporate bottom line by driving usefulness into projects by uncovering unrecognized opportunities by discovering user needs, or by leveraging a deep understanding of the users to design the greatest value into the application up front when the technical and interaction architecture and functionality are first being defined. When I tell the story of how our team should be involved throughout the process, I begin by explicitly stating my assumption that our "normal" role in a project is a beginning-to-end role, from planning through deployment. A chart we have been using that exemplifies this using a Waterfall process is shown in Figure 5.7.

This chart has been so effective in talks and posters because it is framed in a language and structure already used by the organization to describe its software development life cycle. It shows the major deliverables that project managers, developers, and testers already recognize in each phase through the process, and divides them into swim lanes based on the organizations that are accountable for them. By adding a swim lane for user experience, you can show the major linkages between UX activity and the activity of other teams. Teams often ask about what we do and what it impacts. A clear representation of how UX fits within an organization's process lends itself to a narrative that recognizes that while software can be built without a UX team, at each phase of the process UX can make it better and increase the overall chance of project success. I am able to tie the phases of the process to our vision of value driven through the adoption model, and I can show which part of the adoption model is impacted by our engagement during each phase. I can also speak to the iterative user-centered design activity through the development process, pointing to development activities and user research activities during each phase of the life cycle.

For Agile teams, I also have a process chart. In my current organization the teams are inconsistent in how they implement Agile. But I can show a general framework and then negotiate how to adapt it for an individual team. In our context we propose concepts identified from recent literature that we believe are promising. These include the idea of a special scrum team focused on UI quality through the sprints, and moving from a traditional spec to a proto-spec — a prototype that is a living representation of the best guess of the UI design. As the UI is completed, the idea is to update the relevant parts of the proto-spec. This also helps with the challenge of sprints that are too short for traditional usability testing. Rather than a cadence of usability studies through design and development focused on phases (earlier ones being more about shaping the design, and later ones focused on identifying design problems that have crept into the design), we build discount usability methods into the sprints (e.g., heuristic analyses or cognitive walkthroughs), and then schedule scenario-based usability studies periodically using whatever the current version of the proto-spec is at that point in the process.

Mark Detweiler (2007) wrote an excellent summary of the challenges of managing user-centered design within Agile projects. He pointed out that these all fit within a family of newer, presumably more nimble methods that include extreme programming, scrum, adaptive software development, and so on. In general, they are attempts to deal with the accelerated rates of change in the software marketplace and to improve predictability and control in development. Other articles have pointed out that the Agile methods have not been designed to improve the user experience, but they have been created to improve the development process and meet the needs of developers. In the teams I have been in, they tend to get adapted to whatever the teams feel they need (including hybrids like Wagile [Waterfall + Agile], and with sprints ranging from a couple of weeks to several months).

One challenge for the manager that Detweiler highlighted is that Agile projects try to repeat the various phases of a typical user-centered design process within sprints or sets of sprints, rather than across the entire development life cycle. Since Agile projects are under highly compressed timescales users are often only engaged sporadically. Development teams can be smaller (given the time compression tasks that in Waterfall are done sequentially have to be done in parallel), but the demands on the user experience people are greater since they need to be a sprint or two in advance of development while also supporting the team during the sprint. The result is that in some cases the user experience team dedicated to the Agile team has to be larger than would be required for the same feature set in a Waterfall environment. This needs to be reflected in your support estimates for an Agile process. I refer you to Detweiler's article and several more recent papers that have been given at the ACM SIGCHI CHI conference that cover challenges and tips for specific approaches to user-centered versions of Agile.

The goal is to do more than just fit into the process; the goal is to improve the process. In our case the framework used to define our role through the process becomes a tool to drive scalability through the process, and scalability is about growing design thinking across the team and raising the overall quality of the implemented designs. We are building a structure on this framework that engages everyone in user-centeredness.

To achieve satisfaction where the benefits (the usefulness) sufficiently outweigh the costs (e.g., cost of learning) to create a compelling value proposition versus alternative solutions, you need to focus on what you are building to enable users to achieve their most important goals. To do that, you need to understand the contexts in which they have achieved their goals and how they achieve them today. In other words, begin by focusing the entire team on the top user scenarios, which in turn depends on understanding specifically who the users are (in our case represented as personas). When the team buys into this concept, it is easy for them to see how your user research is critical to clarifying who the users are and identifying the relevant aspects of the context that need to be considered in defining the requirements for the solution. In parallel, design explorations that the stakeholders can see and react to create energy on the project that focuses on the user experience vision, and if the visionary explorations create a great user reaction in validation studies it creates a tremendous energy behind the project. Involving stakeholders in those validation studies, therefore, can be very powerful (assuming people like the vision).

They also understand that to come up with a value proposition that is a significant improvement over existing alternatives, a variety of designs need to be explored, prototyped, and tested. Engaging stakeholders from each of the swim lanes in this process creates a common language, a common approach that everyone agrees is the working model (even if details have yet to be worked out), and an effective scoping and scope management of the project. A new step we are implementing is to insert the collaborative prototyping activity in the requirements phase and show it as a new activity that cuts across the swim lanes.

For both Waterfall and Agile design we have focused on supporting end-to-end user scenarios to ensure the complete experience is delivered for users. We focus our core design efforts on the interaction problems associated with the most important scenarios, identify the key screens we will build out in detailed design around those scenarios, and use the scenarios in the formative usability testing. Because all the stakeholders (including UX) are part of defining the scenarios, everyone has a context for how to interpret and evaluate the designs and the user research. Everyone is bought in and excited. We then work with the project managers to create use cases that map to the scenarios and user requirements, building them out of our prototyping and usability work and the interaction design and information architecture that supports it.

When we go into the test phase we argue that we should be part of the plan that Test creates. By being part of it, we can ensure that a variety of experience issues are included that impact experience but that may be beyond traditional design (e.g., the responsiveness of the site). We also engage Test in the user profiles and contextualized scenarios, so even in areas beyond those where we traditionally focus, Test will try to channel the users through the more technical testing of the solutions. This can be particularly important when they need to be engaged to test for accessibility and internationalization. We have also taken the organization's standard bug classification scheme and enhanced it to include the comparable scenario-based experience impact. For example, one of the highest severity bugs is a system crash. Our argument is that if a majority of users cannot complete the target scenarios unassisted, that is equivalent to a system crash. In other words, success is defined from the perspective of the users and not just in terms of whether the program runs. When user experience definitions are equal to the technical definitions, then user experience should have an equal seat at the bug prioritization and management table.

Finally, when the product is shipped, we collect and organize ongoing user feedback around the scenarios. Across the entire process we have baked into the release criteria, which are ordinarily more technology focused, the kinds of scenario-based user experience controls that should help ensure that the user and the design are considered throughout the process. The scenario focused released criteria should also ensure that the experience targeted at the beginning is what comes out at the back end. Furthermore, given that we are part of the standard release criteria, it makes sense to argue that the status of the user experience performance indicators should be reflected in the reports that senior management uses to track progress throughout the project. When this is fully implemented it means that user experience is an equal player in the process and the business success of the experience comes from shared design thinking and interface ownership.

While the user experience teams (mine and the one supporting Human Resources and other internal tools) have been pioneering many of these ideas, the goal is to roll the best practices up to the organization that drives the standards across all of IT. Our two small teams, in effect, will have an indirect influence on products that impact most computer users in the world. All this is through leveraging the process to build user-centered design into the genetics of the organization.

Assessing Maturity

One way to approach organizations is to evaluate their user experience maturity. There have been a variety of approaches to modeling maturity, but one that I am particularly taken with is described by J. Earthy (Earthy, 1998; Earthy, Jones, & Bevan, 2001). It leverages ISO 12207 "Software Life Cycle Processes," the Capability Maturity Model (CMM; from Carnegie Mellon University, Software Engineering Institute), and ISO TR 15504 "Software Process Assessment" as a framework. Building from recognized standards should make it easier to have credibility with some engineers who are comfortable with these models. It also leverages ISO 13407 "Human-Centered Design Processes for Interactive Systems." The maturity model consists of two parts, the human-centered development processes (e.g., the elements included in the user-centered versions of the processes described earlier) and an assessment of where a team or project is for each of the processes (the levels).

The processes include:

- HCD.1: Ensure HCD content in systems strategy
- HCD.2: Plan and manage the human-centered design process
- HCD.3: Specify the user and organizational requirements
- HCD.4: Understand and specify the context of use
- HCD.5: Product design solutions
- HCD.6: Evaluate designs against requirements
- HCD.7: Introduce and operate the system

The levels have a long history (Humphrey, 1990), and have their roots in Deming's quality work with the Japanese after World War II. The levels familiar to CMM users are

- Level 0: Incomplete (not able to carry out process)
- Level 1: Performed (individuals carry out process)
- Level 2: Managed (quality, time, and resource requirements for process known and controlled)
- Level 3: Established (process carried out as specified by organization, resources are defined)

- Level 4: Predictable (performance of process within predicted resource and quality limits)
- Level 5: Optimizing (organization can reliably tailor process to particular requirements)

Humphrey provides several basic principles of process change (Fig. 8.1). In addition, the standard improvement process for moving development organizations through maturity levels according to Humphrey (1990) is:

1. Understand the current status of the development process.
2. Develop a vision of the desired process.
3. Establish a list of required process improvement actions in order of priority.
4. Produce a plan to accomplish the required actions.
5. Commit the resources to execute the plan.
6. Start over at step 1.

I remember in the mid-1980s being at a management workshop at Bell Labs where Joseph Juran (another quality guru and along with Deming responsible for Japan's transformation after the war) attended to observe. We were attempting to implement this process for moving through the organizational maturity model. We reviewed where we were, we brainstormed what we wanted and the required process improvements, and then started to flesh out a plan. In retrospect, the one hidden theme in the discussion was the ongoing "what is doable" that kept a constraining pressure on all the conversation. As we neared the end, proud of all we had accomplished, someone turned to Juran and asked him what he thought of

---

Six Principles of Process Change

- Major changes to the software process must start at the top. Senior management leadership is required to launch the change effort and to provide continuing resources and priority.
- Ultimately, everyone must be involved. Software engineering is a team effort, and anyone who does not participate in improvement will miss the benefits and may even inhibit progress.
- Effective change requires a goal and knowledge of the current process. To use a map, you must know where you are.
- Change is continuous. Software process improvement is not a one-shot effort; it involves continual learning and growth.
- Software process changes will not be retained without conscious effort and periodic reinforcement.
- Software process improvement requires investment. It takes planning, dedicated people, management time, and capital investment.

FIGURE 8.1

Principles of process change (Humphrey, 1990, p. 19).

what we had done. He said, "It strikes me that you are working on the useful many, rather than the vital few!" Wow! Suddenly the balloon began to collapse. But the comment was right on target. This entered my mantra collection along with the principle that Clare-Marie Karat and I kept reminding ourselves of while planning for the CHI 1998 conference, "Keep the main thing the main thing." It is all too easy to zero in on the problem solving and the details and being complete and miss the vital issues that have the largest potential for making a difference.

This applies to moving teams through a user experience maturity model as well as general quality improvements. The idea would be to work with a project team and try to persuade them to assess their own maturity, to set goals for improvement, and to track progress over time. When growing organizations, teams should be led to the conclusion that to move up to higher levels of maturity they may want to consider hiring more user experience people. In our IT user-centered culture change initiative, the argument I have been making to teams even without user experience is that if they move up their UMM (UX Maturity Model) maturity they will find the quality and success of the applications they are building will improve dramatically. The full maturity model is shown in Figure 8.2.

I realized pretty quickly, however, that the system and tools provided by Earthy were too complex for any of the teams to willingly use them. In some ways the process seemed well suited to keeping consulting firms in business doing the assessment.

Process ID	Description	Level0 Incomplete	Level1 Performed	Level2 Managed	Level3 Established	Level4 Predictable	Level5 Optimizing
HCD1	Ensure user-centered design content in systems strategy						
HCD2	Plan and manage the user-centered design process						
HCD3	Specify stakeholder and organizational requirements						
HCD4	Understand and specify the context of use						
HCD5	Produce design solutions						
HCD6	Evaluate designs against requirements						
HCD7	Introduce attend operate the system						

FIGURE 8.2

The UX maturity model.

People wanted to know a simpler number that would just give them a sense of where they were overall. Chances are the processes are likely to be highly correlated so I expected the patterns for teams would be pretty clear. Unfortunately the face validity (or perhaps the practical validity) seemed low to my target audience.

My second attempt is shown in Figure 8.3. I rethought how I was presenting the processes and organized them into categories that already fit strategic initiatives within the organization and priorities that the organization was using. Furthermore, the intent was to use the tool to help larger organizational units compare teams within divisions to ensure that priorities were being set correctly. I also changed the levels to more clearly describe a general team culture, further ensuring that it was likely that all four categories would tend to vary together. People seemed to get the idea, and this led to an effort to further fit a "Build the Right Thing" initiative into a larger Quality Maturity Model. We still have a long way to go to integrate this into an organization's thinking.

There are challenges in applying tools like these and getting traction within organizations. It may be because of the complexity of the tools and the challenge of making actionable sense out of the results, or it may be that these kinds of tools just do not fit well within real-world corporate cultures. If a project is low in maturity there is not a lot of motivation for them to highlight the fact to someone else. If they are motivated to address user experience issues, they typically just go ahead and hire UX people. The UX professionals, when they come on board, have little incentive to do this exhaustive formal assessment since the bad news can alienate the people who were good enough to bring them on and to try to make an improvement.

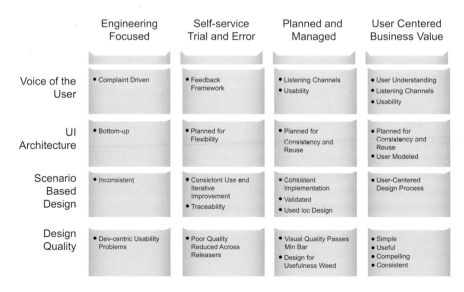

	Engineering Focused	Self-service Trial and Error	Planned and Managed	User Centered Business Value
Voice of the User	• Complaint Driven	• Feedback Framework	• Listening Channels • Usability	• User Understanding • Listening Channels • Usability
UI Architecture	• Bottom-up	• Planned for Flexibility	• Planned for Consistency and Reuse	• Planned for Consistency and Reuse • User Modeled
Scenario Based Design	• Inconsistent	• Consistent Use and Iterative Improvement • Traceability	• Consistent Implementation • Validated • Used for Design	• User-Centered Design Process
Design Quality	• Dev-centric Usability Problems	• Poor Quality Reduced Across Releasers	• Visual Quality Passes Min Bar • Design for Usefulness Weed	• Simple • Useful • Compelling • Consistent

FIGURE 8.3

An alternative maturity model.

Human Factors International recently published their own survey of maturity (Straub, Patel, Bublitz, & Broch, 2009). They built their evaluation on a set of dimensions described in Eric Schaffer's (2004) book *The Institutionalization of Usability: A Step-by-Step Guide*, and had 1,123 respondents complete the entire survey. They found that across the industry, "stable, visible, internal usability and user experience groups with executive support have become significantly more prevalent since Schaffer (2004) outlined the elements of a mature usability/user experience practice. But having a presence is not the same as having a practice." They found that common challenges included having no real executive champion, no centralized function (see centralization vs. distribution in Chapter 3), lack of strategy, and failing to leverage reusable work.

DEVELOPING THE PORTFOLIO OF WORK

Anyone can look for fashion in a boutique or history in a museum. The creative explorer looks for history in a hardware store and fashion in an airport.

Robert Wieder

A great way to think about the work on your team is to imagine it as a portfolio. For most of my teams, roughly 50 to 60% of the work is usually aimed at nearer term benefit and the immediate needs of the teams we are supporting. The value they experience is usually so great, that if that is all they received they would still be happy and feel the team's existence was justified. This work consists of the usual prototypes, usability studies, design activities, and so on that are the standard deliverables for a UX team through the development process. Another 20 to 30% or more is work that we have identified as being critical to the business and users, but that we are still evangelizing with the sponsors. By its nature, there is a little more risk, but when it hits it results in "ahas" that have a tremendous value far outweighing the effort invested. In several groups, the ethnographic work we have been able to drive to deeply understand the users has fallen into this category along with the exploratory design work. This shows what the future of an experience might be like and to stimulate discussions of the technical evolution that will be needed to support the designs. For many members of my team learning to identify these opportunities and to deliver them successfully is a key part of their career and skills growth. The remaining effort is often aimed at things that we know will be important, but the importance might not be seen for awhile. Some of the design patterns work, incubations, and support of emerging work that is likely to turn into a major source of work falls into this category.

As a manager, I am also always looking to see what the current strategic priorities of the business are. I am looking for those areas where the business value is high, and where the user experience is going to be critical to attaining that business value. I created the engagement model tool described in Chapter 3 to drive the conversation about value and prioritize resources on projects based on these ideas. The importance is assessed and then based on the assessment teams can determine whether they need full support, partial support, or just consulting support from UX. I use this thinking to also identify areas that we want to move into and projects that we want to join. Once targeted, I then apply the skills honed during my consulting days to work my way into the project.

When sitting in senior management meetings or large organizational gatherings you can listen for pointers to strategically important projects. When you hear of something promising, you should try to learn as much as you can and then track down someone within the project (or even the senior executive who first spoke about the project) to talk about the potential value that user experience can bring. You can look for pointers in corporate newsletters, in press reports, and in announcements coming through the management chain. Executive decks that get circulated are also good sources. Once you have established a network of friends and colleagues who have their ears to the senior executive doors, periodically touch base with them to talk about what is going on and potential roles. It was through a contact like this, for example, that I learned of an effort to re-envision our intranet. It was being sponsored by the CIO, and clearly was a place where user experience could play a leadership role. I volunteered to lead the visioning process, and one of my colleagues who manages the user experience team that supports the HR organization got involved in the research to support it. This was a perfect place for user experience to make a mark and provide influence across the entire company.

At Ameritech, I experimented with Delphi studies. I created a pool of experts in technology, business planning, marketing, and user experience, and had them generate a list of emerging technologies that might offer new product opportunities for the business. I then had them rate the technologies based on their potential for business impact and their readiness for being turned into product. I iterated with them by sharing the ratings with the raters, and allowed them to change their ratings. We went through iterations until the ratings stabilized. Originally the intent was to build a plan to develop our own design skills and to guide our prototyping priorities, but the CTO adopted the results to drive the technology plan for the company. Because we were working with the CTO office, additional projects that we could participate in and add to our portfolio of work opened up and we were able to expand our influence within the company.

Getting into a Project

My memories of September 11, 2001, are still vivid. I was at a Sapient training class in Cambridge, MA. The class was just about to begin when someone called us over to look at a newscast streaming on a computer screen as the planes flew into the World Trade Center. I remember the jets flying over Cambridge as I walked along the Charles adjusting to what had just happened and the feeling of being isolated from my family who were back at home in Colorado. An odd side effect was that the experience served to seal the training into my memory as well.

We were learning basic sales techniques to be more effective consultants. Those techniques made explicit things I had been doing more instinctively over the years, and have been useful when identifying a targeted project and going after it. The key idea was that there is a network of people that you need to develop to work your way into a project. They are the coach, the champion, the influencer, the decision maker, and the approver. There are variations on this list, but the language is fairly common among those in the sales area.

The coach is the person who helps you understand the context of the project, who the players are, who are playing the different roles, their needs and desires, and how to position your story to best describe how your team will enable them to be successful. The champion is someone who will work on your behalf to get in the door, the person who will send the e-mail or that you can reference to get a meeting. The influencers are the people that the decision makers listen to, and they are the ones you need to meet with and persuade with your case. The decision maker is the person who actually says yes, you can work on the project (and hopefully funds you). The approver may or may not be the decision maker, but is the final person in the chain.

These strategic projects also become showcase projects for the team. The right projects get visibility across the executive ranks and become examples of the impact that user experience can have. Often other executives will see a project and realize they want something like it, and as a result will want to engage user experience themselves. These projects become something that may get shown to customers (winning business) and at conferences (potentially winning job candidates and providing another source of recognizing good work from the existing team).

STANDARDIZATION AND REUSE

The pressures we are often under are focused on the immediate problem we are facing. We are designing for the project and we are testing prototypes to improve the design on which we are working. Each project may be treated as independent of every other project. As described earlier, the biggest levers we have to increase impact are in our choice of project and our choice of what to do for the project. If you can grow your intellectual capital across projects you may be able to increase your team's productivity over time. Monty Hammontree, a colleague who runs the Visual Studio UX program, has suggested that one way to look at the design process is that we are attempting to match design patterns with behavior patterns. In the former case, inconsistency between how users interact with applications when they have to use the applications together guarantees efficiency and effectiveness problems, and will hurt business value. It is also costly to develop and redevelop the same functionality with variations in how the users interact with it.

At both Bell Labs and Ameritech we built guidelines that we used to bring consistency across our designs so we could concentrate our design cycles on new design problems rather than those we have already solved. The standards and guidelines we created were a combination of more traditional standards and guidelines, and a universal style guide that we could apply across projects. Over the last few years there has been more and more energy around design patterns. I will not go over the concept of patterns here since there are several books available on its evolution from architecture to software and design and its application to the Web. But what we are doing in my current team is creating a full structure to drive consistency and reuse.

We started with a user interface (UI) architecture for our application set. This described the technology road map we intended to use, and the assumptions we were making about how the applications would be delivered. It also described how the UI layer connected with the middleware capability layer and the foundational data model and systems. This architecture then allowed us to embrace a structure of existing standards and guidelines, as well as software that already embodies some of these standards. Not too surprisingly, this guidelines stack and the associated APIs and SDKs build on the operating systems, leverage application platforms constructed on them (like Office), and specify the space where we will further constrain and drive consistency across the experiences.

Across the company we participate in efforts to drive more consistency to ensure this stack works together in the appropriate way. Admittedly, we all know we have a long way to go and the culture of the company impedes progress. We have created a common set of UI requirements that impact design, but are not actually designs. The approach to branding, accessibility requirements, responsiveness and performance requirements, and so on all fall into this category. We are then building a guidelines framework that serves as an index of common design guidelines and specific style guide implementations. The framework helps designers and developers to find the relevant patterns, controls, and assets and understand when to apply them. Pointers then take them to a database that contains a more detailed description of the pattern and the code that supports it as well as a code sample that developers can use. We can track downloads to measure the usefulness of the patterns and code. We also put change control around the requirements, guidelines, and code, and people can write bugs against them to drive continuous improvement in quality.

Our vision for the development environment we are trying to create is similar to the process of design used in some companies in the auto industry. There is rapid prototyping up front where virtual UI teams can grab wireframes and other design elements that make up these guidelines and patterns, and assemble them into design that can be validated and tested with users and stakeholders. Right now we do this rapid prototyping with the existing tools (e.g., PowerPoint, Visio, and Excel), and others that are emerging in the marketplace. We would like a tool to support the evolution of the prototype as the fidelity increases. Ideally this should connect to a tool that is optimized for detailed visual design and that connects with the tools used by the developers. It should be possible to produce XAML or other code used by development. The tool should be able to pull in the code samples (or just import the libraries) from the code pattern library. As the design evolves, it should be possible to annotate its evolution with the feedback obtained (e.g., from user research), and the team should be able to move through the evolution to find why the design changed at any given point. This would allow us to create a proto-spec, and ideally we would be able to automatically output redlines for inclusion on the documented specification (so the designers can work on design, rather than on text, but not require the design to be translated by a project manager, for example). Microsoft is working on tools as part of the Expression suite to support many of these capabilities. A very exciting one is called SketchFlow. It meets many of these requirements and is rapidly evolving to satisfy more. When I was at Bell Labs, my team designed and built an early prototype that embedded design best practices into an intelligent tool so that as designers and developers used the tool advice would appear at the appropriate place and adjust sketches appropriately (if desired) to fit the guidelines and standards.

External Standards

The setting of one story I have told periodically is a candid lunch with one of the managers I had at Ameritech in order to get feedback on how to personally improve and how to increase the effectiveness of my team. I was also making a pitch for more resources for research. My boss, Joel Engel, leaned across the table, looked me in the eye, and asked "Don't you guys actually *know* anything?" He is an engineer and was used to principles derived from science, and applying the principles to new engineering design problems.

There is debate among some about how much we do know in UX. I have long been involved in the UX certification effort and I believe there is a body of knowledge that, if known, helps designers and user researchers to be more effective. I have also long been involved with the development of ANSI and ISO standards and guidelines. When I was in the telecommunications area, many of those standards were under CCITT (Comité Consultatif International Téléphonique et Télégraphique). There are also standards and regulations such as those for accessibility (255, 305) and the Web (W3C). In some areas there are platform standards and guidelines that have emerged from industry best practices.

Some argue that designing within the constraints of standards and guidelines overly constrains creativity, when working with engineers the upside is that arguing from existing standards makes it clear that we really are in a discipline that shares genes with engineering. We do know things and have a scientific basis for much of what we do, and leveraging the external standards and research can help to argue persuasively for a given point of view (or as a reality check against which to test our arguments). There are times when we push into new areas or innovate in a significant way; in those cases there may be reason to violate a guideline. When we do it, we do it with our eyes open, forcing a conversation about what the underlying principles are behind the guidelines. Chances are if there is evidence in favor of an innovation, the problem with the guideline is that it was written at the wrong granularity level.

An example of how standards can be leveraged to advance the cause of user experience within the organization is the Common Industry Format (CIF) effort. Anna Wichansky (2007) described the process that was followed in the article "Working with Standards Organizations." Known by some as the CIF project and others as the Industry Usability Reporting project, this article was about trying to reach consensus on how to represent usability data. Several of us got involved in the beginning as a result of thinking about how we could transform the industry and make it more user focused. Our idea was that if we could get a major purchaser of applications like the government to demand user data on the usability of applications, large suppliers would provide it. If they provided it, they would start using the data in their sales efforts and this in turn would raise the consciousness of the public, stimulate their competitors to follow suit, and cause other purchasers to follow the lead of the government and demand the data.

The recommended standard became a formal International Organization for Standardization (ISO) standard (ISO/IEC 25062:2006), and spawned a follow-up effort to define an approach to the requirements tested and reported within the standard. Researchers have used the standard as a way of not only reporting summative data (e.g., in a user acceptance test), but also as a structure for reporting formative data based on the scenarios and use cases we are driving through the process.

SCALING UP AND DESIGN THINKING
Training Others

The need for user experience work is often greater than the staffing for user experience can possibly support. More important, great user experiences are a collaborative effort. They are not owned only by UX people. They require the full range of design and user research skills and require project management skills. Project management can serve a role similar to that of a producer and gather the resources needed for great design and help remove barriers. Project management not only keeps the UI work on track and ensures that the implementation supports the experience, but project managers may also lend a hand with some of the tasks (e.g., defining and documenting scenarios and wire framing). A great experience requires knowledgeable developers with a specialization in user interfaces who not only take the output from design and turn it into code, but who may need to take models of designs and style guides and build out areas of the user interface that the designers have not been able to touch. They also need to be able to partner with the designers and researchers, and together they need to be able to negotiate the appropriate compromises that achieve the goals of the design and satisfy the needs of the users. They need to do this while also ensuring the design is implementable with high-quality code that is easy to maintain and extend in the future. Increasingly designers and developers need to be able to use tools that support and interface with each other. Testers also need to be able to ensure that the goals of the design are

---

HINTS FROM EXPERIENCED MANAGERS

Be open to accepting where you stand today, and working with peers to persuade them to move towards your goal.

Keith A. Butler, Affiliate Professor and Principal Research Scientist, Human Centered Design and Engineering,
University of Washington, Seattle, WA

---

delivered and the specifications are implemented correctly as well as understanding the personas and scenarios and how to reflect them in the planned test cases.

In my current environment there has been intense encouragement to not only grow skills among those who partner with user experience, but to also grow the skills of teams that do not include user experience people. This is a controversial topic as there are those who are absolutely convinced that teams should not be encouraged to feel they can design user experiences without user experience people. Many of us have been in situations where the developers or the project managers saw nothing special about design or user research, felt they understood what users need, and believed that they could create perfectly fine user interfaces. This is complicated by the fact that often the implementation and optimization orientation of many engineers is at odds with a discipline that lives in the world of generation and conceptualization. At times this attitude makes the funding tight or even nonexistent for user experience work. The feeling of some, therefore, is that not using user experience people should be discouraged.

On the other hand, another way to look at this is to agree that in some sense they are right that we do need to be careful in how growing design thinking is approached. User interfaces are being created every day without UX people. It may often be badly designed software that eventually fails, but it is being created. More often than not, however, when people learn about user experience they go from thinking they are instant experts to often becoming more humble. They discover what they do not know and begin to demand support by professional designers and researchers. Certainly when we think about the larger goals we are fighting for, it seems clear that we should be trying to grow design thinking within organizations and we should be trying to help even those without user experience support to do a better job of designing easy-to-use and useful software. Training in UX should result in better collaboration with our teams as the collaborators speak the same language. In Chapter 5, I talked about building in metrics to track the user experience. I believe we can leverage making the experiences visible to drive the feedback loop that makes it clear that more UX professional work is needed while empowering people and enabling them to do a better job with the user experiences they are creating.

It is almost certain your team will will need to drive formal and informal training for your larger organization and the teams you support. When I was at Sapient we created training in information architecture for teams across the company (under the direction of my manager, Lillian Svec), and one of my last projects there was to create a user-centered design class for Cisco. Most recently I have been inspired by the notion of training for Six Sigma quality black belt certification, and have been thinking more systematically about what an internal user experience curriculum might be like.

Eric Schaffer (2004), in his book *The Institutionalization of Usability: A Step-by-Step Guide*, distinguished knowledge training and skills training. In knowledge training people learn the what, but in skills training they acquire what they need to know to exercise the how. In a recent curriculum we put together we created a mix of courses to address both knowledge and skills training in appropriate venues and for different audiences. There were introductory courses that were designed to help teams collaborating on the user interface to work together more effectively, mid-level courses designed to provide more skills that non-user experience people could use to take on more substantive tasks, and higher level courses for those who may want to eventually move into user experience or who may be on teams where there are no user experience people at all. There were general introductory courses that educated people about the goals we were hoping to achieve, resources that were available, and a common language that all could use when talking about user experience work. There were also courses focused on design and courses specifically about user research. There were introductory courses, and courses to help people go deeper in the skills they were developing.

Your mission is actually doing great design and research, and not to be a training organization. One way to advance such a program is to focus on things you will do anyway and just open the opportunity to learn to a broader audience. You can leverage best practices and materials you are creating in the course of your work. You hopefully can leverage the resources of your training organization to develop and customize training for your needs. Another option is to leverage current video technologies to capture live training and to turn it into simple self-service training. Finally, to drive the training out more aggressively you should consider persuading senior management to build relevant topics into the objectives of the engineers working with your team on the user interfaces you are developing.

8.1 IS USABILITY ROI STILL RELEVANT? WAS IT EVER?

By Daniel Rosenberg, SVP User Experience, SAP

As recently as last month (May 2010) I was asked in an e-mail from an HCI professional I had never met before if I still believe that usability ROI calculations are a waste of time. He sent this e-mail after re-reading the infamous "7 myths of usability ROI" article I published in September 2004. He did not say why he was asking but I fear it was precipitated by some unenlightened manager above looking at a budget spreadsheet.

Well, it is 6 years since that infamous article (and the flack it generated), and I am still in management leading a global UX team of approximately 200 professionals and I still have not been asked for ROI analysis to justify the existence of my organization. Nor was I asked to present an ROI analysis to our new SAP CEO when he allocated additional budget to significantly increase the size of the global UX team over the next few years. Of course budgets needed to be prepared for the financial controller, but this is not an ROI analysis. It only measures the outflow. It was almost assumed as an act of faith that usability is a must-have for any forward-looking product strategy in today's market.

So, what has changed in 6 years and what has remained the same?

Six years ago my primary assertion was that usability in the enterprise arena was best measured by Total Cost of Ownership (TCO). Enterprise systems historically were large and had lengthy deployment cycles often with heavy training for specialists. Then came a wave of self-service enterprise applications directed at the everyday corporate employee so they could manage their own purchasing, hiring, budgeting, and travel. For these applications little training was assumed. In addition, the advent of the Internet changed people's expectations. All of a sudden, the benchmark for usability shifted from competitive enterprise software products to the consumer experience of the Web. For example, all enterprise procurement applications were suddenly judged against Amazon.com's shopping experience. However, what did not change at the same exact time was the corporate buying center of power. Regardless of who actually used the product, the decision to purchase and implement it was generally made by the IT department and, in particular, the CIO who was still focusing primarily on TCO only to find out that they were becoming out of sync with their internal user communities quality expectations.

Then another significant change started to take place around 2007. This was the advent of on-demand software vendors. One important early example was the CRM vendor SalesForce.com. Their success was quickly followed by applications in procurement and human resources from other startups. The major impact of the move to on-demand software delivery with regards to usability was that the buying power center changed. It was now possible for a single individual or a department to make a business software application purchase decision because they were free of the stranglehold of the IT department for infrastructure support.

It is clear now in 2010 that an alignment of the consumer's expectation for usability in conjunction with their ability to make autonomous corporate software procurement decisions has changed the rules of the game. It reduces the significance of the TCO metric, although not entirely. But does this change revitalize the relevance of usability ROI calculations?

I still believe the answer is "no" but now for a slightly different, but even older reason.

In February 1994, Lawrence Fisher (then the preeminent technology writer for the *New York Times*) published an article about Borland's famous spreadsheet Quattro Pro and how its extreme usability allowed it to survive a price drop from $495 to $49 a copy, which generated a very large pool of new users. Many Borland executives, including myself, were quoted in this article. As every product category matures there are only three criteria relevant to its mainstream success. These are price, reliability, and usability (experience). What has changed in the last 6 years is that the enterprise software market has finally converged with the consumer market due to the change in delivery model.

Does any consumer product company ask for usability ROI before launching a new product? Somehow I think it very unlikely that Apple performed a usability ROI analysis before funding iPad development. So, at least if you are a UX practitioner in a product-centric business the smart approach in my opinion remains to focus on great design and not the post hoc justification of UX organizational budget.

8.2 DEFINING YOUR VALUE TO THE ORGANIZATION

By Carl W. Turner, Human Factors Engineer, Railinc Corp., Cary, NC

Management perspectives on creating and building user experience departments was the subject of a panel discussion at the Human Factors and Ergonomics Society 2010 Annual Meeting in San Francisco. The five panelists shared their lessons from having created and built user experience (UX) teams within large organizations.

Ravi Adapathya of GE Healthcare spoke on the need for UX teams to create product solutions that were not only easy and satisfying to use, but were differentiated from other solutions in the market and held special meaning for customers.

Mark Hoffman of the Business Strategy Group discussed the challenge of remaining current with new technology while still delivering solutions that meet business and marketing requirements.

Arnold Lund of Microsoft posed a list of questions that aspiring managers should answer for themselves as they move into their new roles: Should the job be about being a creative director or about managing people and their assignments? What are the top three to five things I should focus on and never let slip? How do I influence senior level managers with my vision of what needs to be done to drive user-centered design?

Consultant Ronald Shapiro spoke on the new manager's need to give up the comfortable role of idea generator and lead designer, and to put one's energies into developing other people to be design leaders. This lead to a discussion, unresolved, about whether to protect people from corporate politics or to develop them by encouraging them to deal with the politics initiated by others in the company.

Leslie Tudor at SAS Institute talked about the importance of building capabilities internally, working with others, and promoting the team's work within the organization. She described an initial success in expanding the team's role by moving into idea generation and new product development.

Panel Chair Carl Turner at Railinc Corporation raised the issue of building trust in the workplace and its importance to UX managers for successfully leading teams and building partnerships.

Two topics in particular generated a great deal of discussion. The first question from the audience was, "How do you show return on investment for the time spent on UX activities?" Perhaps as a tribute to Bias and Mayhew's excellent 1994 book *Cost-justifying Usability*, practitioners tend to think of quantifying their responses to this question in dollar amounts. As several panelists pointed out, however, UX practitioners' value is not simply in the creation and evaluation of design artifacts. UX practitioners who perform user research also develop detailed knowledge of customers, their preferences, and their patterns of usage. This value is not easily and unambiguously translated into dollar amounts. A UX manager needs to understand and articulate his or her team's real value to be able to sell its value to the organization.

A second question was raised, "How do you talk to other managers?" On the one hand there is a need to educate others in the organization about UX value, concepts, and processes. That implies at least some exposure of senior business managers to the unfamiliar ideas of usability and user-centered design. At same time, UX managers need to learn the concerns and language of the business areas that the UX team serves and to be able to translate its value into others' language. Senior managers in operations, marketing, engineering, and finance have their own needs, priorities, concepts, and language for expressing them. A new UX manager must understand the business area's needs and priorities, and be able to cast the UX team's value in terms senior management will understand.

8.3 SUCCESSFUL COLLABORATION ACROSS THE ORGANIZATION

By Keith A. Butler, PhD, Affiliate Professor and Principal Research Scientist, Human Centered Design and Engineering, University of Washington, Seattle, WA

Have you ever seen a real-world problem packaged with a neat little invitation that says, "Come to the UX project," or "…database project," or "…network…?" Neither have I. Most disciplines evolved around technologies and a cluster of skills to work on them. On the other hand, most important problems I've seen are messy and require multiple disciplines to produce an effective solution for the user community who owns them. Unfortunately, the default is for disciplines to compete. She who moves fastest appears to lead. The situation has lots of implications, most of them difficult, for UX managers who must continually position their groups to contribute conspicuous value. If you don't lead, then you're vulnerable on important projects that quickly reach the point where the software design is too constrained for UX to contribute much.

Concurrent Engineering

To counteract the default I've adopted a project management method over the years that's based on Concurrent Engineering (CE) principles.[1] I'd seen CE applied with great success at Boeing to build-in "maintainability" for the highly successful 777 airliner. Before the 777 the cost of maintaining an airliner over its life was about as much as buying one. Maintenance was awkward because it was not considered until the airplane design was nearly frozen. That all changed with the 777. Maintainability was built-in — designed concurrently with the traditional disciplines, the cost of operating a 777 was drastically cheaper, and the airlines loved it and bought them by the dozens.

How does CE work in a software project? The short answer is, "Really well!" So here is one of my IT case studies to illustrate. It's one of my first for simplicity, but the principles are valid to help you lead your next project toward CE. One of the advantages of CE is that it can bring incremental benefits even if you don't achieve nirvana in the first few tries.

Employee Timekeeping System (ETS)

My personal experience trying CE on software began when Boeing introduced a new IT application for recording labor time. Federal rules required accurate labor reporting. So, every day ~160,000 employees dutifully turned in paper time cards allocating their labor hours to the various projects they'd worked on. The paper-based system was slow and expensive. When Boeing got its (then) new TCP/IP network the solution was obvious, an electronic time card called ETS. To enter your time you just went to a PC, opened the ETS application, and a window popped up with your time card. The UI looked like a simple weekly calendar. It was obviously the right solution. What could possibly go wrong?

When I tried actually using ETS I found out. The only use case with intuitive procedures was the one for making the initial entry of time on the current day. But people had to shift from job to job all the time, so the initial entry had to be changed. The procedures to edit a prior entry or navigate to earlier weeks and then change entries required arcane combinations of keys. It was a very error-prone design. The most treacherous part was that users often didn't know it when they'd failed to make a correcting edit.

A False Start

I called the manager who was responsible for Timekeeping, making sure to begin by complementing him on a valuable process improvement that could really save on costs. Then I explained that I was pretty sure it could be made even better if the UI could be modified. Much to his credit he invited me to his next staff meeting. When I got there about twenty-five people attended. They listened politely while I carefully laid out how usability engineering worked and ETS's need for it. At the end the manager thanked me for an interesting presentation, then matter-of-factly said thanks, but usability engineering was not in their near-term plans. We left the meeting on good enough terms. About six months later a lot of time-correction notices were being sent out every week. The manager, who I hadn't talked with since, called. The Help Desks were swamped; Boeing's big defense programs were refusing to adopt ETS because it would jeopardize labor audits. ETS was planning a new release. Was I still interested in helping?

Getting Organized

Our usability lab began formative testing quickly based on our best guess of the frequent or critical use cases for ETS. At the same time I found out the key leads for release 1.0 were database, application, and infrastructure architecture. Initially we met one on one. When we met I complimented their earlier work, told them what I'd heard, then asked what the next release needed to accomplish. Even though it seemed obvious, it was important to get their buy-in and have them reach their own conclusion that ETS needed an improved UI. The conversations focused more on establishing the common goal then on the technical steps to reach it. Then I requested the first meeting with the leads as a group.

None of us worked for the other or reported to the same boss. We met as peers on a virtual team. In the first meeting I just repeated what we'd all agreed on separately, but added a briefing on what the usability tests found. Basically, the UI had a number of "gotchas" — design-induced errors that disrupted key use cases. Less than half the test users successfully changed a prior entry! I suggested that a good objective would be a new ETS version that tested with a high task-completion rate by sample users. If we did that, the data accuracy problems should be corrected. As the meeting ended I tried a technique that had worked well for managing the organizing committee of the CHI'91 conference. I asked everyone to sketch the work stream of their respective team's plans for this objective and share them in a few days.

Essential Collaboration

The next meeting turned out to be the first in a weekly series that ran for five months. As each of the leads stood up and walked us through their plan, the others began seeing their own dependencies and potential conflicts. At first, people hesitated to point the conflicts out, but as the meeting wore on it became pretty routine. To deal with them we adopted another practice from CHI'91: if you can easily resolve the conflict, do it on the spot; if not, hold a one-on-one to figure it out before the close of business. We got about halfway through everyone's plans, and people really seemed to like the way it was working, so we continued the next day. By the end of the week we had a multidisciplinary plan with clear roles and responsibilities, and each lead knew their interdependencies of their work stream with the others. They included such diverse fields as usability testing, infrastructure architecture, database, UI design, application programming, and security. Cutting across them all, reliability was a major requirement because ETS had to work 24/7. All the planning took about two weeks.

Every Monday morning we held a 30-minute progress meeting. Rather than sit, we all stood to encourage brevity and focus. Afterward, I would drive over to the Timekeeping manager to summarize status and ask for any help we needed. This technique kept him involved at the right level. He felt informed and we had the latitude to work as peer collaborators.

As the project unfolded the leads got the knack of tailoring their communication: who needs to hear what and when, and how to tell it to them. The more we worked on the project the more we learned. But the great thing about this team was they knew their interdependencies and how to communicate efficiently. So, when things didn't go exactly to plan, the affected leads didn't need top-down direction: They met to decide the needed changes, let the rest know, and carried them out. The more they worked this way, the more they learned who to inform and how to tailor communications succinctly. Trust was the by-product of making commitments and keeping them. Relationships were relaxed and cordial, but very focused. We were developing confidence that we had a plan to deliver a high-quality product, and a style of working that could get there sooner than anyone imagined.

Like Welders on Submarines

When the database interface testing finished we were ready to assemble the alpha version. The question came up, "Who's going to test it?" A few weeks earlier I'd met a colleague's husband who was a welding supervisor at the Navy submarine base at New London. Among the fascinating things he told me was the tradition of submarine welders to go out on the first dive. Now there's motivation to get your job right! I told the team that if we really believed in our work on ETSweb then we should be willing to get paid through it. About 20 tech staff and managers had worked on the project over five months, and each was willing to bet their paycheck it would come out right. The alpha went smoothly enough for a month, and after minor bug fixes we were ready for beta. There were 300 users invited by random for beta and the Help Desks were notified to get ready. When the first week closed with a total of one call everyone knew we had a winner. ETSweb was launched, first adding 1000 a month, then 2000, and after 18 months virtually all ~160,000 were using it.

Benefits and Beyond

ETSweb produced an operational cost-savings that was documented at $40M for the first two years. Last summer I heard that after fifteen years they were finally planning to replace it. It was very satisfying when people said it was one of the best projects they'd ever worked on. There were some other important benefits beyond Timekeeping: It opened the door to more usable Web-based designs for many critical systems. It was the first time usability engineering was applied to a company-wide critical system at Boeing. The credibility helped establish a usability group in another division that's still going strong. CE has helped me on numerous projects since, and spawned significant research to enable it.[2]

Of course, the details of this case may not resemble yours, and they are only here to illustrate the principles:

Three Key Questions

The answers to these can help everyone converge on a vision of a new system: Whose work will it improve? Will it be technically feasible to build and support? Will the value of the new work processes be worth much more than the system's cost? You can bring some clarity to these with a fast usability test on a low-fidelity prototype. Keep them at the forefront of every important session.

Invest in Relationships

Early on, look beyond your own responsibilities to the overall project. Understand how it is supposed to work. Identify your counterparts on the project that you'll have to depend on or support. Invest in relationship building with the other disciplines. Learn what they need to know, when they need it, and how best to tell them. Ask for the same. This can be difficult if you are not hitting it off, but all the more important to keep at it. Don't avoid *the difficult conversation* about a persistent obstacle. There's a valuable, short book, *Getting to Yes: Negotiating Agreement Without Giving In,*[3] which provides powerful tools to negotiate difficult conflict by depersonalizing it. Even if another manager is peripheral, notice if she is negative, neutral, or positive. Make your case initially by focusing on your team's role and responsibilities to achieve the common goal; afterwards describe your plan.

Learn to Tolerate Ambiguity

One of the most difficult stages for collaboration is getting started. The project probably has a core team assigned, and they are being asked for a schedule of deliverables. Everyone should understand they are approximations. If you don't know more about what your project should be doing after several months you haven't been paying attention. Keep investing in relationships. They can be the one constant when things inevitably don't go as expected. When things change be the manager with a plan to make lemonade. The relationships will allow you to provide leadership to decide how to respond to unexpected challenges.

Play to Your Strengths
You are the discipline that knows how to talk to users. If you begin a point with the assertion, "Users say . . ." it can carry a lot of weight. Getting data and feedback on low-fidelity prototypes can give you the leverage to initiate leadership. More than anything, develop a vision of how the product will benefit users, how the project should unfold, and tailor your message to communicate it effectively.

[1]Swink, M.L., Sandvig, J.C., & Mabert, V.A. (1996). Customizing concurrent engineering processes: Five case studies. *Journal of Product Innovation Management,* Vol.13, Issue 3, 229–244.
[2]Butler, K.A., Zhang, J., Hunt, A.J., Huffer, B., & Muehleisen, J. (2010). Ontology models for interaction design: Case study of online support. In: *Extended Abstracts CHI 2010,* ACM.
[3]Fisher, R. & Ury, W. (1981). *Getting to Yes: Negotiating Agreement Without Giving In.* Boston: Houghton Mifflin.

8.4 DEVELOPING A PORTFOLIO OF WORK

By Robert M. Schumacher, PhD, Managing Director, User Centric, Inc., Oakbrook Terrace, IL

Comedian Steve Martin once said that if you want to become a millionaire, the secret is "First you find a million dollars." This reminds me of the conundrum faced by most small companies who are striving to develop a portfolio of work. In order to build a portfolio, you have to have work. But how do you build a portfolio without a portfolio? In many ways, this is a bootstrapping exercise to pull yourself along one step at a time until you notch enough wins to demonstrate a credible portfolio.

In working toward portfolio building, your small company needs to be a little like a blowfish; you have to seem bigger than you are without being deceptive. You need to be capable of doing things in a way that will make big companies willing to take a risk on you. There are strategies for accomplishing this. One is to give away some work, which will show your competence with minimal risk. The risk is that this may be seen as a little desperate and should be done with some care. Another approach is to do studies of your own that may be of interest to a given market, a technique we've used successfully at User Centric. We've done the research, then published the results in white papers and put them out as high visibility press releases. This draws attention, drives traffic to our Web site, and shows our knowledge and credibility to potential clients. Another method is to find opportunities to provide services to an organization (e.g., non-profits) in exchange for promotion and/or publication. Working with a high-profile organization also can link your company with other potential clients. One thing to bear in mind is that any work you show needs to have approval from the client. This is not easy, but often it's worth the effort.

Early on, you need to determine what it is you're good at, and just what service it is you're trying to sell. It can be tricky as there may be a particular kind of work you want to do or an industry you'd like to work in, but you may not have the experience. You also must understand what your market wants to buy, and be able to show your company's strengths and abilities in delivering it.

Once you land a client or two, the next step is simply to work your tail off to foster a good relationship and do excellent work on their behalf. The best marketing any company can have is its past work, so starting small and building a good reputation in the industry is key.

In user research, process is the essence of *what we do,* but *ultimately outcome is what we sell.* So while you must be able to clearly articulate to clients each step of the process and demonstrate the impact of your intervention, the most important thing is to show how your solution to a business problem resulted in more than a marginal return on investment. Any portfolio must emphasize the bottom-line impact so customers will know that what we do has value, and see very clearly that spending on user experience is worth their investment.

Evangelizing UX

COMMUNICATION PLAN

The meaning of a communication is the behavior that results.

John Gall

When the ROI discussion arises it often is not about ROI. It is really about understanding what that user experience is doing, and if the person asking the question understands how he will benefit. The answer is different for people at different levels in the organization. What the general manager needs to know is different from what the developer wants to know. The problem is not that we do not have the answers; the problem is often that we are just so busy working that we forget to actually tell people what we are doing and about its impact. The manager does a little of this as he shares individual success stories and presents the work. You can have more impact if you sit back a little and think through a communications plan and align your messaging around it.

The communications plan illustrated in Fig. 9.1 consists of several parts. It includes:

- The area you want to communicate about
- The audience you want to reach
- Your goal in reaching them and the forum you are delivering the message over
- The owner of the messaging
- The frequency of communication

When written up in more detail, you may include the messages that you want to weave through the communications as well. These may be the total cost of ownership messages, mission and vision messages, or others. The goal of this plan is partly to clarify ownership so you can make sure it is happening and does not fall through the cracks, and partly to make sure that you have explicitly thought through what

Category	Forum	Owner	Audience	Purpose	Medium	Frequency
Rhythm of the Business	1:1 w/Directs	Arnie	Directs	Status, risks/issues, asks from management, career development	Face to face	Biweekly, and as needed
	Project Coordination 1:1	Karen	Projects Overseeing	Ensure cross-project communication, coordination, budget and resource management, and so on	Face to face	Biweekly, and as appropriate
	Design Critiques	Arnie	Team (P1), and PM, Dev, Test (P2)	Improve design quality, resolve design problems, increase consistency across designs	Face to face	Weekly (as needed)
	Clinics	Sindhia	PM, Dev, and Test	Improve design quality, resolve design problems, increase consistency across designs	Face to face	Bi-weekly (as needed)
	Research Meeting	Alexander	Biz, SD, PM	Maximize impact of research, identify gaps	Face to face	Monthly
	Platform Panel	Karen	Biz, SD, PM, Dev, Test	Increase consistency across user experiences	Face to face	Semiannually to quarterly
	Status Reports (general)	Karen, All	Team, Funders	Status, blockers, asks	SmartDash, Email, Team meetings	Weekly
	Status Reports (supplement)	Karen, All	Arnie, Karen	Status, blockers, asks (confidential)	Email, Face to face	Weekly
	Platform Research Plan	Karen	Funders, UI v-team	Align expectations and support planning	Document, Email, Project sites, Team site	As appropriate
	Research Reports	Researchers	PM, Dev, and Test; SD and Biz	Engage stakeholders in user understanding; and validate and improve designs	Email, Streaming video, Live observation, Reports, and Face to face	
	Working Design Catalog	TBD	Team, PM, Dev, Test	Visibility into design direction, best practice examples	Project sites, Team site	Ongoing
	UX Scorecard (KPIs)	Arnie	Funders, RXD LT	Health of project UIs	Surveyor report	Monthly
	Status Reviews	Karen, All	Funders	Status, blockers, asks, feedback on engagement	Face to face	Quarterly
	Success Stories	TBD, All	RXD	Examples from projects demonstrating generalizable best practices	Brown bag, Newsletter items, Briefs	As appropriate
	MBRs	Arnie	RXD LT	Monthly Business Review status and blockers	Face to face	Monthly
	Deep Dives	Arnie	RB, RXD LT	Detailed status of projects and direction	Face to face	As appropriate
	Partner Satisfaction	TBD	Funders	Feedback on performance	Consensus survey	Semiannually
	Engagement Model and SLA	Arnie	Funders, Pot Funders	Clarity of roles and responsibilities	Face to face, Team site	One time with updates
	Budget Tracking	Karen	Funders, Finance Contact	Rationalize budget, actuals and planned activity	Face to face, Report	Monthly
	Project RACI	Leads	PM, Dev, and Test	Clarity of roles and responsibilities	Face to face, VSTF, Team site	Project kickoff

FIGURE 9.1

Example of a communications plan.

you want to say and its impact. Your communication plan is the intentional part of the branding you create.

GROUP BRANDING

In some ways, every contact people have with your UX team forms a kind of brand identity around the team. You are arguing that there is something unique and special about what you provide the projects you support, and the people who engage with you can have specific expectations about excellence, creativity, timeliness, or the attributes of the vision in your strategy.

A common milestone is naming your team. It may seem trivial, but it can be more important than you would expect. Your name becomes part of your branding. We are currently debating how to change our name given a new position within the organization. Do we want to identify ourselves as a user experience team supporting the entire division (the RXD User Experience team), or do we want to associate ourselves with a specific team inside the organization and signal that we are sharing their charter? A full name is pretty long, however, to put on posters and other communication. Often you will just want to use an acronym for your team, and possibly associate the acronym with a logo.

HINTS FROM EXPERIENCED MANAGERS

Translate any tasks, words, or deliverables into the language of your intended audience (business, technical, etc.), and you will be much more effective than speaking in "human factors tongues."

Luke Kowalski, Vice President, Corporate Architecture Group, Oracle

---

We have also thought about a general palette of colors and a look that can be used for our various communications. With an acronym, possibly a logo, and general stylistic elements you can create a consistent identity system. You can apply it to the various items included in your communications plan, including artifacts such as:

- PowerPoint templates
- Newsletters
- Posters
- White papers and reports
- Team social networking page
- Guidelines
- E-mail signatures
- Team Web site

The brand image you associate with your team also contributes to its identity. The logo shown in Fig. 9.2 represented my Ameritech team very effectively. It connected with the new corporate brand, and tied to the ad campaign that was

FIGURE 9.2

Ameritech UX logo.

featuring our work and the unique approach we were taking to the design and research. At many companies teams have defined logos and the identity system for their teams, and these have brought their teams together as well as represented the team to the rest of the organization. One note of caution is that the corporate branding people often try to forbid teams from creating logos and their own branding inside the company. They argue there are already too many and that it dilutes the corporate brand.

Your name, logo, and identity, and the way you use them across your various communications vehicles should convey a consistent representation of your team. Done well, they convey the vision and mission in your strategy. They can shape the design of the space in which you work, and extend your presence into the work areas frequented by the organizations you support. They inspire your team, and like product brands set the expectations of those who view your various forms of communication.

MANAGING UP

In the modern world of business, it is useless to be a creative original thinker unless you can also sell what you create. Management cannot be expected to recognize a good idea unless it is presented to them by a good salesman.

David M. Ogilvy

Jeremy Ashley (2007), in a recent article, correctly pointed out, "As user experience professionals in management roles, we inevitably need to work with the top executives within our companies." I have to admit, one of the things I am not very good at is schmoozing and politicking. One piece of advice I received from a valued boss and mentor is that I need to work harder at taking key influencers out for drinks and the occasional cigar. It probably would help if I smoked.

I am very comfortable talking with whomever I need to talk with about the importance and wonders of user experience. I developed an excellent relationship with the CEO of Ameritech (who later become the CEO of Qwest). I have talked with CEOs at several companies where I have worked, and talked user experience with people up and down the management chain. But my style is by nature and nurture to come across as more of a thoughtful and patient person. I am not one of the arm wavers and more theatrical types. I often wish I was, but I am not, so I have had to identify influence approaches that work for me.

Bloomer and Croft (1997) pointed out:

Every organization has a number of different groups that need to be convinced about usability. Each group has different concerns and needs to hear not only different messages about usability, but messages delivered in different ways. To win these groups over you need to develop carefully targeted usability messages. You need a pitch.

They argue it will be important to sell your message to senior managers, potential allies, developers, clients and users, and other internal groups. The senior managers are where you find the champion or angel that is the source of the funding for your program. Your allies are evangelists for your effort. Bloomer and Croft made an excellent suggestion that you need to identify the hot buttons for each group, and need to tailor your messages to address them. You need to help the audience understand how you will be enabling them to achieve the goals that matter to them. Knowing the usability myths that may be held by different audiences allows you to dispel them and make way for your positive messages. With an effective strategy targeting the audiences you are after, you are in a position to implement it and drive transformation. Keep the entire organization informed about your successes and engage them in the process. Also, keep demonstrating value and enroll people in driving and growing that value.

HINTS FROM EXPERIENCED MANAGERS

Promote Your Experience Designers as the Experts They Are

If you are managing a team of experience designers, you are likely to encounter business stakeholders who have very strong ideas about design and who, on occasion (or even as a rule) disagree with design decisions that your experience designer(s) have made. These stakeholders may even lobby you to override the designers' decisions in favor of their own ideas. While it is important to respect each stakeholder's point of view — he or she may have domain expertise or insights that yield legitimate (even great) design alternatives — it is also important to respect and empower your team members, especially your most experienced designers. They are familiar with your experience vision and have probably thought deeply about best practices, your design standards, the end-to-end experience and detailed design requirements in making their design decisions.

Having worked in an escalation oriented environment, I have experienced this type of lobbying many times and found it best to avoid the "executive override." Such overrides undermine the leadership capabilities of your team and encourage gratuitous escalations.

As an alternative approach, consider this. First, respectfully listen to and understand the stakeholder's point of view while firmly positioning your team member as an expert with that stakeholder. If necessary, review the situation with your team member off-line and allow him/her to craft a response. (Perhaps some changes in approach are warranted; perhaps not.) Finally, empower your team member to lead by bringing his/her recommendation back to the stakeholder with your support. This approach will help you position your experience designers as experts, it will empower them to be independent decision makers, and it will discourage gratuitous escalations.

Marilyn Salzman, User Experience Strategist, Salzman Consulting, LLC, Louisville, CO

The advice I give to my team is the advice I try to use myself. If I do not know what people are doing, I cannot evaluate it. If others do not know what you and your team are doing they cannot value it. You need to keep your boss informed about where you are heading and your experiences getting there, as well as the impact of the results or lessons learned from the failures. I can honestly say, however, that it is as hard for me as it is for my team. I am used to being pretty self-sufficient and I enjoy being given free reign. I am confident in what I am doing and the impact it will have, so mostly I put my head down and just do it. That means there are probably too many times when my management does not fully appreciate what they have until after it is gone.

My favorite type of manager is one who has let me chart the way, but who has both challenged me and has been there to help when I needed it. Managing upward with those managers has partly been to help them achieve their goals, as I achieve mine, and to help them see the relationship between the two. We have been able to have candid, open conversations and I have grown as a result. My team has reaped many rewards as a result of my boss' (and their boss') awareness of the work.

HINTS FROM EXPERIENCED MANAGERS

If your manager is not a UX person, spend time getting them invested in the field. Educate them on the importance of the user experience. Get them to help you carry the torch. If that is unlikely, try to find other influencers who will help you. You need organizational support.

Susan Boyce, Principal UX Lead, Microsoft, Mountain View, CA

The senior management that never quite gets it, or does not like what they do get, is a problem. I have had managers who are not around to learn what we have done, but who also explicitly do not want e-mail or other communication telling them what has been done. I have suspected in these cases that the problem is even if they have a vision of what they want, it is so far from the kind of value we deliver that they would rather have UX go away. This is where you really need a good mentor, someone who can help you figure out how to manage to your boss' priorities (or who can help you and your team to escape, if escape is necessary).

I suspect another approach is to try to find someone on your team who has a stronger sales personality, and to leverage them to influence your management team. Selfishly, you probably should make sure they are not the Machiavellian type, but assuming they are truly committed to your leadership and your team's goals, it may be possible to leverage them to help. I have to say I am just speculating here since I have not been able to make this approach work.

Another challenge is when your management chain changes frequently. In my most recent job I have averaged more than one manager per year, and changes above my managers have been nearly as frequent. That can be very hard both on your personal career as well as on advancing your UX agenda. You have to continually be in education mode, and be ready to adjust your tactics as needed.

Ashley (2007) wrote an interesting article called "Working with C-level Executives." He lays out five principles for dealing with senior executives, which include:

- Know thy executive. This principle is related to the strategic approach to ROI. It is about understanding what is truly important to the executives. He points out that every executive is held accountable to make a profitable product on time and within budget. It makes sense then to position your work within those motivators.
- Set expectations. I found this one very interesting, and it is one of the battles I feel I am continually fighting with executives. The idea is to ensure that the executives' expectations are realistic. Jeremy points out that increasingly executives get the general idea and are willing to fund the work. But many of us find that they see it as a "magic happens here" situation, and they can expect instant results. They do not always understand that they need to stand behind the efforts that will be needed, and be patient in seeing them fulfilled. On the other hand, the issue may be that their management is not always patient when they are trying to put their plans in place.
- Present fact-based recommendations. The third principle that Jeremy offers is based on the power of what we do. It is to make sure that the design and the recommendations presented are research based, and that they are grounded in organizational, user, and customer data.
- Be part of the team. This one is also reflected in the strategic approach to ROI. The idea is to be seen by the executive as a partner in his success. This is true for managing your immediate manager as well as senior executives. At Ameritech this was the principle that I used to sell our work into new areas as executives were coming on board and looking for innovative solutions to their goals. There is one challenge to be aware of — executives who take credit for the user experience success without sharing credit, and indeed letting the user experience people hang out to dry despite the success.
- Get it done. The final principle is to keep pushing and pushing until the job gets done. Ashley has a nice quote for this: "Working with C-level executives is not about glory and personal visibility; it's about getting the job done repeatedly over an intense product development cycle."

One way to drive influence is by selecting projects that are already strategic priorities for the business, and placing yourself in the middle of them. Another is to identify projects that represent the heart of your user experience vision and that you are confident will deliver business value, and advance those as well. A recent example is accessibility. The corporate accessibility team launched an updated set of requirements and a new corporate policy calling for all products to achieve the new requirements in a specified period of time. As we listened to their presentations, it became clear that while the designs my team was creating were accessible, many applications have not been as accessible as we want them to be. We began to evangelize the potential negative business impact of not being accessible, and through these and other efforts accessibility became one of the top three priorities for one of the vice presidents. A new standards board had been created within IT, so I proposed that we create a standard for how to more consistently implement the corporate accessibility requirements, and the standard was sponsored by this vice president. The CIO and CTO were clearly supporters of the effort. Through the process of creating the standard the UX vision and accessibility within it was exposed to senior executives throughout IT, and is becoming a case study of IT UX impact.

BOOKS TO SHARE WITH SENIOR MANAGERS

A common step in building influence with executives is sharing particularly compelling books. The books serve to educate and motivate, as well as to give you a common basis for communication. Listed here are a few of my favorite books to share with senior management:

- Buxton, B. (2007). *Sketching User Experiences: Getting the design right and the right design*. Boston, MA: Morgan Kaufmann. This is my current favorite; it speaks especially well to the early parts of the design process.
- Cooper, A. (1999). *The Inmates Are Running the Asylum: Why High Tech Products Drive Us Crazy and How to Restore the Sanity*. Indianapolis, IN: Sams.
- Diller, S., Shedroff, N., and Rhea, D. (2006). *Making Meaning: How Successful Businesses Deliver Meaningful Customer Experiences*. Berkeley, Calif.: New Riders.
- Kelley, T. (2001). *The Art of Innovation*. New York, NY: Currency and Doubleday. Kelley provides an excellent discussion of design thinking and the environment that supports it.
- Landauer, T. (1995). *The Trouble with Computers: Usefulness, Usability, and Productivity*. Cambridge, MA: MIT Press. An older, but excellent book motivating what we do.
- MacKenzie, G. (1998). *Orbiting the Giant Hairball: A Corporate Fool's Guide to Surviving with Grace*. New York, NY: Viking. This is an amusing book that speaks to creativity in the enterprise.
- Norman, D. A. (1998). *The Invisible Computer: Why Good Products Can Fail, the Personal Computer Is So Complex, and Information Appliances Are the Solution*. Cambridge, Mass.: MIT Press.
- Norman, D. A. (2002). *The Design of Everyday Things*. New York, NY: Basic Books. This is still a classic, and probably one of those books that is most often shared with managers.
- Norman, D. A. (2004). *Emotional Design: Why We Love (Or Hate) Everyday Things*. New York, NY: Basic Books. This speaks to an area that isn't often addressed in design.

- Shneiderman, B. (2002). *Leonardo's Laptop: Human Needs and the New Computing Technologies*. Cambridge, Mass.: MIT Press.
- Tufte, E. R. (2004). *The Visual Display of Quantitative Information*. Cheshire, Conn.: Graphics Press.
- Tufte, E. R. (2006). *Beautiful Evidence*. Cheshire, Conn.: Graphics Press.
- Tufte, E. R. (2006). *Envisioning Information*. Cheshire, Conn.: Graphics Press. Tufte is one of those who manage to communicate well to a broad range of people.

CORPORATE COMMUNITY BUILDING

When I started my career at AT&T Bell Laboratories we had several hundred people in the UX community across the company. While there was some contact between teams when there were shared interests (e.g., I remember my first meetings with Mary Carol Day were over her research in LCD coding when I was interested in a similar application for voice and data indicators), often people just worked in their own silos. There was a behavioral sciences organizing committee that attempted to work on cross-organizational interests. The most common one was to drive a periodic internal conference — Behavioral Sciences Days — that brought the community together to share ideas and to network. But it also was a forum where we could collaborate on specific issues that transcended any individual team. One issue was the fact that salaries for people in the behavioral sciences area were significantly lower on the average than for engineers of similar levels of experience and training. As a result of the efforts of a couple of key people, an excellent survey pulling together all the data, and an executive or two willing to listen, we were able to move salaries to be more comparable between user experience people and the rest of engineering.

At various companies I have been at we have had user experience leadership teams with many of the most senior user experience people across the companies and representation from each of the key user experience areas. Such teams work on things like the career ladder for the discipline, growing the future leadership within the discipline, and overall strategy while also sponsoring internal conferences and events, reviewing areas of common interest like the lab infrastructure, and other initiatives.

In general, user experience is often culturally quite different from the more dominant disciplines in many companies (certainly within technology companies). There are definite advantages in gathering user experience people into a community for the stimulation, networking, and mutual support it brings. Sharing as professionals contributes to a sense of mutual support and growth. While you may not have the budget to directly do many things, just working together enables you to become a voice to be reckoned with and a voice that can accomplish things that will advance user experience for the benefit of your customers, your business, and the community itself. Working together can create an atmosphere that lets each of your teams be more successful in implementing its strategy. Plus, it is often an excellent excuse to get a bunch of people together, drink beer, and talk design and user research.

9.1 MANAGING UP: IT'S ABOUT SPEAKING THEIR LANGUAGE AND TAKING THEIR PERSPECTIVE

By Nelson Soken, PhD, Sr. Program Manager, Medtronic, Inc., Mounds View, MN

You have been assigned the responsibility by a senior vice president to accelerate the number of offerings within your company. Specifically, your task is to create the user experience strategy. You have been given some freedom in how the strategy is developed and executed. What an opportunity! After the initial excitement and exhilaration, reality sets in and the challenges loom large as you start to create your plan.

What becomes evident fairly quickly is that the details of the plan are not the primary challenge. You know what needs to happen from a user experience standpoint. The biggest challenge is communicating your strategy to the key stakeholders in a way that resonates and "sticks" with them. Garnering strong and ongoing support is critical to success. Are you up for the challenge?

Merriam-Webster defines influence as "the act or power of producing an effect without apparent exertion of force or direct exercise of command" (www.merriam-webster.com). The concept of influence is critical for those involved in strategy and management of user experience organizations and initiatives, because it is typically the primary and predominant mode of decision making. Very rarely does the user experience manager have direct and complete control over decision making.

It's All About Perspective-Taking

One of the first things to recognize if we are to influence executives is that we need to shift from a self-centered perspective to one that takes into account the perspective of others. Jean Piaget (1970), a child psychologist, described the phenomenon in the preschool years called egocentrism, which is the tendency to judge everything from one's own perspective because of an inability to see another person's point of view. It's all about *my* thoughts, *my* beliefs, *my* feelings, and *my* needs and desires. In fact, the confirmation bias is people's tendency to perceive information that supports what I believe and dismiss, ignore, and/or distort information that does not fit with my beliefs. Well, guess what, I would argue that these biases are alive and well in the workplace, don't you think?

Beyond our individual bias, we create group viewpoints that can work at cross-purposes. What does marketing think? What does engineering think? What does management think? It's not unlike John Godfrey Saxe's poem, *The Blind Men and the Elephant*, in which six blind men touch different parts of an elephant and come to different conclusions about the characteristics of an elephant. Everyone is looking at the problem from their functional perspective and assessing the situation. In order to successfully sell a user experience strategy, the user experience manager needs to *herd the cats* and get the stakeholders to realize that they are blind to the other parts of the elephant, or recognize that they need each other to truly understand and create a superior user experience. Keep the eye on the prize or the vision and don't get derailed right away by the loudest voice or the person that seems to be the most important or powerful. Make sure the cats are herded and keep the goal in mind. Tear down the silos and turn barriers into opportunities!

Piaget (1970) described a concept called *decent ring*, which is the transition from being self-centered to considering other points of view. Successful influence management requires the user experience leader to create a shared vision of what constitutes a superior user experience for the company.

Success requires user experience managers to deliberately and skillfully manage perspectives. Rather than focusing on a "my way or the highway" and "what don't they get" attitude that dismisses other people's viewpoints, they need to shift to putting themselves in the shoes of others and asking themselves "why do the stakeholders think the way they do and what do I need to provide for them to see my point of view?" Are you ready to see the world through others' eyes and speak their language?

What Do I Need to Do to Succeed?

Roger Martin (2009), in his book *The Design of Business: Why Design Thinking is the Next Competitive Advantage*, represented the executive stakeholder influence challenge for user experience managers.

Key takeaways:

- Turn your attention to learning about your own "customer environment"
- Learn the language and mind-set of management
- Obtain and maintain momentum and commitment to the strategy

Ultimately, success in user experience is a balancing act and requires us to balance between executing on today's issues and to seek out future opportunities.

Sidebar References

Piaget, J. (1970). Piaget's theory. In P. H. Mussen (Ed.), *Carmichael's manual of child psychology*. New York: Wiley.

Martin, R. (2009). *The design of business: Why design thinking is the next competitive advantage*. Boston: Harvard Business Press.

Conclusion

10

> While you are preparing to go on a journey, you own the journey, but after you have started the journey owns you.
>
> **Chinese Proverb**

LEADERSHIP

> Perhaps those who are best suited to power are those who have never sought it. Those who, like you, have leadership thrust upon them, and take up the mantle because they must, and find to their own surprise that they wear it well.
>
> **J. K. Rowling**

I have had people working for me who became frustrated because I wouldn't order the people under them to do whatever they say. I did this because I wanted to help them grow into being a leader rather than just being a manager. At its core, being a leader is about being the kind of person that others want to follow. I worked on formal career ladders both at Sapient and Microsoft, and at both companies it was clear that moving up the management ladder and moving up the individual contributor ladder involves showing and growing leadership skills.

The relationship between management and leadership is described in a variety of ways. Some refer to management skills as a subset of leadership skills; others argue that one of the skills managers need is leadership. I found that the best managers are leaders, and the best leaders can also manage. Leadership is about knowing where to go and getting others to join you in the journey. Leaders have followers. Management is about creating and executing the plan to get there. Being a manager is a formal designation, and it is about having subordinates. A good manager wants

---

Leadership

- Leaders infect others with vision and generate enthusiasm.
- Leaders communicate, and communicate well.
- Leaders are trusted, and trust themselves
- Leaders handle uncertainty and stress with grace and calm
- Leaders are proactive, goal oriented, and go after exciting challenges, rather than only being reactive.
- Leaders respect and value their followers and those with whom they work.
- UX leaders fight for users, inspire with design, and yet never lose sight of business value.
- Leaders embrace feedback and get better.
- Leaders inspire others to be their best and to improve, and mentor them.
- Leaders know how to leverage people's strengths, and how to work around or manage weaknesses.
- Leadership is hard work, but leaders get in the flow.

FIGURE 10.1

The attributes of leadership.

to turn the subordinates into followers by providing the vision and effectively leading them to success. Great UX managers are able to define the UX vision and have the management skills needed to achieve that vision; they also have the leadership skills to bring the team along in achieving that vision. One part of the job is to do the right thing for users and the business, and the other part is to do it right.

Management is in large part about the set of responsibilities that make up the formal role, but what makes management exciting and important is the juice that comes from leadership. You can create a plan and require people to follow it through formal management. To really make something important happen, to move the dial on the impact of user experience within an organization, you need to be a leader. Even if you are not a manager and do not want to take on those formal responsibilities, your ability to achieve great impact is going to be enhanced if you are an effective leader.

What makes a leader? I have listed some of the characteristics in Fig. 10.1. Many of the attributes I noted earlier in the best managers are really about their leadership. They have a compelling vision that people want to rally around. They are able to lay out the plan for how we would get there, and apply their management skills to align us to the plan. They are trusted, and that requires an appropriate level of transparency. This can be hard at times for a manager, since part of being a manager is that you are not only leading a team, but you are implementing corporate strategy. A good leader knows when to be transparent, how transparent you can be, and how to communicate that you have been as open as you can be without violating your corporate responsibilities. Wanting to follow a leader also involves wanting to believe that at some level he cares about me, my success, and my team; we are all united in the vision and what achieving the vision will mean. Leaders are often trusted because their judgment is sound, but they are also willing to take appropriate risks. They are flexible in how they move forward when the risks occasionally do not pay off.

Part of leadership is modeling the right behaviors, as well as articulating the vision that you are inspiring others to follow. The kind of person that people want to follow is the person who clearly cares about them as people, and values and leverages the diverse skills and experiences they bring to the table. The Adaptive Path workshop in August 2008 (Adaptive Path, 2008) identified best practices that included cultivating emotional intelligence (presumably helping to communicate that valuing); articulating and communicating the vision and thinking big picture; the ability to define a plan, to get people to follow it, and to manage it over time; and finally to define clear roles and responsibilities and identify and manage expectations. For people to feel fully bought in they want to believe in the end result of the big picture and they want to see how their part contributes to that vision.

HINTS FROM EXPERIENCED MANAGERS

Leadership is not about merit or title, but earned through respect. So much can be learned in simple places, such as Boy/Girl Scouts, that are applicable to many management and leadership scenarios.

When establishing policy (HR or otherwise), the key is not about the exact policy because this can be surprisingly vague to many. What one needs to do is provide the rationale and allow this information to generalize and cover what the words of a policy may not. People generally make good decisions. Give them information to generalize to novel situations rather than use explicit rules.

Avoid micromanaging!

Gavin S. Lew, Managing Director, User Centric, Inc., Chicago, IL

Lead through example. Be passionate about design and your approach to projects. If you're excited they'll be excited.

Susan Boyce, Principal UX Lead, Microsoft, Mountain View, CA

Andreas Hauser (2007) pointed out that to drive the appropriate changes through a development process it often requires a change of mindset, and I would argue often a change of culture. As Hauser pointed out, part of the role of the user experience manager is to be a leader in driving this change as well as a catalyst to create a design process that creates a truly collaborative relationship across all those sharing ownership for creating a great user experience.

SHOULD YOU BE MANAGING?

A good manager is best when people barely know that he exists. Not so good when people obey and acclaim him. Worse when they despise him.

Lao-Tzu

One question worth thinking about is "Do you really want to manage? Or do you want to focus on leading as an individual contributor?" Many of the concepts discussed thus far can apply in either situation. While most of my career I have been in management, I have moved back and forth between management and being an individual contributor as my interests and goals have changed. Even as a manager, I defined a role for myself that has typically included an ongoing set of research and design activities and hands-on work.

HINTS FROM EXPERIENCED MANAGERS

Be sure you want to be a manager for the right reasons, not because you think you have to do it to (a) get ahead or (b) because no one else on your team wants to do it or (c) you can't stand the thought of someone else being your manager.

Kent Sullivan, Principal UX Researcher, Microsoft, Redmond, WA

As a manager you are in a unique position to make a difference, and to do your part to change the world. In Wiklund (1994), the author states that to seriously move the usability bar for products companies need to "hire a fairly senior individual with exceptional experience at related design challenges to assume the role of usability 'guru' or 'evangelist.'" He argues that the senior people should be brought in at a level high enough to garner respect among senior executives, and to bring them in at least at the level of team leaders for product areas. The idea is to bring senior people in at a level that shows the commitment to user experience in the organization, and that usually is in the role of manager.

You, however, may find yourself almost anywhere in the organization such as hired in at a senior level; the first user experience person in a company, and are now being told to hire in people under you; an individual contributor whose leadership is being recognized; or working in another role such as project management or as a development lead or manager, and either proposed or been told to start building a user experience team. If you are not already a senior user experience person high in the organization, part of your goal for your career as well as for your UX team may be to get there. Looking across the case studies in his book, Wiklund concluded that the long-term success of a UX program depends on the quality of the leadership of the organization. Leaders are challenged to do the work of a design specialist and be both an educator and a promoter. They need to constantly sell and resell, and to tell the story of the value that user experience delivers. They need to work collaboratively with people across the functions that share ownership for the experience, and they need to build and manage an effective team.

It is worth spending time to explore the different types of leadership, and think about the situation in which you find yourself. Do you see yourself in one or more types of leadership, and do they fit the situation in which you find yourself? How comfortable are you in moving from one style to another? I have run across many different types of managers. There are those who are laser focused on moving up the management chain to higher levels, with each level bringing more recognition and prestige. Often they relish the political side of management, and dwell on who they can influence and how to take another step or to get their way; unfortunately sometimes they do not worry about who they step on to make a move. I was in a management training program a few months ago where one senior manager said that virtually every one-on-one he had with his boss was spent brainstorming how to move higher in the influence ladder. I have definitely had one or two colleagues where I always checked the chair they offered before I sat on it.

HINTS FROM EXPERIENCED MANAGERS

1. There is no cookie cutter management style — every employee is different and you must be flexible to find a style that works for each of your directs.
2. Be honest, be open, don't wait to communicate.
3. Take time to know each person.

Marcella Rader, User Experience Manager, Microsoft China

There are those who are at the other extreme, and are focused on the task at hand. In this situation they are still virtually an individual contributor, and the people under them are truly extra hands to get things done. They lean toward micromanagement to implement their specific vision. Most of us hate working in groups like that, and it does not seem like this style gets you very far as you hit your own limits. Certainly managers who make detailed decisions when their team members have the greater expertise are not doing all they could to help users or the business. There are those who are more *laissez-faire* managers, who mostly focus on the administrative tasks and just assume everyone under them is figuring out what needs to be done and is doing it. My very first manager was a little like this. He was a great guy who introduced me to chicken liver sandwiches, but as I learned later he did not add much to my success. There are those who are more visionary, set a general direction, and then support those under them as they work toward the vision. You will have your own additions to the list.

An interesting exercise is to search for leadership styles on the Internet. You find terms like the inward, the outward, the exemplar, the eccentric, the facilitator, the authoritarian, the participative, the delegative, the servant, and others. Lewin, Lippit, and White (1939), in their seminal work on leadership styles, summarized them in three categories whose properties follow well from their names: authoritarian, democratic, and *laissez-faire*. At a recent management training class I attended, they laid out the situational influence model (www.smsinc.com). In the model there are four styles of influence used by the different categories of leaders: asserting, attracting, bridging, and persuading. In situational leadership, managers can move between the styles as needed depending on the circumstance. I have to admit that the managers I have had the most challenge working for have spent most or all of their time working in the authoritarian mode. If I cannot work for a UX professional, then the person I usually like to work for is closer to the *laissez-faire* type who trusts me to do my job, who will also lend a hand when I request it and praise successes, and who acts as an evangelist working on my team's behalf. Education here is critical, however, because they cannot be good evangelists unless they truly understand what you are trying to do and what your team is delivering.

The kind of manager I strive to be is often known as having a transformational leadership style. The teams I have enjoyed being in and leading are those where we were all inspired by a shared vision of the future. It has been the most fun when I feel like I am in close communication with the members of my team and can see how they are running with and adding their special sauce to the general, strategic direction I have provided and supported. In that close relationship, if a specific tweak is needed, it feels more collaborative in how it is implemented. It is less about leading from the front, since responsibility in general is delegated. In the best situations, I have had at least one member of the team who was detail oriented in a way that complemented my own strengths and growth areas.

For example, I currently have a senior person on my team (Karen) who does not have a formal user experience background, but has tremendous project management and general management skills and business knowledge. She came to the team to grow her UX skills and get closer to customers as part of her career journey. Many of her preferred skills are not mine and vice versa, but we collaborate particularly well. Together we have been able to have a great impact in very challenging situations. We have been successful partly because we each have worked at mastering situational leadership and adapted what we do to what is needed as well as to what the other is doing.

It is generally recognized that the skills needed to start something new are different than those needed to run the factory once the pipe has been laid. Transformational leadership is especially important in growing a new team and moving into a new area. Transactional leadership, which is more about implementing and optimizing, is more appropriate to keep the factory going.

At several of the companies I have worked, there has been a leadership training or a fast track program designed to identify people with leadership characteristics and to nourish them to quickly move up the management track to reach those lofty heights quicker than they otherwise might. At AT&T, for example, Douglas Bray ran a study called the Management Progress Study, which began in 1956. Bray provided organizational guidance to a variety of major American companies after being at AT&T. In his study he found 422 managers and followed their careers over 20 years, testing them in a variety of ways. One important finding that has been replicated in different contexts is "The most significant general conclusion of the study so far is that a person's total satisfaction and happiness with life appears to be almost totally unrelated to whether he or she is successful at work." As noted in Chapter 1, this has been true through my experience as a manager. Success has been a valuable metric to tell me how I am doing, but what has driven me from job to job has been finding the work that brings me joy and fulfillment. My hope is that success will follow when the result is recognized, but the reason I have taken management jobs has been to make a difference in areas that I felt were important at the time. It has been about exercising the management philosophy that feels right. It has been about working in an environment and for people who enable my team to be our very best.

In many of the technology companies I have worked, the Peter Principle holds. People rise to their level of incompetence. People move up often because they are excellent as individual contributors, and they move almost independent of whether they are likely to be good managers. When I was at Bell Laboratories, a colleague who had started in human factors and moved into systems engineering created a survey to do a more local version of the corporate survey to predict success within the organization. It turned out that across the systems engineering organization one of the best predictors of success was that you had started out as a human factors professional. Fearing a little organizational backlash, this study was discretely suppressed. On a post hoc basis, however, it made sense. There is a premium in UX on being able to solve problems, to think in a systems manner, and to communicate effectively. All of these characteristics are useful for systems engineers *and* UX managers and leaders.

I have had the privilege of knowing many excellent UX managers. Of course excellence is partly in my own eyes, and partly from what I heard from people who have worked with them. What has struck me is that in addition to the styles that have been discussed, these excellent UX managers have several common characteristics:

- Point of view. In general, they each have something to say, something they are passionate about. They typically are trying to drive an agenda that they believe will make a big difference for the user and the impact of the design.
- Business judgment. In general, their point of view tends to be a good one. As it is implemented by their team it does make a difference for their team, for users, and for the business. They don't sweat the small stuff; and they keep the main thing the main thing.
- Communications skills. They are able to articulate their ideas effectively and persuasively, in public situations (including formal presentations), as they write, and as they express themselves through sketches.
- Empathy. They genuinely and deeply care about their team. They have strong emotional intelligence.
- Customer focus. They visibly are passionate about the users.
- Design focus. They evangelize great design, the importance of design, and design thinking across the organization.
- Passionate curiosity. They love to ask questions and to understand before pontificating about their point of view.
- Creativity. They are able to produce lots of ideas for solutions to tough problems, whether in real time or after a little thought.
- Urgency. They are motivated to get things done, and to have an impact.

- Risk taking. They are willing to take risks partly for the challenge, and partly because of the big results they can bring. The risks, however, are in the zone of optimal development, and while clearly risks (and therefore sometimes bring failure), the risks are worth taking.
- Self-awareness and learning. At one of my management trainings, a phrase was used to capture this. "Feedback is a gift. Embrace it." The best see it that way, go after it, and act on it.

A FINAL COMMENT

Throughout this book the focus has been on you as a leader and often on you as a manager. The goal has been to provide a window into what it means to be a leader or manager if you are thinking about moving in that direction, and to provide guidance about some of the things you should think about as you start to step into the role. Much of the advice should be useful if you are an individual contributor trying to make a difference. It should enable you to have a point of view beyond your level. In other words, it should help you as you advance your career. For those leading virtual teams as well as those with direct reports, this book contains ideas that can be applied to enable teams to work more effectively together to achieve your mission and vision. For those starting teams, inheriting teams, or even in early management this book contains a framework to become more effective. Experienced managers may even find fresh points of view that challenge assumptions and can be built upon to drive more UX management innovation.

All of this discussion has been in the service of my fundamental belief that what you do when you manage and lead teams is important. You have the ability to take the best of who you are and leverage the creative power of others to amplify it. You are not only representing yourself; you are representing the field. You really can move the world to a better place, starting with your world. My very best to you on your journey!

10.1 MANAGEMENT OBSERVATIONS

By Barry L. Lively, Manager of the User Interface Design Group (retired), Lucent Technologies Consumer Products

The way I approached managing what at the time was a human factors group came out of my experience as a member of technical staff (MTS) at Bell Laboratories. I started at the Labs in Holmdel, NJ, in 1976 with "dual citizenship" in two departments: a human factors department headed by John Karlin, the original human factors expert hired at Bell Labs, and a systems engineering department in the switching systems area of the company. It was the job of the switching systems people to write requirements for new systems. They recognized that the user interface (whether for the telephone operator or the customer) was crucial to good design and they wanted people dedicated to their work.[1] At the same time, they recognized that one human factors engineer sitting exclusively with systems people might become isolated and it would be useful to have that subject matter expert sitting with human factors people as well. The way it worked out was that I had my desk in the human factors department and reported to two managers, one in each department. This gave me easy access to other human factors people and the lab facilities in the human factors department. On the whole this worked well. For lack of a better term, a spirit of generosity existed on both sides of the arrangement, which reduced friction to a negligible level, if it existed at all, and given that I was the first one through with this kind of arrangement, there was willingness all around to give the arrangement some space to see how it would develop. It worked and I was offered a promotion as a result.

The promotion in 1980 was to manage a human factors group in Indianapolis where consumer products such as telephones were developed. The range of products grew over time to include answering systems, security systems, pay telephones, and other products.

The group had been started a few months before I arrived. A department head had already hired two people, both of whom I would have hired had I been there.[2] The prototypical human factors engineer of the day had a PhD in experimental psychology. That was my training and the training of just about all of the human factors MTSs back in Holmdel. Whether they had earlier studied human visual perception, memory, the behavior of rats in mazes, or the design of instrument panels, these people shared a core set of skills in the design of experiments and studies, an understanding of statistical methods, and an appreciation for the value of empirical data to resolve issues. Of course there is a far wider range of people with appropriate skills and at some level we knew that. But as university teaching positions were not getting more numerous and in many cases were shrinking, there were lots of very good experimental psychologists looking for work and we could get highly qualified people with all the basic skills quite easily. Thinking back on it, if I offered someone a job they almost always took it. If they didn't, it was to go to a group much like ours.

I suppose there are other lessons I could share but I'm going to bring this section to a close with just one lesson, which to me is the greatest one of all. It's a painful lesson that only became apparent the hard way. Our part of AT&T, and then Lucent Technologies, was going to be closed and sold. Consumer products were no longer making money for the company the way they had been. Those at my level, and other levels of course, did the best we could to save money, work smarter, and do all those things that in the larger picture are good but aren't going to make the difference between success (profit) and failure (lack of profit) for the entire division of the business. It was coming to a close and I felt that all the work we had done to save the division was as if we were writing in the sand just above the low tide line. The tide came in and all that work was washed away. But that threw into relief the truly large lesson: the difference you will make in the long run is how well and fairly you treat your people. You are a coach. This means helping them grow in the job by expecting more and rewarding them when they do grow, not perhaps monetarily but certainly in how you treat them. You can count on their going on elsewhere after they leave your group and the question will be "What did they learn from you?"

---

[1] This wasn't just lip service. In the end, the requirements for the forerunner to the directory assistance system you experience today were prepared by a systems engineer and me.
[2] There was another human factors group in Holmdel that had been working with the Indianapolis developers. They advised on these hires.

Appendix

PROFESSIONAL SOCIETY CONFERENCES

ORG	Actual conference
DMI	http://www.dmi.org
PMN	http://www.pmn.co.uk/mex/
BCS	http://www.bcs.org
UPA	http://www.usabilityprofessionals.org
Mobile HCI	http://www.mobilehci.org
UbiComp	http://www.ubicomp.org
Siggraph	http://www.siggraph.org
TED	http://www.ted.com
SIGCHI	http://www.sigchi.org
EPIC	http://www.epiconference.com/
IDSA	http://www.idsa.org
AAA	http://www.aaanet.org
AIGA	http://www.aiga.org
ACM	http://www.hotmobile.org.main/
HFES	http://www.hfes.org
MIX	http://www.microsoft.com/events/mix/default.mspx
DPPI	http://www.utc.fr/dppi09/
IFIP	http://www.dexigner.com
IXDA	http://www.ixda.org/
SIGACCESS	http://www.sigaccess.org/
STC	http://www.stc.org

OTHER RECOMMENDED MANAGEMENT BOOKS

Several of the experienced managers I have consulted for this book have recommended additional resources they have found useful in their management careers. There is a thriving industry in these books, but the following are worth considering. Nelson Soken's list was included in his presentation on getting a seat at the table at the 2009 HFES conference, and from recommendations he made in his book *Lead the Pack*.

- Blanchard, K. H., & Johnson, S. (1982). *The one minute manager*. New York, NY: William Morrow & Co.
- Blanchard, K., Fowler, S., & Hawkins, L. (2005). *Self-leadership and the one minute manager: Increasing through situational self-leadership*. New York, NY: HarperCollins.
- Christensen, C. M. (2003). *The innovator's dilemma: What new technologies cause great firms to fail*. New York, NY: Harper Paperbacks.
- Christensen, C. M., & Raynor, M. E. (2003). *The innovator's solution: Creating and sustaining successful growth*. Boston, MA: Harvard Business School Press.
- Collins, J. (2009). *How the mighty fall: And why some companies never give in*. New York, NY: HarperCollins.
- Collins, J. (2001). *Good to great*: Why some companies make the leap...and others don't. New York, NY: HarperCollins.
- Heath, C., & Heath, D. (2007). *Made to stick: Why some ideas survive and others die*. New York, NY: Random House.
- Johansson, F. (2004). *The Medici effect: Breakthrough insights at the intersection of ideas, concepts & cultures*. Boston, MA, NY: Harvard Business School Press.
- Kay, B., & Jordan-Evans, S. (2008). *Love 'em or lose 'em: Getting good people to stay*. San Francisco, CA: Berrett-Koehler Publishers..
- Kim, W. C., & Mauborgne, R. (2005). *Blue ocean strategy: How to create uncontested market space and make the competition irrelevant*. Boston, MA: Harvard Business School Press.
- Lafley, A. G., & Charan, R. (2008). *The game-changer: How you can drive revenue and profit growth with innovation*. New York, NY: Crown Business.
- Lencioni, P. (2002). *The FIVE dysfunctions of a TEAM: A leadership fable*. San Francisco, CA: Jossey-Bass.
- Lundin, S. (2008). *CATS: Nine lives of innovation*. New York, NY: McGraw-Hill.
- Moore, G. A. (2002). *Crossing the chasm*. New York, NY: The Penguin Group.
- Moore, G. A. (2008). *Dealing with Darwin: How great companies innovate at every phase of their evolution*. New York, NY: The Penguin Group.
- Patton, B. M., Ury, W. L., & Fisher, R. (1992). *Getting to yes: Negotiating agreement without giving in*. New York, NY: Penguin.
- Ressler, C., & Thompson, J. (2008). *Why work sucks and how to fix it*. New York, NY: Portfolio.

- Senge, P. (2006). *The fifth discipline: The art & practice of the learning organization*. New York, NY: Doubleday Business.
- Soken, N., & Wengert, W. (2008). *Lead the pack: Sparking innovation that drives customers wild*. Minneapolis, MN: Mill City Press.
- Thompson, C. (1992). *What a great idea*. New York, NY: Harper Perennial.

Nelson Soken Recommendations
Executive Summaries of Business Literature
- www.GetAbstract.com

Periodicals and Web Sites
- *Harvard Business Review*
- *MIT Sloan Management Review*
- *Forbes*
- *Fortune*
- *BusinessWeek*
- *FastCompany*
- *Wired*

Training and Skill Development
- Exercising Influence: Building relationships and getting results. Barnes and Conti Associates, Inc. www.barnesconti.com.
- Intelligent risk-taking: From vision to Action. Barnes and Conti Associates, Inc. www.barnesconti.com.
- Managing Innovation: Driving ideas from strategic initiatives to value creation. Barnes and Conti Associates, Inc., and Francis, D. www.barnesconti.com.
- Speaking to the Big Dogs. Powerspeaking.com.
- Patterson, K., & Grenny, J. (2007). *The influencer: The power to change anything*. New York, NY: McGraw-Hill.
- Madson, P. R. (2005). *Improv wisdom: Don't prepare, just show up*. New York, NY: Bell Tower.
- Kotter, J., & Cohen, D. S. (2002). *The heart of change: Real-life stories of how people change their organizations*. Boston, MA: Harvard Business Press.
- Heath, C., & Heath, D. (2010). *Switch: How to change things when change is hard*. New York, NY: Random House.
- Morrell, M., & Capparell, S. (2002). *Shackleton's way: Leadership lessons from the great Antarctic explorer*. New York, NY: Penguin.
- Lundin, S. (2008). *CATS: The nine lives of innovation*. New York, NY: McGraw-Hill.
- Sutton, R. I. (2002). *Weird ideas that work: 11-1/2 practices for promoting, managing, and sustaining innovation*. New York, NY: The Free Press.

Books

- Christensen, C. M. (2003). *The innovator's dilemma: What new technologies cause great firms to fail*. New York, NY: Harper Paperbacks.
- Christensen, C. M., & Raynor, M. E. (2003). *The innovator's solution: Creating and sustaining successful growth*. Boston, MA: Harvard Business School Press.
- Collins, J. (2009). *How the mighty fall: And why some companies never give in*. New York, NY: HarperColllins.
- Friedman, T. L. (2005). *The world is flat: A brief history of the twenty-first century*. New York, NY: Farrer, Straus and Giroux.
- Gladwell, M. (2002). *The tipping point: How little things can make a big difference*. New York, NY: Little, Brown and Company.
- Gladwell, M. (2004). *Blink: The power of thinking without thinking*. New York, NY: Little, Brown and Company, 2005.
- Heath, C., & Heath, D. (2007). *Made to stick: Why some ideas survive and others die*. New York, NY: Broadway Business.
- Heath, C., & Heath, D. (2010). *Switch: How to change things when change is hard*. New York, NY: Random House.
- Hamel, G. (2002). *Leading the revolution*. New York, NY: Plume.
- Johansson, F. (2004). *The Medici effect: Breakthrough insights at the intersection of ideas, concepts & cultures*. Boston, MA: Harvard Business School Press.
- Kelley, T. with Jonathan Littman. (2005). *The ten faces of innovation: IDEO's strategies for beating the evil's advocate & driving creativity throughout your organization*. New York, NY: Currency Books.
- Kelley, T., Littman, J., & Peters, T. (2001). *The art of innovation: Lessons in creativity from IDEO, America's leading design firm*. New York, NY: Currency Books.
- Kim, W. C., & Mauborgne, R. (2005). *Blue ocean strategy: How to create uncontested market space and make the competition irrelevant*. Boston, MA: Harvard Business School Press.
- Kotter, J., & Cohen, D. S. (2002). *The heart of change: Real-life stories of how people change their organizations*. Boston, MA: Harvard Business Press.
- Lafley, A. G., & Charan, R. (2008). *The game-changer: How you can drive revenue and profit growth with innovation*. New York, NY: Crown Business.
- Lundin, S. (2008). *CATS: The nine lives of innovation*. New York, NY: McGraw-Hill.
- Martin, R. (2009). *The design of business: Why design thinking is the next competitive advantage*. Boston, MA: Harvard Business Press.
- May, M. (2009). *In pursuit of elegance: Why the best ideas have something missing*. New York, NY: Broadway Business.
- Moore, G. A. (2002). *Crossing the chasm*. New York, NY: Harper Paperbacks.
- Moore, G. A. (2005). *Dealing with Darwin: How great companies innovate at every phase of their evolution*. New York, NY: The Penguin Group.
- Morrell, M., & Capparell, S. (2002). *Shackleton's way: Leadership lessons from the great Antarctic explorer*. New York, NY: Penguin.

- Rogers, E. M. (2003). *Diffusion of innovations* (5th ed.). New York, NY: The Free Press.
- Schwartz, P. (1996). *The art of the long view: Planning for the future in an uncertain world*. New York, NY: Currency Paperback.
- Senor, D., & Singer, S. (2009). *Start-up nation: The story of Israel's economic miracle*. New York, NY: Twelve.
- Silverstein, M. J., & Fiske, N. (2003). *Trading up: The new American luxury*. New York, NY: Portfolio.
- Soken, N. (2008). *Lead the pack: Sparking innovation that drives customers wild*. Minneapolis, MN: Mill City Press.
- Sutton, R. I. (2002). *Weird Ideas that work: 11-1/2 practices for promoting, managing, and sustaining innovation*. New York, NY: The Free Press.
- Taylor, W. C., & LaBarre, P. (2006). *Mavericks at work: Why the most original minds in business win*. New York, NY: HarperCollins Publishers.

ADDITIONAL HELPFUL RESOURCES

- Creative Good's Councils (http://creativegood.com/councils/) — A peer-network of experience leaders and executives. A great place to share challenges, ask questions, and receive guidance.
- Russell Wilson's Executive/Senior Group
- *UX* (published by UPA)
- *Interactions* (published by ACM SIGCHI)
- *Ergonomics in Design* (published by HFES)
- Dilbert (http://www.dilbert.com/)

References

Adaptive Path. (2008). <http://managinguxteams.com>.

Ashley, J. (2007, May/June). Working with C-level executives. *Interactions*, 29–30.

Basadur, M. S. (2004). Leading others to think innovatively together. *Leadership Quarterly*, *15*, 103–121.

Basadur, M. S., & Gelade, G. (2003). Using the creative problem solving profile (CPSP) for diagnosing and solving real-world problems. *Emergence Journal of Complexity Issues in Organizations and Management*, *5*(3), 22–47.

Bloomer, S., & Croft, R. (1997, November/December). Pitching usability to your organization. *Interactions*, 18–26.

Bodine, K. (2006, September). The people who make great Web sites. *Forrester Best Practices,* September 13.

Brown, T. (2008, June). Design thinking. *Harvard Business Review.*

Buckingham, M., & Coffman, C. (1999). *First break all the rules: What the world's greatest managers do differently*. New York: Simon and Schuster.

Changing. (2009). <http://changingminds.org/disciplines/change_management/kubler_ross/kubler_ross.htm>.

Cheskin & Sapient. (1999). *eCommerce trust study*. <http://www.cheskin.com/cms/files/i/articles/17__report-eComm%20Trust1999.pdf>.

Colfelt, A. (2007, November 27). *Building the UX dreamteam*. <http://www.boxesandarrows.com/view/building-the-ux>.

Creating. (2002). Creating a work climate that motivates staff and improves performance. *The Manager*, *11*(3), 1.

Csikszentmihalyi, M. (1982). Towards a psychology of optimal experience. In L. Wheeler (Ed.), *Review of personality and social psychology* (pp. 13–36). Beverly Hills, CA: Sage.

Davis, F. D. (1989, September). Perceived Usefulness, perceived ease of use, and user acceptance of information technology. *MIS Quarterly*, 319–340.

Davis, F. D., Bagozzi, R. P., & Warshaw, P. R. (1989). User acceptance of computer technology: A comparison of two theoretical models. *Management Science*, *35*(8), 982–1003.

Desmond, K. (2007, May/June). What makes UX successful form the executive perspective? An interview with Mark Vershel. *Interactions*, 31–33.

Detweiler, M. (2007). Managing UCD within agile projects. *Interactions*, 14(3), 40–42.

De Young, T. (1996). Organizational support for software design. In T. Winograd (Ed.), *Bringing design to software* (pp. 253–267). Reading, MA: Addison-Wesley.

Dumas, J., & Redish, J. (1999). Appendix A: Setting up a usability laboratory. *A practical guide to usability testing* (pp. 384–394). Portland, OR: Intellect.

Earthy, J. (1998). Usability maturity model: Processes. IE2016 INUSE Deliverable D5.1.4p. <http://www.lboro.ac.uk/eusc>.

Earthy, J., Jones, B., & Bevan, N. (2001). The improvement of human-centered processes — facing the challenge and reaping the benefit of ISO 13407. *International Journal of Human-Computer Studies, 55,* 553-585.

Gatlin, J., Wysocki, A., & Kepner, K. (2009). Understanding conflict in the workplace. HR024, the University of Florida IFAS Extension (http://edis.ifas.ufl.edu).

Goleman, D. (2000). An EI-based theory of performance. In G. Cherniss & D. Goleman (Eds.), *The emotionally intelligent workplace* (pp. 27-44). San Francisco, CA: Jossey-Bass.

Gray, W., & Salzman, M. (1998). Damaged merchandise? A review of experiments that compare usability evaluation methods. *Human-Computer Interaction, 13*(3), 203-261.

Grudin, J. (2005). Why CHI fragmented. *Proceedings of CHI* (pp. 1083-1084). Portland, Oregon.

Hauser, A. (2007, May/June). UCD collaboration with product management and development. *Interactions,* 34-35.

Hendrick, H. (2010). *It all begins with self: how to become a more effective and happier you!* Salt Lake City, UT: Millennial Mind Publishing.

HFES. (2010). *2010-2011 Directory & Yearbook* (pp. 1-3). Santa Monica, CA: HFES.

Hill, C., & Jones, G. (2001). *Strategic management.* Boston: Houghton Mifflin.

Humphrey, W. (1990). *Managing the software process.* Reading, MA: Addison-Wesley.

Innes, J. (2007, May/June). Defining the user experience function: Innovation through organizational design. *Interactions,* 36-37.

ISO 9241: Part 11. (1998). <http://www.iso.org/iso/iso_catalogue/catalogue_tc/catalogue_detail.htm?csnumber=16883>.

ISO/IEC 25062. (2006). <http://www.iso.org/iso/iso_catalogue/catalogue_tc/catalogue_detail.htm?csnumber=43046>.

Israelski, E., & Lund, A. M. (2002). HCI work in telecommunications. In A. Sears & J. Jacko (Eds.), *The human-computer interaction handbook* (pp. 772-789). Mahwah, NJ: Lawrence Erlbaum Associates.

Karat, C. M., & Lund, A. (2005). The return on investment in usability of Web applications. In R. Bias & D. Mayhew (Eds.), *Cost-justifying usability, second edition: An update for the Internet Age* (pp. 297-316). San Francisco, CA: Morgan Kaufmann Publishers.

Kelly, T. (2001). *The art of innovation: Lessons in creativity from IDEO, America's leading design firm.* New York, NY: Currency and Doubleday.

Kelly, T. (2005). *The ten faces of innovation: IDEO's strategies for beating the devil's advocate and driving creativity throughout your organization.* New York: Doubleday.

Kleinfield, S. (1981). *The biggest company on earth: A profile of AT&T.* New York: Holt, Rinehart and Winston.

Kübler-Ross, E. (1969). *On death and dying.* New York: Macmillan.

Lewin, K., Lippit, R., & White, R. (1939). Patterns of aggressive behavior in experimentally created social climates. *Journal of Social Psychology,* 271-301.

Lindgaard, G. (2004, May/June). Making the business out business: One path to value-added HCI. *Interactions,* 12-17.

Lindgaard, G., & Millard, N. (2002, April 20-25). The business value of HCI: How can we do better? *Proceedings of CHI 2002.* New York, NY: ACM, 928-929.

Lund, A. (1994a). Ameritech's usability laboratory: From prototype to final design. *Behavior & Information Technology, 13*(1 and 2), 67-80.

Lund, A. (1994b). How many human factors people is enough? *Ergonomics in Design, 1*, 36–38.

Lund, A. (1996a, November/December). Are we having fun yet? *Interactions*, 24–30.

Lund, A. M. (1996b). Advertising human factors: A case study of an ad campaign. *Ergonomics in Design, 4*(4), 5–11.

Lund, A. (1997a). Another approach to justifying the cost of usability. *Interactions, 4*(3), 49–56.

Lund, A. (1997b). Expert ratings of usability maxims. *Ergonomics in Design, 5*(3), 15–20.

Lund, A. M. (1998). Damaged merchandise? Comments on shopping at outlet malls. *Human-computer Interaction, 13*(3), 276–281.

Lund, A. (2000). *Interviewing for a job.* <http://www.hfes.org/Web/Students/Lund.pdf>.

Lund, A. (2001). Measuring usability with the USE questionnaire. *Usability Interface, 8*(2), 3–6. <http://www.stcsig.org/usability/newsletter/index.html>.

Lund, A. (2006). Post-modern usability. *Journal of Usability Studies, 2*(1), 1–6.

Lund, A. (2007). Usability ROI as a strategic tool. *User Experience Magazine, 6*(2).

Lund, A. (2010, May). Creating a user-centered development culture. *Interactions*, 34–38.

Marcus, A. (2002). User-interface design, culture, and the future. *Proceedings of the working conference on advanced visual interfaces.* New York, NY: ACM, 15–27.

Mayhew, D., & Tremaine, M. (2005). A basic framework. In R. Bias & D. Mayhew (Eds.), *Cost-justifying usability, second edition: An update for the Internet Age* (pp. 41–101). San Francisco, CA: Morgan Kaufmann Publishers.

Miller, C., North, R., Gawron, V., Wichansky, A., Beith, B., & Chappell, S., et al. (2002). HF/Es place in the parade: Should we be drum majors or toot our own horns [panel]? *Proceedings of the human factors and ergonomics society 46th annual meeting.* Santa Monica, CA: HFES, 1693.

Mok, C. (2000). Experience design *GAIN, 1*(1), 1–2.

Monitor. (2008). <http://www.csmonitor.com/2008/0128/p13s03-wmgn.html>.

Morrison, T., Conaway, W. A., & Borden, G. A. (1994) *Kiss, bow, or shake hands: How to do business in sixty countries.* Avon, MA: Adams Media Corporation.

Nair, R. (2006). Climate studies and associated best practices to improve climate issues in the workplace. *Proceedings of the 2006 WEPAN conference.* <http://www.haygroup.com/tl/Downloads/Leadership_booklet.pdf>.

Nielsen, J. (1994). Usability laboratories: A 1994 survey. *Behavior & Information Technology, 13*(1–2). <http://www.useitcom/papers/uselabs.html>.

Nielsen, J. (2008). <http://www.useit.com/alerbox/roi.html>.

Pruitt, J., & Adlin, T. (2006). *The persona lifecycle: Keeping people in mind throughout product design.* (pp. 369–379). San Francisco, CA: Morgan Kaufmann.

Rohn, J. (2007, May/June). How to organizationally embed UX in your company. *Interactions*, 25–28.

Rosenbaum, S., Rohn, J., & Humburg, J. (2000). A toolkit for strategic usability: Results from workshop, panels, and surveys, *Proceedings of CHI 2000.* The Hague, The Netherlands.

Rosenberg, D. (2004, September/October). The myths of usability ROI. *Interactions*, 23–29.

Rosenberg, D. (2007, May/June). Introducing the 360° view of UX management. *Interactions*, 22–24.

Rosenhead, J. (2006). IFORS Operational Research Hall of Fame: Stafford Beer. *International Transactions in Operational Research, 13*, 577–578.

Rosson, M. B., & Carroll, J. (2002). *Usability engineering: Scenario-based development of human-computer interactions.* San Francisco, CA: Morgan Kaufmann.

Schaffer, E. (2004). *The Institutionalization of usability: A step-by-step guide.* New York: Addison-Wesley.

Scholtz, J., Belloti, V., Schirra, L., Erickson, T., DeGroot, J., & Lund, A. (1998, January). Telework: When your job is on the line. *Interactions*, 44–54.

Schumacher, R. M. (Ed.), (2009). *Handbook of global user research.* Burlington, MA: Kaufmann Publishers/Elsevier.

Schwartz, A., Thomson, L., Seifert, C., & Shafto, M. (1996). Can a usable product flash 12:00? Perceived usability as a function of usefulness. *Proceedings of the human factors and ergonomics Society* . Santa Monica, CA: HFES, 313–317.

Schwartz, B., & Riley, C. (1988). Evolution or extinction? A case study of decentralized human factors in a telecommunications R7D company, *Proceedings of the 12th international symposium on human factors in telecommunication* (pp. 1–11). Amsterdam: Elsevier.

Senge, P. (2006). *The fifth discipline: The art & practice of the learning organization.* New York, NY: Doubleday Business.

Spool, J. (2007, December 10). *Assessing your team's UX skills.* <http://www.uie.com/articles/assessing_ux_teams>.

Straub, K., Patel, M., Bublitz, A., & Broch, J. (2009). *The HFI UX Maturity Survey — 2009, Findings, HFI white paper.* <www.humanfactors.com/UXMaturitySurvey.asp>.

Stringer, R. (2002). *Leadership and organizational climate.* Upper Saddle River, NJ: Prentice Hall.

Tichy, N. (1997). *The leadership engine: How winning companies build leaders at every level.* New York: Harper Business.

Venkatesh, V., Morris, M. G., David, G. B., & David, F. D. (2003). User acceptance of information technology: Toward a unified view. *MIS Quarterly*, *27*(3), 425–478.

Watkins, C. (2000). The leadership program for serving headteachers: Probably the world's largest leadership development initiative. *Leadership and Organizational Development Journal*, *21*(1), 13–20.

Wichansky, A. (2007, May/June). Working with standards organizations. *Interactions*, 38–39.

Wiklund, M. (1994). *Usability in practice: How companies develop user-friendly products.* Boston, MA: AP Professional.

Index